ANDRÁS TÖRÖK

BUDA PEST
A CRITICAL GUIDE

Illustrated
by András Felvidéki

ZEPHYR PRESS
Boston
PARK PUBLISHING
Budapest
1992

TO FLÓRA AND LILI

my daughters

ENGLISH VERSION

by Peter Doherty and Ágnes Enyedi

ACKNOWLEDGEMENTS

The author would like to express his gratitude to everyone who encouraged and helped him.

Special thanks to

DR ZOLTÁN SZENTKIRÁLYI and DR BALÁZS VARGHA

who were kind enough to go through the manuscript as consultants and to

ANDRÁS BARABÁS

who improved on the text and who could possibly write a much better book on Budapest

PETER DOHERTY

who comes from Dublin and who knows best what to enjoy and laugh at in Budapest

The author and the illustrator are also indebted to a large number of people, first of all, to their

CORRESPONDENTS:

George and Julie Gábor   László Lugosi Lugo
András Nyerges   Róbert Sarlós

also to Márta Aczél, Ferenc Bodor, Éva Blaschtik, Mária Borbás, Klára D. Major, Zoltán Erő, Katalin Farkas, Ádám Fischer, Doris Fischer, András Fűrész, Zsuzsa Gáspár, Tibor Frank, Robert Hetzron, György Kassai, László Kis Papp, Pál Kövi, Miklós Molnár, Ádám Nádasdy, Vilma Nádasdy, Ágnes Padányi, István Rév, Klára Péter, Anna Szemere, István Teplán, Lionel Tiger, Ágnes Tompa, Benedek Várkonyi, Anna Veress, Tibor Vidos, Péter Virágvölgyi.

Revised with the assistance of András Nyerges
This revised edition went to press in December 1991

A NOTE

Few travel books are without errors, and no guidebook can ever be completely up to date, for telephone numbers and opening hours change without warning, and restaurants come under new management, which can affect standards. This is especially true in Budapest nowadays. While every effort has been made to ensure that all information is accurate at the time of going to press, the author and the publishers will be glad to receive corrections and suggestions for improvements, which can be incorporated in the next edition. See last page card.

ISBN 963 77 37 04 9 (Hungary)
ISBN 0-939010-24-0 (U.S. & Canada)

Contents

Introduction
to the Second Edition

Budapest, my native city has not changed much for the tourist during the last three years, since I finished the manuscript for this edition. More luxury restaurants, more and nicer shops, together with Vienna prices in some places.

It has changed for me — beyond recognition. That meek and mellow dictatorship has given in: melted away in front of our very eyes.

You should know that this regime was different from all the others in Eastern Europe. We did not cry out against it every day after getting up; on the contrary, we had to remind ourselves of what kind of a regime we are living in, at the weekend. We laughed at the ignorant "politicians", and detested money. We wore ragged blue jeans from twenty to thirty and our hair was reluctant to follow the Zeitgeist into a shorter and shorter style. We read a lot of books, but very few papers, always trying to read between the lines. We didn't expect this world to disappear in our lifetime. We were conditioned to irreverence and to having absolutely no responsibility outside the family.

Being born in 1954, I didn't have any memories of the revolution in 1956. My best friend, a poet and scholar did. He kept on telling me the story about the Cow.

He explained that in the dark 50s his family didn't think the régime would last. They felt that a big dark cow that was grazing over a beautiful meadow (i.e. Hungary) suddenly sat down. But that darkness, they thought, cannot last forever: it is the very nature of cows that one day they get up. And the Cow did get up. For only twelve days — a glorious but short time. After that nobody thought that she would ever leave. Some people — including me — thought it was not a cow just a cow-shaped piece of solid rock. And it is possible to live under a rock — if you are some species of fungus.

Around 1982 the government decided to introduce some "reforms": after inventing lukewarm water they opted for inventing hot water. Letting small businesses start and flourish was going to erode the remaining ideological features of the system. Earlier, a district hall official could turn down a permission for a shoemaker's shop just by saying that there are enough shoemakers in a given neighbourhood.

That made a slow but dramatic impact on Budapest. There were better and better shops. The gentrification of the Inner City started again, first making the tourist reservation just a bit bigger, later spreading throughout within the Grand Boulevard. That slowly changed my generation as well. Some of us felt that it was worth earning money so as to spend it in an intelligent way. You could be, if not happy, free. Some of us were not interested in money at all - they published the half a dozen underground papers, for a couple of thousand people. Some were interested in both. Some in nothing. But everyone thought that the régime cannot become more liberal than it had become. Common sense was infiltrating everyday life more and more, though. Not so much, though, that one of the stupidest laws — my favourite — was abolished. Until the autumn 1989(!) if you had a car younger than 3 years old, you could only sell it to the state, at a depressed price. Thus, a three-year-and-one-day-old car was much more expensive than a three-year-old car...

But who now remembers these days? Suddenly, to our astonishment, the Cow started fidgeting, and slowly, very slowly it was getting up. It was a slower and much less dramatic event than in the countries around Hungary; nobody was killed and there were hardly any demonstrations, the world press showed much less interest.

One of the most important consequences of the departure of the Cow for you is that you will not be able to use your maps if not brand new, and printed in Hungary. Several dozens of street names were restored plus a couple of cinemas. No more Red Star and May 1 cinemas, no Spark cinema and no Victory. No Lenin körút or Majakovszkij utca.

There is a free Parliament, free business, even a free press. (Even my friends and I could start a literary monthly; see Café New York, p. 124).

In a couple of years' time Hungary might become one of those smaller, prosperous, boring countries. Not yet though.

The patch of grass where the cow was lying still shows signs of "fatigue". Hopefully, regeneration will not last for the 400 years of the old English joke about grass.

You should check it out from time to time.

October 1990

Introduction
to the first edition

BUDAPEST, my birthplace, used to be compared to Vienna by visitors. "The Danube, the ring boulevards, the many eclectic and neostyle buildings — the city is a second Vienna, in a more modest edition", they would say. "True, Mother Nature has been more generous, but as regards historic buildings, it cannot even hold a candle to Vienna. On top of that, the Hungarian language does not resemble any other European language."

Budapest now has earned a higher reputation among the young who come from Paris, Amsterdam, Warsaw or Leningrad. There are many back-packing tourists in Budapest but the number of "non-package" independence-loving visitors, who arrive in their own car, has also much increased recently. Those friends of mine, mostly my age, whom I have shown around in the last ten years have usually sung the city's praises beyond the point of politeness.

They said they found Budapest to be truly cultured, truly European. They said that from certain points of view it has better preserved the old, humane qualities of days gone-by than many other cities, where development has swept the past away. They remembered staircases, badly needing renovation, locksmith's workshops with wooden floors, and the smell of oil and small suburban family-run restaurants. They were fascinated by the large, uniform riverbank, and the beauty of the three bridges in the middle. They also said that the historic buildings seemed to be familiar to them (perhaps because quite a few of them are copies?) and were very accessible. It is not so much the grandeur but the prettiness of the buildings that captivated them. They even said that the city was like a Sleeping Beauty still hidden from the eyes of Europe. My friends who have returned after two, three or more years have said that Budapest has changed a lot. New shops and restaurants have opened, and now you can even get a taxi. They noticed some nice modern buildings. They found their money still went a long way, though not as far as it had done.

"We would not have got too far without you", my friends said. And that was more than a simple compliment. The spirit of the city had revealed itself to them, a spirit which can get close to you only with the help of a native.

THIS BOOK tries to combine three types of guides with the advantages of all three: the Baedeker type, the critical guidebook and the alternative guidebook. Obviously it will not be exhaustive in any single type.

THERE IS a Hungarian saying for things which seem impossible: "an iron ring made out of wood". Even if this book cannot overcome the language difficulties, it is designed to put the visitor at ease when making his own plans to discover the city. After all, it is easier to get help with the language from friends, business-partners, interpreters or hotel receptionists, than to get ideas for spending one's time.

Believe me that Hungarian is not an ugly language. Here is the list a Hungarian poet made of what he thought are the most beautiful words in our language: *láng* (flame), *gyöngy* (pearl), *anya* (mother), *ősz* (autumn), *szűz* (maiden), *kard* (sword), *csók* (kiss), *vér* (blood), *szív* (heart), *sír* (grave).

October 1988

A CITY

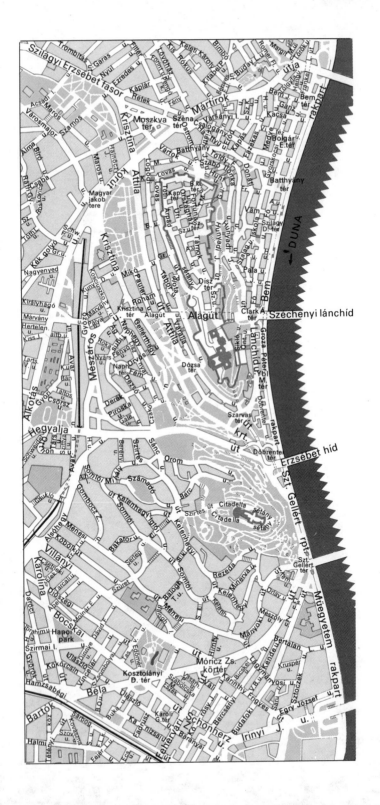

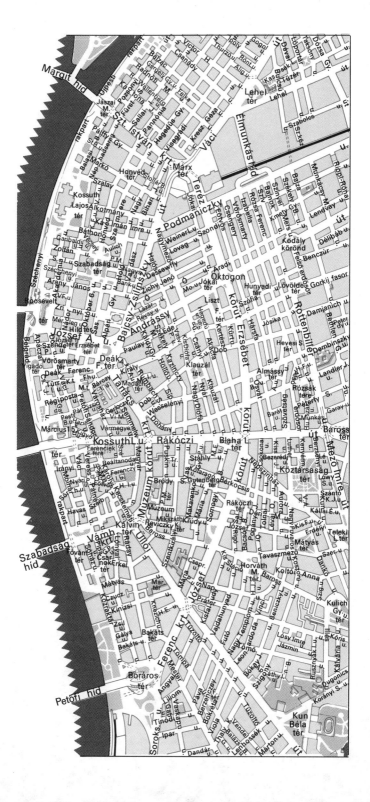

General Information

Visas — Customs — Registration — Money and Changing Money — News, Newspapers — Telephones, Telegrams — Weather

Visas

As a consequence of recent changes, visas are not required for citizens of European countries. The exception, at the time of going to press is the Soviet Union (if you are not a packaged tourist). They (and citizens of the non-European countries, with the exception of the USA) should obtain a visa from the Hungarian consulate abroad. (Prices change with rates.) A visa is valid for six months and entitles the holder to a stay of up to 30 days. For a longer stay, the visitor must extend the visa at the local police station. (The Budapest police stations are listed below, see Registration.)

Visas can also be obtained at road frontier crossing points or at Budapest Ferihegy Airport. There visas cost somewhat more. Passengers arriving by train or boat must buy their visas in advance.

Customs

The foreign visitor can only bring 100 Ft in coins. Articles for personal use, not in commercial quantities, may be brought in free of duty. Duty-free allowances for alcoholic drinks and tobacco are 1 litre of spirits, 2 litres of wine and 250 cigarettes (or 50 cigars). These allowances are only available to those over 16 years of age. Presents to a total value of 5,000 Ft are free of duty — once a year. On other occasions, within the same year only 500 Ft's worth is free of duty. The rest should be declared. All articles of significant value should be registered on entry to ensure no complications on leaving the country. When leaving, goods to the value of 3,000 Ft are free of export duty. Goods bought in a hard-currency shop, whose purchase can be proved with a receipt, are also free of duty.

Articles which are prohibited by law are drugs, fire-arms, explosives. Hunting weapons, ammunition and CB radios require a permit on entry.

Registration

Foreign visitors are no longer required to register with the police, provided their stay is for 30 days or less. If they wish to stay longer, they should go to their local police station.

BUDAPEST POLICE STATIONS BY DISTRICT

I. Pauler utca 13.
South side of the park called Vérmező. Access: Tram 18; Buses 2, 4, 5, 78. T.: 175-8722.

II. Rómer Flóris utca 6.
In line with Margit híd, on the Buda side. Access: Bus 91. T.: 115-0270.

III. Tímár utca 11.
Opposite Margitsziget, near the Danube. Access: Szentendre HÉV to Tímár utca stop; Buses 6, 86, 111. T.: 168-9420.

IV. Árpád út 87.
Close to main square of Újpest. Access: Trams 10, 12, 14; Buses 20, 30, 43, 84. T.: 169-3500.

V. Szalay utca 11—13.
Close to Parliament. Access: Second (Red) Metro to Kossuth Lajos tér; Tram 2;
Bus 15; Trolleys 70, 78. T.: 118-8466.
VI. and VII. district together:
VII. Dózsa György út 18-24.
Trams 44, 67, Bus (black) 7. T.: 131-6998.
VIII. Víg utca 36.
Near Rákóczi tér. Access: Trams 4, 6; Bus 12. T.: 134-0380.
IX. Haller utca 7—9.
Access: Tram 24; Bus 33. T.: 134-1560.
X. Harmat utca 6—8.
Near Szent László tér. Access: Trams 13, 28; Buses 62, 68, 85, 185. T.: 147-3760.
XI. Zsombolyai utca 4.
Trams 47, 49. Buses 7, 7A, 41. T.: 166-7833.
XII. Maros utca 3—5.
Close to Moszkva tér. Access: Second (Red) Metro; Trams 18, 59, 61; Buses 12,
21, 39; T.: 155-6766.
XIII. Teve utca 6.
Access: Third (Blue) Metro to Árpád híd. Tram 1; Buses 33, 43, 55, 84, 120, 132.
T.: 120-1640.
XIV. Stefánia út 83.
Access: Trams 44, 67; Bus 7; T.: 183-4380.
XV. Czabán Samu tér 1.
Access: Tram 12; Buses 24, 25, 70, 96, 104, 104A, 177. T.: 169-0922.
XVI. Veres Péter út 101.
Corner of Jókai Mór utca. Access: Kerepesi út HÉV to Mátyásföldi repülőtér;
Buses 45, 46, 92. T.: 252-8455.
XVII. Ferihegyi út 79.
Access: Buses 61, 62, 69, 69A, 80, 97, 98, 161, 162, 198. T.: 127-0699.
XVIII. Üllői út 438.
Near Kossuth tér. Access: Tram 50; Bus 93. T.: 157-1122.
XIX. Ady Endre út 29.
Access: Tram 42. T.: 127-3050.
XX. Török Flóris utca 78—82.
Access: Trams 30, 31, 52; Buses 23, 48, 59, 66, 166. T.: 147-0570.
XXI. Szent Imre tér 23.
The main square in Csepel. Access: Csepel HÉV to Tanácsház tér. Buses 38, 38A,
38B, 48, 51, 52, 59A, 71, 148, 159. T.: 157-2411.
XXII. Városház tér 7.
Access: Trams 9, 47; Buses 3, 14, 58. T.: 226-0022.

All callers at a police station are handed a stamped metal disc by the policeman
at the door; this should be returned on leaving. Losing it inside the building is
not very advisable.

Money and changing money

The Forint (Ft) became the Hungarian currency in August 1946, after a period of extremely high inflation was brought to an end. There is no compulsory amount of money to be exchanged; credit cards and hard currency
are accepted in a growing number of shops. Forints left over may be re-ex-
changed on leaving the country up to a limit of half of the total bought and
to a maximum of $100. (Certificates of exchange are needed.) A total of 400
Ft in denominations of 100 Ft may be taken out of the country.

The rate of exchange is exhibited daily in banks. It is difficult to offer global
advice on how much to change. Hotel rates are close to those of Western
Europe while restaurants and food prices are considerably cheaper. So too
are ticket prices for theatres, cinemas and concerts.

Visitors will no doubt be solicited to change money in the street at a better
rate. Don't! Apart from being illegal, there are a large number of con-men
walking the streets: some pass on forged notes but most simply work a

switch whereby the tourist finds himself with a heap of toilet paper bundled up in genuine notes at either end of the roll.

Money can also be changed at OTP branches — the initials stand for National Savings Bank.

Most of the larger travel agency branches also change money. Every transaction is covered with a print-out, though you may well have to queue during the high season. The service in the hotels is the quickest but the commission charged is higher (usually 1 %).

Banks handle most travellers cheques, for which there is a 2 % charge. Eurocheques may be written in Forints (HUF).

For any problems connected with credit cards turn to IBUSZ Bank at XIV., Ajtósi Dürer sor 10., where they have a credit card section (T.: 252-0333, ask for the **hitelkártya csoport**).

The denominations of notes are brown 5,000 Ft with Count Széchenyi, the early XIXth century aristocrat and reformer, on it, the green 1,000 Ft with Bartók, the composer, the purple 500 Ft with Endre Ady, the poet, the red 100 Ft with Kossuth and the brown 50 Ft with Ferenc Rákóczi II, who led an unsuccessful struggle for independence against the Hapsburgs in the early 18th century. The blue 20 forint note has the picture of György Dózsa, the leader of a XVIth century peasant revolt. You can still see the green tenforint-note, with Sándor Petőfi, the poet.

Coins come in denominations of 20, 10, 5, 2 and 1 Ft. You may find some **fillér** coins in your change, but there is now nothing you can buy for less than 1 Ft.

The reverse of the new 5,000 note is, in its own way, a historical document: in front of the Academy building, the designer has parked a selection of East European made cars.

Newspapers

All newsagents and hotels downtown sell the important foreign papers. You should get hold of a **Budapest Week,** a companion while in town. About a year old, it's edited & published by half a dozen young Americans. It includes a comprehensive listings section and some good columns. My favourite is "Sam Worthington at large". It is beginning to establish itself as an independent voice in Budapest. I should add that the "Best of Budapest" column is mine, and I see it ass an extension of this book.

The New Hungarian Quarterly is a prestige review, notable for its translations of modern short stories and poetry and with a lively review section, through which the more committed reader can obtain insight into the country and its history. Difficult to get, but is well worth the trouble, even to the point of subscribing to it.

See also *Entertainment/Radio and television* for broadcast news.

Telephones, telegrams

Local calls are made with a 5 Ft coin in public call-boxes. In the city centre you are likely to fird the huge, blue, vandal-proof, push-putton sets, imported from South Africa. They communicate to you in English. Between 7 a.m. and 6 p.m. the unit is 3 minutes, outside these hours and at weekends, 6 minutes.

On lifting the receiver wait for a dialling tone (a long single note) then drop a coin in. You will come across phones where you cannot get a coin in because the box is full. You will have to look for another call-box. In many booths you will only find a piece of paper with the following words: "A telefon rongálás miatt nem működik." (The telephone doesn't work because it has been destroyed.) No card phones yet.

Places where there are many public phones located together are the Marx tér subway and behind the Belvárosi Telefonközpont next to the Main Post Office, alongside the church. (On the first floor of the centre are telephone directories from all over the world.)

FOREIGN LANGUAGE INFORMATION T.: 117-2200 (Weekdays from 7 a.m. to 8 p.m.)

Most countries can be directly dialled. Enquiries can be handled in English, French, German and Russian and even in Esperanto.

Telegrams can be phoned through to 02 and some operators can speak German or English. It is safer to write out your telegram in person. Everyone thinks that bigger post offices are quicker because they have more staff — they do, but they are also busier and queues are long. Try the smaller post offices. Since our walks begin at Vörösmarty tér, note the position in a side-street at the northern end of the square:

POST OFFICE 51 V. Dorottya utca 9. T.: 118-6441.

24 HOUR POST OFFICES are located besidĕ two of the rail terminals:

NYUGATI PÁLYAUDVAR (62.) VI. Teréz körút 51—53. T.: 112-1200.

KELETI PÁLYAUDVAR (72.) VIII. Baross tér 11/c. T.: 122-1099.

You will notice that some addresses are given beginning with their district number, in Roman, and some with a four digit post-code in Arabic. For speedier delivery of letters, the postcode should be used. The correct way of addressing an envelope is:

KOVÁCS JÁNOS

BUDAPEST
King Kong utca 6
H-1052

The logic of the post-code is that the H indicates the country, the 1 indicates Budapest, the next two digits the Budapest district and the final digit, the sorting-office's division of the district. The same address would be found under V. King Kong utca 6. in an address list.

Only one other European country has fewer telephones in relation to the population than us — Albania. Waiting for installation literally lasts years. In the old Parliament a deputy made an ironic suggestion that telephone applications should be made inheritable.

Various services are provided by the telephone: they include alarm calls and bedtime stories — in Hungarian, of course. The only service for which you don't need the local dialect is an "A" for tuning: 117-1822.

Weather

In Hungary we celebrate name-days which are usually the feast days of a saint of that name. The name-days of Sándor, József and Benedek fall between March 18th and 21st and, according to the saying, they "bring the warm weather in their bags". Indeed this is usually the time when spring allows us to shed our winter topcoats — a good time for a visit too. A really heavy fall of snow is somewhat rare, but it is followed by slush and filthy piles of frozen snow pushed to the edges of the pavement. Dusk falls early in winter, between 3.30 and 4.30 in the afternoon and the sun is rarely seen. However, the other three seasons make up for this. Stormy days total about 30. Summer is warm, temperatures of 30°C are by no means unusual. Nevertheless raincoats or umbrellas should not be left behind, especially if it rains on Medárd Day (June 8th). Tradition has it that the next 40 days will also bring rain.

Finding Your Way

Tourinform Office — Maps — Orientation — Vantage points — Taxi — Metro (Underground) — Buses — Trams — Trolley buses — Other transport — Car hire

The greatest help for visitors to Budapest is a friendly office just half a minute's walk from the junction of the three underground lines, the

Tourinform office: 117-9800

Right in the heart of the city, at Sütő utca 2, the office is open from 8 a.m. to 8 p.m. seven days a week. You can get virtually all information here in German, English, Russian and French, sometimes even in Italian. The office has the most up-to-date information on transport, accommodation, activities, sights, on everything a tourist might be interested in, and it's all on their computer. They will help you to get accommodation only in certain special cases but they will always help you with the necessary addresses and telephone numbers. They keep a range of travel brochures here as well. There are about 20 people on its changeable, but remarkably experienced staff, who are willing to pass on their own knowledge of the city. They will also do some detectivework to find out where some special goods can be bought. I spent a whole morning in this office checking on various data and was struck by their enthusiasm. In need you can always rely on them.

Maps

In hotels and travel agencies you are given a miniature one-page map — a highly insufficient one. The absolute minimum is the

Budapest: The Inner Part — Budapest belső területe

Under the not very attractive, greenand red cover there is a very practical, easy-to-use map. The back shows the inner city areas in such detail that even the numbers of the buildings are indicated at the corners of the streets. (Scale: 1:7500!) There is a street index including the streets of the maps on both sides.

The Map of Budapest

A map showing the whole city, the districts of the city are in different colours — which is sometimes of help even to a foreign visitor. All tram and bus routes are indicated. Full index. Includes a very well designed inset map of the centre.

Euro City Budapest

A red, spiral-bound booklet, very clearly and cleverly designed, somewhat expensive, though. It must nave been designed far from Budapest — it covers a very large area of Pest, but very little of Buda. Full, easy-to-read index.

The Atlas of Budapest

A 14 x 25.5 cm hard covered book with an attractive cover showing a lamp beside Parliament, this is the map used by taxidrivers. The area of Budapest is shown on 29 separate pages with lots of overlapping parts. A separate detailed map of Margaret Island, the Castle District, the Inner City, the main roads of the city and of the surroundings of the capital. A little large to carry in your pocket but it has a full index. There is a lot of information at the back of the book, which is useful, even though difficult to look through.

Budapest Információs Atlasza

New street names only on the four most detailed sections of the 62 sections of the map. The sections were designed haphazardly — it is never indicated to which section you should refer if the street you are tracking happens to lead off a page. Map section numbers are so tiny you can hardly read them without your eye an inch from the page. To its credit, housing estate blocks are more clearly drawn than on any other map of Budapest, except perhaps the military ones. Half of the spiral-bound book is full of advertisements, which one would think should make it cheaper. It does not.

There are two foreign-produced maps which are usually available in map shops (VI., Bajcsy-Zsilinszky út 37.; VII., Dohány utca 29.) and in the two foreign language bookshops (V., Felszabadulás tér 5. in the arcade called Párisi udvar; V., Váci utca 32.).

Budapest Falk

The usual, beautifully printed map which you can unfold at home and leaf through in the street. It shows clearly the structure of the city. The inset map shows such a small area that it is almost useless. Full street index. Attracts muggers.

Cartographia's Budapest (in a transparent plastic folder)

Basically a brand new, locally edited version of the Falk map, simply printed as a traditional flat map (i.e. you cannot leaf through it). New street names. Separate section details metro system. Full index on the back. Landmark buildings in primitive but useful 3-D drawings. Closest to "best buy".

Budapest Hallwag

A traditional folded map with red cover, printed on grey paper. Indicates car parks. Full street index.

The best buy is without doubt **Budapest: The Inner Part** which also suits best the present book. It is so cheap that you do not hesitate to jot down your notes in it and is very clear, especially its back page. But those who arrive with a **Falk** need have no worries.

Orientation

Now let's lay out a map in front of us and try to keep the structure of the city in mind.

It is very rare that a city has two parts that are so different from one another. The hilly part in the west is Buda; across the river, twice in size and totally flat, is Pest. In the Middle Ages the two were independent, in fact it was just over 100 years ago that they joined with Óbuda to form the modern city. In the 15th century, when Buda was first in its heyday, it was considerably larger and more important than Pest. The number of its inhabitants is estimated to have been about 24,000, whereas Pest had only 4,000. (After the Turks were driven out, towards the end of the 17th century, Buda had about 600 and Pest about 300 inhabitants.)

The Danube, which is strictly speaking the main thoroughfare, divides the capital in two as it flows southwards. At the northern limit of the city the river is almost a kilometre wide, a little further down it encircles two islands. Downriver from Margit (Margaret) Island the Danube narrows considerably. It is at its narrowest at the foot of Gellért Hill, only 230 metres wide. Its average water-level is 96 metres above sea level. The hills of Buda are between 150 and 500 metres in height and, with the exception of Gellért Hill, rise gently. The higher peaks form a semicircle some 8 or so kilometres from the city centre. Even Pest is not as flat as it seems to be, since it rises steadily and the X. district, Kőbánya, is at the same height as Castle Hill. All this explains why we get such a magnificent view of Pest from the vantage points in Buda. Since the rise on the Pest side also forms a semicircle, with some poetic exaggeration, Budapest can be compared to a gigantic amphitheatre, the stage being Castle Hill in Buda. All the hills offer a marvellous view of the city; Budapest could compete with Naples or Rio de

Janeiro in this respect. It is also rare that a large city provides the characteristic landscapes of the whole country. To the west, beyond Buda, there are
the hills and valleys typical of Transdanubia, whereas to the east, not so far
from Pest, behind some small hills the Great Hungarian Plain stretches out
perfectly flat. True, to the north there are mountains, though with the highest
peak at 1,015 metres, they are not very high.

A lot more will be said about the history of the six bridges over the Danube,
and we will also have a close look at them during our walks. Just now, let's
find them on the map. In this book they will always be referred to by their
Hungarian names. (Remember that 'híd' is the Hungarian for 'bridge'.)
There is an island between two of the bridges. The bridge south of the island
forms an obtuse angle in the middle. This is Margit híd. Let's take this as
our starting point, or, as we say in Hungarian, the stove which we always
start out from.

The historic centre of Buda can still be seen today on Castle Hill, from that of
Pest hardly anything has survived. The historic city centre of Pest used to be situated between Lánchíd and Szabadság híd; that is, between the first and the third
bridges south of Margit híd. This is what we call the city centre or downtown
even today; officially it is the southern part of the V. district. The edge of this
district is flanked by the Kiskörút (literally the 'small boulevard'), which consists of József Attila utca, Károly körút, Múzeum körút and Vámház körút.

The main street in the city is Váci utca. Halfway along this street there is
the Pest end of Erzsébet híd, the only modern bridge in the city. On the Buda
side, the road from the bridge turns sharply to the right and starts climbing
steeply. It leads straight onto the motorway to Vienna and to Lake Balaton.
Before the turn of the century, Buda hardly developed at all, while an
enormous amount of construction took place in Pest. From the Pest end of
Margit híd runs a semi-circular avenue, built after the Parisian pattern. This
is called the Nagykörút (literally the 'great boulevard') and reaches the
Danube at both ends, joining Margit híd in the north and Petőfi híd in the
south. This avenue consists of Szent István körút, Teréz körút, Erzsébet
körút, József körút and Ferenc körút. The semicircle continues on the Buda
side, although not quite as regularly as in Pest. Thus the circle is completed
by Irinyi József utca, Karinthy Frigyes út, Villányi út and Mártírok útja, and
there we are again at Margit híd (most of this can be travelled on by the number 6 tram). It is more or less true to say that Budapest was built within this
circle by the turn of the century, with some additional building along main
roads running out of town such as Andrássy út, which ends in Városliget in
the east. The bridge north of Margit híd, Árpád híd, is the beginning of an
outer semicircular ring. Its parts are Róbert Károly körút, Hungária körút
and Könyves Kálmán körút. The latter does not reach the Danube again in
the south, though in a few years' time the semicircle will be completed when
a new bridge, Lágymányosi híd, will be built here, right beside the present
rail bridge, Déli Vasúti Híd. Pest had spread more or less this far by the
beginning of World War II. Beyond the outer semicircular road, there is not
much that would attract a tourist. The semicircular roads are connected by
five major roads that carry traffic from the city towards the suburbs: Váci
út, Andrássy út, Rákóczi út which continues in Kerepesi út, Üllői út and
Soroksári út. Underground lines run all along but the last.

Budapest, with an area of 525 square kilometres, is the home of more than
2 million people, one in every five citizens of this country.

Vantage points

The most famous vantage points, Castle Hill and Gellért Hill, are included
in our first and third walks. Some more places worth visiting are:

The look-out tower on János-hegy (Erzsébet Tower)

The tower is situated at the highest point over the city, on top of the 529 metre
high János-hegy. Four platforms, one above the other, encircle the wall of the

tower. On an average day visitors can see places 75 kilometres away from here in all directions, but on especially clear days some have even seen the High Tatra Mountains which are 215 kilometres away! The best way to get there is by the 190 bus and the chairlift.

The terrace of the restaurant Bellevue, Intercontinental Hotel
(on the bank of the Danube)
The restaurant is on the 10th floor of the hotel.

The look-out tower on József-hegy
(II. Józsefhegyi út)
This small look-out tower, built in brown stone, is neither very well known, nor in very good shape. There is a full view of the city with all the bridges, the Danube Bend and all the Buda hills. The easiest way to get there is by 91 and 191 bus. I hope the neo-nazi graffiti will have gone by the time you get there.

Margit híd—the "elbow"
At the 'elbow' of the bridge, opposite the island, as close to the river as possible.

Martinovics-hegy (at the top of XII. Gaál József út)
From this 259 metre hill there is an unusual view of the city, especially of Castle Hill. In fact the top of the hill is a nature reserve almost directly above the busy Moszkva tér. It is also a favourite rendezvous for dog owners and their dogs. Dusk, when streetlamps are being lit, is an especially pleasant time to walk up here. 15 minutes from Moszkva tér on foot.

Árpád tower
Best to get there by 11 bus and then walk up Látó-hegyi út from the terminus. It is one of the most beautiful spots of the city. The tower echoes folk architecture.

Taxi

Budapest can be explored much more easily by public transport than by car. Since visitors are usually short of time, a word on taxis is in order. As opposed to the grim situation of some years back, nowadays you can get a taxi at any time and in almost every part of the city within minutes and there are also a number of taxi companies waiting for your telephone call. There used to be two state companies only but from the early 1980s anyone who has had a driving licence for over a year and with a car which is less than 6 years old can apply for a taxi-driver's licence.

So nowadays there are Budapest taxis which belong to a state company, and there are private taxis, some of which have formed cooperatives. The cooperative drivers are connected to a central office by radio. In the streets you hail a taxi. It is for hire only if the "TAXI" sign is lit up on top of the car. By phone, you have to give the address, then your full name and telephone number. Almost all the taxi companies take orders in English.

A WORD OF WARNING. Avoid the "hyenas" queueing at hotels and at the railway stations. The worst are those working at the airport. Insist on the meter being turned on — and on paying in forints. At the airport the situation is so bad, you are better off taking the coach or, if you are staying in a downt own hotel, a new hotel feeder bus. At hotels insist on the receptionist ordering a taxi for you. If not, you can be sure of going on a zigzag route, of being overcharged and fooled.

Budataxi: 120-0200
A cooperative of private taxi drivers with about a thousand taxis. They take orders in German or English and will send a non-smoking driver by request.

Citytaxi: 153-3633
Another cooperative of private taxi drivers with about 800 taxis. Orders are taken in German or English as well.

Főtaxi: 122-2222

A state company with long traditions, Főtaxi has 120 taxi ranks in Budapest, over a thousand cars, not all of which have radios. Forty drivers are available as guides for sightseeing tours. (This guide service can be arranged on 113-0242.) The company holds lost property found in their taxis for 5 years.

Gábriel taxi: 155-5000

Two small companies have recently merged, and adopted this name: that of a symbol of one of the insurance companies. It claims to be able to send you drivers with a working knowledge of several European languages. You can even buy an insurance scheme in their cars.

Rádió taxi: 127-1271

A cooperative of taxi drivers with about 600 taxis.

Volántaxi: 166-6666

A state company with about 600 taxis. Orders are taken in English or in German but some of the drivers speak some Russian, French or Italian. They do a 3 hour sightseeing tour.

Taxi drivers in Budapest are generally outgoing and talkative people and actually do circulate the latest news and know about everything. It is worth asking them if they can speak any foreign languages. And remember to check whether the meter is on. You are not supposed to pay if it isn't.

Most locals remember the telephone number of the first and at one time the only (state) taxi company; however most of their best drivers, who used to know the city inside out, have gone private. (Look for the taxi driver's 'badge of honour' on the dashboard: a plaque given for 1/4, 1/2 and 1 million accident-free kilometres.) One of the oldest of taxi driver jokes: A driver drives straight through all the red lights without hesitation. When he arrives at a crossing where the traffic lights are green, he stops immediately. "Can't we go now?" asks the customer, who is shaken up from the ride. "No way", the driver says. "This is when the taxis are coming from the right."

Taxi drivers turned out to be a well organized class when in October 1990, as a protest against unexpected, several times denied, brutal hike of the price of petrol, they blockaded all the bridges and motorways for 3 days. As a consequence of their civil disobedience movement, the price of petrol was liberalized.

Metro (Underground)

Most people travel by underground with a monthly pass. Those who do not have this (or a day ticket) have to buy a tram ticket in the ticket office of the station. You have to say: "Kérek egy villamosjegyet" (Kheh-rekh-edj vil-lah-mawsh-yed-yet). You have to put your yellow tram ticket into the slot of one of the orange ticket-punchers, which will cut off a corner and time-stamp your ticket. You can use this ticket for an hour on one line only; you can interrupt your journey if you wish.

The first underground line, coded yellow, runs between Vörösmarty tér in the city centre (all our walks start from this square) and the terminus at Mexikói út. The journey takes just over 10 minutes. The entrances to most stations and the notices on the walls are copies of the originals; it was only in the 1970s that the old trains were replaced by more modern cars.

On this line there are no punchers on the stations, you should punch them in the cars, just as on board trams or buses.

The second line, coded red, takes passengers from a large housing estate in the east of Pest to the centre of Buda to Moszkva tér and to the Déli Railway Station. The line crosses under the river, between the Parliament and Lánchíd. The journey takes about 20 minutes. In the rush hour, trains run at 2 minute 7 second intervals.

In all stations, there is a rubber strip on the edge of the platform. You may not step on this until the train has stopped in the station. If you do stray onto it, a voice will, with increasing hysteria, start coming over the loudspeakers: "A biztonsági sávot kérem elhagyni". Naturally, most foreign visitors do not understand the warning, which will be repeated until a Hungarian passenger taps the visitor on the shoulder, showing him to step back.

The third line, coded blue, is the newest. It takes 28 minutes to take passengers from an industrial district in the south-east through the downtown area to the northern part of the city. In the rush hour the trains on this line are at an interval of two minutes 20 seconds.

The three lines have a busy junction at Deák tér. Tickets are available at every station, until about 8 p.m. at the regular "pénztár". After that time you can get one in the section called "forgalmi ügyelet." There you can have a look at the not very state of the art black and white monitors the network is followed on.

Underground trains run between 4.30 a.m. to 11.10 p.m.

The 78 night bus serves most of the route of the second underground line, while the 182 night bus follows the route of the third line.

Buses

Most people in Budapest travel by bus, some 40% of all passengers. There are more than 200 bus routes in the capital. All the buses which run on these routes are Hungarian made with automatic gears. They are manufactured at Ikarus, which is the fifth largest bus factory in the world. Perhaps half of them are articulated buses — a landmark of Budapest not less than the double-deckers of London. On busy routes, buses whose number is in red are the fast buses; the route is the same as that of the buses whose number is in black but they stop at far fewer stops. Boarding these buses should be given careful consideration. Bus numbers in red which are also followed by a red letter E (e.g. 73E) are express non-stop services. These buses stop only at the two termini. Most bus stops indicate the stops on the route on a board. Substantially subsidized bus tickets are blue and cost 15 Ft at the moment. After boarding the bus, passengers must look for a punch-machine to validate their tickets. You put your ticket into the slot of the machine upside down and pull the rim of the slot firmly towards you. The machine punches the ticket or, at least, indents it and such tickets are accepted by the Inspectors, who either wear a uniform when getting on the bus or disguise themselves as housewives carrying large shopping bags. In either case an Inspector states: "Kérem a jegyeket ellenőrzésre" (Keh-rem ah yedj-e-ket el-len-owr-zesh-re) i.e. Show me your tickets for checking. Inspectors are often tolerant of confused foreigners. City buses are traditionally blue; advertisements have appeared on them only quite recently but, on the request of the police, are painted only on the side of the buses, so as not to distract other drivers. You can board the bus through any door. The bus stops only if there is someone waiting to get on or to get off. If you wish to get off, you signal to the driver by pushing the button above any of the doors. People do not queue at bus stops: you board the door nearest you when you can.

Trams

There have been trams in Budapest for more than a century, the tracks laid by competing companies, all of which had their trams in their own livery. Until only fifteen years ago there were still various types of trams and people had various sentiments towards certain types. Some trams had an open platform and more adventurous passengers, or those who could not find any room inside the tram, stayed outside. Most Budapest children naturally preferred the platform, which provided the sense of being master of a ship as the tram swayed along.

Nowadays all the trams are yellow and all have doors that close automatically. A few years ago many tram routes were replaced by buses but this trend has now stopped and a new tram line was even laid (the number 1 tram: Thököly út—Lehel út—Árpád híd—Bécsi út). Yellow tram tickets have to be validated in exactly the same way as bus tickets. If the tram is packed, you pass your ticket over to someone beside the punch and they will punch it for you.

Trams start running early in the morning, some as early as 3 a.m. Information on the first and the last trams on a route can be read at every stop. (Utolsó kocsi indul = The last one leaves).

A WORD OF WARNING: You cannot buy tickets on trams or buses. You have to buy them in underground stations or at the busier tobacconists.

Trolley buses

There have been trolley buses in Budapest since 1949 and there are 13 routes at present. Their numbers allegedly start from 70 only because it was on Stalin's 70th birthday that the first line started operating. (A line briefly operated between the wars: it didn't have any number of course). You can travel on trolley buses with tram tickets. The current-collectors of trolley-buses frequently come loose, providing a favourite piece of street-theatre when the driver jumps out of her seat, assembles a long pole, catches the loose current-collector with it and puts it back onto the overhead wire. (Trolley buses and trams are usually driven by women.)

Every bus, tram and trolley stop has a sign which shows when the last vehicle starts from the terminus on that route, usually between 11 and 12 p.m. You can find information on all-night trams and buses which run even after midnight in the chapter "Weekends and Nights." For a visitor the best value is a daily ticket. There are two kinds: a general pass, and a cheaper one that is not valid on buses.

Other transport

Boat traffic is special in Budapest in the sense that it has only a minimal role. It is a pity, as travelling by boat is a real experience even if you just cross the river. There is a longer run which can be covered by boat, information on this is given in the chapter "For Children". There are three points where the boats shuttle between the two banks. Tickets are available from the kiosks on the bank or on the boats themselves. Boat trips start from Vigadó tér on weekday afternoons and evenings; at weekends and on holidays there are excursion boats in the morning too. Call 129-8844 for information.

The cog-wheel railway (Fogaskerekű) began running in 1874 and has since been electrified. It climbs up into the Buda hills, starting from Városmajor near Moszkva tér and reaching Széchenyi-hegy station in 16 minutes. The distance between the two termini is 3.7 kilometres and the difference in height is 327 metres. The trains run from 4.25 a.m. to midnight and bus tickets must be used.

The Pioneer Railway starts from where the cog-wheel train line ends up on the hill. The trains run on an 11 kilometre narrow-gauge track and provide an enchanting trip through the woods. What is special about it is that the line is run by children, naturally with adult helpers in the appropriate positions.

The chair lift runs 8 metres above the hillside from a valley called Zugliget up to the highest peak in the city, the look-out tower on János-hegy. There is a 262 metre difference in height between the two termini and it takes 12 minutes to make the journey. It is in operation between 9.30 a.m. and 4 p.m., in summer between 9 a.m. and 5 p.m. There is no service on the weekday following holidays and Sundays.

The cable car (Sikló) train was re-opened in 1986, entirely reconstructed after damage suffered during the war. It takes visitors from the Buda end of Lánchíd up to Castle Hill in 1 minute. It carries prams and wheelchairs as well. Tickets on the spot.

Car hire

In Hungary anyone between 21 and 70 years of age who has had a driving licence for more than a year can hire a car. The registration number of hired cars begins with XX. As I have never rented a car in Budapest, I have only heard my friends complaining about rented cars, and less than impeccable services. The firms with the better record, in alphabetical order:

Avis
V. Aranykéz utca 4—8., T.: 118-4158. Ladas, Toyotas, Volvos, Mercedeses and other makes. Volvo and Volkswagen vans are also available. 15 % discount when organized by IBUSZ Travel Company.

Contrex
I. Alkotás utca 20—24. T.: 156-3485. And: 1016 Mészáros utca 56/a. T.: 175-2058. BMWs, Golfs, vans, etc.
Reservation: (361) 156-3485.

Budget/Pannónia
I. Krisztina körút 41—43. T.: 156-6333. Ladas, Volkswagens, BMWs, Mitsubishis. Also small buses.

Főtaxi
VII. Kertész utca 24—28. T.: 111-6116. Hire Ladas, Peugeots, Mazdas or BMWs. Weekend reduced rates between Friday noon (12.00) and Monday 9.00 a.m. A wide range of credit cards are accepted.

Hertz
V. Aranykéz utca 4—8. T.: 117-7533 or 117-7788. Ladas, Opel Kadetts, Peugeots, Volvos.

Europcar
IX. Vaskapu u. 16. T.: 133-4783.

Driving

I wouldn't recommend it to anyone who doesn't know the town very well. Not even the occasional emigré who comes back for a visit. A couple of factors make it hell to drive in Budapest.

Cars are more than nine years old on the average, many driven by a two-stroke engine. Pollution is unbearable. Huge oil spots on the sidewalks everywhere cars happen to have parked. Oil is dripping from every conceivable part of the cars.

Cars double, even treble-park. Parking lots, garages are scarce, parking at a meter is too cheap. Fines are impossible to collect. The former regime was strong in politics but the totalitarian state — perhaps it's not common knowledge — was weak in everyday life, unable to enforce its petty rules (traffic, parking, housing, building, etc. regulations). The young, energetic mayor (38), a former dissident, might soon put an end to all that.

Vans load in daylight, at high noon, causing bottlenecks at every corners. Also cars go wrong, including my middle-aged (fivish) beige Lada (registration plate: GO 55-20 — if you dent it, just leave your check under the wipers.)

Traffic manners are non-existent. The bigger (more "Western") car you have, the more aggressive you are.

Women drivers are considered easy game. If you want to see Budapest driving at its best (worst), try the Pest side of the Lánchíd (Chain Bridge). There is only one lane of the three around the square (the middle one) that entitles cars to get onto the bridge. Stand at the corner with a gas mask and watch the Ayrton Senna manoeuvres to get into that lane; within five minutes you are guaranteed a fine display of mutual recrimination when fender meets offender.

So take a taxi. Or take a tram. But above all: walk.

BUDAPEST BESTS :: BUDAPEST BESTS

Péter Lengyel, reclusive novelist, short story writer, a living classic*

My city is that kind of city. (Among the characters who appear in my fiction she is always to be found.) For her visitors can do no better than to move through her. Those of us who were born in here can do no more if we want to have a true relationship with her.

Plan your day. Go up to the Castle's Tárnok utca, there to see her other guests and the petticoated plastic peasants. Perhaps computer technicians working on the black. Turn around whatever strikes you — not the spurious. If it is swarming humanity that you crave, take the underground to Keleti and go into the streets around Garay tér. From there go on to Mátyás tér one morning and see the city that does not show itself to strangers. Slip into her subways, and feast on the bazaars of seven nations. At Marx tér (still named so), Astoria, Batthyány tér. Put your money in your most secure pocket and, madame, if you do not have any such, sew it in somewhere right away. The pickpockets' favourite hunting grounds are Váci utca and Petőfi Sándor utca. They are of world class. Beware of those who offer their services, whether of their bodies or their bank rates — the cost is more usually greater to you than not.

Take a 17 tram from the Buda side of the Margit bridge all the way to Óbuda. Get off at Szépvölgyi út stop. Buy some fruit at the Kispiac on your right (standing now but condemned to destruction). From Lajos utca cross Evező utca, turn into Uszály utca and stroll among the Bauhaus buildings, amid the three-story high trees. From Dereglye utca go to the banks of the Danube. Sit quietly on a bench in Kispark under the tallest of the willow trees and contemplate the 950 years of Uszály utca. Street kids — just like I did — play tig by the garage doors and foot tennis at the top of the street. "Aotó!" they shout and the game stops until the car has passed. It's a fine thing to play in the street.

Return to the market to take a number 6 bus and watch the streetkids on their way to school. Get off at the first stop on the Pest side and walk on up to Szemere utca. You're tired. Sit down at the Kis Itália. I recommend a minestrone followed by a spaghetti milanese with a Roquefort salad, accompanied by beer and topped off by a coffee. For two that's 950 Fts plus a 10 per cent tip. If you think that's cheap, bear in mind the average wage.

*His celebrated masterpiece, "Macskakő" has just been published in English, by Readers International, London.

Accommodation

An office round the clock — Five star hotels — Four star hotels — Three star hotels — Inexpensive hotels — Pensions — Camping sites — Bungalows — Youth hostels — Paying guest service — Rented apartments

The following list is not a critical guide to possibilities: sorry, I have never stayed in a hotel in Budapest.

Budapest has approximately 55,000 beds for visitors, which is by far not enough. They range in price from 300 Ft to 8,000 per person in a double room. (The former is for a paying-guest room, the latter for a room in a five star hotel.)

An office round the clock

IBUSZ Hotel Service
V. Petőfi tér 3. T.: 118-5776. Open 24 hours.
Try to break through the ranks of landlords offering their apartments. You tend to find cheaper supply, greater choice inside.

Five star hotels

All these are new, having been built within the last fifteen years.

Atrium Hyatt
V. Roosevelt tér 2. T.: 138-3000. With 356 rooms, 28 apartments. Town centre.

Duna Intercontinental
V. Apáczai Csere János utca 4. T.: 117-5122. With 340 rooms, apartments. All rooms overlooking the Danube.

Hilton
I. Hess András tér 1—3. T.: 175-1000. 323 rooms. Superb location on Castle Hill, overlooking the Danube. Remains of a XIIIth century convent are built into this fine building. See First Walk for details.

Thermal
XIII. Margitsziget. T.: 132-1100. 205 rooms. On the island in the Danube, the hotel offers a wide range of services.

Four star hotels

Béke Radisson
VI. Teréz körút 43. T.: 132-3300. 246 rooms. Recently modernized hotel on the city's main thoroughfare. Well served by public transport.

Buda Penta
I. Krisztina körút 41—43. T.: 156-6333. 400 rooms. Close to Déli rail terminal in Buda. Rooms have a fine view of Castle Hill.

Flamenco
XI. Tas vezér utca 7. T.: 161-2250. 336 rooms. A lesser known hotel, close to the centre with quiet grounds and an artificial lake. Large indoors tennis facility.

Forum
V. Apáczai Csere János utca 12—14. T.: 117-8088. 408 rooms. On the Danube close to Lánchíd — windows overlook the river.

Gellért

XI. Szent Gellért tér 1. T.: 185-2200. 460 rooms. Traditional grand hotel with windows looking on the most beautiful of the bridges, Gellérthegy and its own large swimming pool.

Helia Thermal

XIII. Kárpát utca 62—64. T.: 129-8650.
Just opposite the middle of Margaret Island, in the immediate vicinity of a pre-fab housing estate. Thus, half the rooms have superb, the other half lousy views. Don't forget to inquire when reserving a room. Water from the springs of the island. Swimming-pool of course. Brand new. Near a station of Metro 3.

Grand Hotel Hungária

VII. Rákóczi út 90. T.: 122-9050. 528 rooms. Ten minutes walk from inner city. Some rooms looking onto Keleti rail terminal. Entirely rebuilt in 1985. Largest hotel in the country. Excellent food in Fiaker Söröző, huge paper aeroplane out of ceramics in the foyer.

Korona

V., Kecskeméti utca 14. T.: 117-4111. An unmistakable, much discussed building on key downtown site, on busy, noisy Kálvin tér (special, treble windowpanes). See Walk Three. It is obviously more pleasant to look out of this building than to look at. 440 rooms, plus small conference facilities on two sides of a street, with a "Bridge of Sighs" between the two parts. Excellent access to all the sights, 3 minute walk from the river. Pleasant atrium enclosing the reception desk.

Nemzeti

VIII. József körút 4. T.: 133-9160.
Traditional splendour of the Grand Boulevard days, when cars didn't yet spoil this crossroads, when the National Theatre, pulled down in 1966, spilled its fashionable crowd to the restaurant of this hotel. 75 rooms, a suite and a conference room. Built over an underground station: Blaha Lujza tér (Line 2).

Novotel

XII. Alkotás utca 63—67. T.: 186-9588. 324 rooms. On road leading to Erzsébet híd, surrounded by hills, completed at the beginning of eighties. Beside it stands the Budapest Convention Centre, also a concert venue.

Olympia

XII. Eötvös út 40. T.: 156-8011. 172 rooms. Located in a favoured walking part of the hills, some 20 minutes from town by car.

Three star hotels

Aero

IX. Ferde utca 1—3. T.: 127-4690. 139 rooms. Ten minutes from centre by Metro on road leading to airport. Built in the sixties. Favoured by truck drivers and smugglers.

Alba

I. Apor Péter utca 3. On the corner of Hunyadi János út. T.: 175-9244.
A 95 room brand new hotel in Buda, at the foot of the Castle hill. No panorama, but couple of stairs. Very good access to main sites.

Astoria

V. Kossuth Lajos utca 19. T.: 117-3411. 128 rooms. Landmark in centre — the crossroad here is named after it — and recently redecorated retaining its old-fashioned style.

Budapest

II. Szilágyi Erzsébet fasor 47. T.: 115-3230. 153 rooms. Unmistakeable landmark, built as a cylinder. Ten minutes from centre in a very pleasant Buda area.

Emke
VII. Akácfa utca 1—3. T.: 122-9230. 70 rooms. Central location which also houses the city's best cabaret, Maxim.

Erzsébet
V. Károlyi Mihály utca 11—15. T.: 138-2111. 123 rooms. Modern hotel in the heart of Pest, close to the Erzsébet híd.

Európa
II. Hárshegyi út 5—7. T.: 176-7122. 163 rooms. Tower block in one of the wooded areas of the Buda hills. About 20 minutes from centre by bus.

Liget
VI. Dózsa György út 106. T.: 111-7050. A singularly pleasant, though not very silent site, opposite the side of the fine arts museum and the Zoo, that is to say, the City Park (Városliget). Brand new. Nice post-modern building with a sauna and gym.

Normafa Hotel
XII. Normafa utca 52—54. T.: 156-5373. A 53-room small establishment, with a swimming pool, a bowling alley and medical service. Lotus Oriental Massage Salon, "with all kinds of services."

Palace Austrotel
VIII. Rákóczi út 43. T.: 113-6000. 93 rooms. An interesting Art Nouveau building on one of Pest's main thoroughfares. Used to be the property and after World War II the headquarters of the Social Democratic Party.

Rege
II. Pálos utca 2. T.: 176-7311. Modern hotel in Buda, about 25 minutes from the center. 164 rooms, 8 suites, a conference room. Swimming pool, gym, beauty parlour, also a major disco.

SAS Club Hotel
XI. Törökbálinti út 51—53. T.: 181-1953. A 42-room small Buda hotel. Swimming-pool, gym, sauna. Pets are welcome. 25 minutes to centre by car.

Stadion
XIV. Ifjúság utca 1—3. T.: 163-1830. 379 rooms. Part of the sports complex around the Népstadion. Very good public transport connections.

Taverna
V. Váci utca 20. T.: 138-4999. 224 rooms. Impossible to be more central and in Pest's main shopping street. Discussed in the First Walk in connection with its postmodern style.

Victoria
I. Bem rakpart 11. T.: 201-8644. Right on the Buda riverbank, overlooking the old Chain Bridge. In fierce legal battle with the city hall: the proprietor just added one more floor, hoping that in these turbulent times it will go unnoticed. It didn't. Brand new.

Volga
XIII. Dózsa György út 65. T.: 129-0200. 308 rooms. System built hotel in northern Pest, 4 Metro stops from town.

Inexpensive

Citadella
XI. Gellérthegy, Citadella sétány. T.: 166-5794. 11 rooms. On the rocky summit of the hill in part of old fortress. See Third Walk.

Expo
X. Albertirsai út 10. T.: 184-2130. 160 rooms. In the grounds of the Budapest International Fair, at the edge of town. Five minutes on foot to racetrack and fifteen by car to centre. Modern building.

Ifjúság
II. Zivatar utca 1—3. T.: 115-4260. 100 rooms. In one of the nicest parts of Buda, Rózsadomb. See Second Walk. About 10 minutes on foot to Margit híd.

Metropol
XII. Rákóczi út 58. T.: 142-1175. 102 rooms. On busiest shopping street in Pest.

Panoráma
XII. Rege út 21. T.: 175-0522. 41 rooms. Styled as a hunting lodge on the summit of Széchenyi hill, which is reached handily by the cogwheel railway. Five acre pine forest around it and about 20 minutes by car to centre.
It was originally called "Golf", later "Vörös Csillag" (Red Star), until recently.

Villa Pax Corporis
XI. Hárs-major utca 1. T.: 162-0190. 11 rooms. On south-east edge of town but good bus service reaches town in 10-15 minutes.

Wien
XI. Budaörsi út 88—90. T.: 166-5400. 110 rooms. On the feeder road for the Balaton and Vienna motorways and ten minutes drive to centre. Good bus connections.

Pensions

With no more than a dozen or two rooms, these are a more modest form of accommodation. Normally with twin bedded rooms, a further bed can be added on request. Hot and cold running water in bathrooms, (in some places) telephone and porter.

Bara Panzió
I. Hegyalja út 34—36. T.: 185-3445. 21 rooms with garage. Halfway to the top of Gellért hill, on the road leading to Vienna.

Cinege Pension
XI. Csipke utca 4. T.: 175-7260. Forty rooms, garage, tennis, sauna. Pets are welcome.

Gyopár Panzió
II. Gyopár utca 8. T.: 116-7890. Seven rooms: family atmosphere.

Korona penzió
XI. Sasadi út 127. T.: 185-1646. 9 rooms. On the hill called Sashegy, not far from the Novotel. Tennis courts quite close and 5 minutes from centre by car.

Marika Panzió
II. Napvirág utca 5. T.: 176-4564. 17 double rooms, with TV and fridge. Parking facilities.

Panoráma Panzió
II. Fullánk utca 7. T.: 176-4718. Only three rooms in a nouvau riche housing estate.

Pál Vendégház Panzió
III. Pálvölgyi köz 15. T.: 188-7099. 8 double rooms, very near the Pálvölgy Dripstone Cave, a first class attraction.

Rozella Panzió
II. Gyöngyvirág utca 21. T.:175-7329. 22 rooms, not all with bathroom. Groups are welcome.

Siesta Villa
II. Madár utca 8/a. T.: 142-1404. Three rooms and a small bar.

Sport penzió
II. Szépjuhászné út 9. No phone. 5 rooms. Pleasantly located in Buda hills. About 25 minutes by car to centre.

Strand penzió
III. Pusztakúti út 3. T.: 167-1999. Open 15 April to 15 October. 18 rooms.

Trió-Jager penzió
XII. Ördögorom út 20/d. T.: 186-5472. 5 rooms. On the western fringe of town near a nature reserve. 30 minutes to centre by car.

Unikum penzió
XII. Bod Péter utca 13. No phone. 5 rooms. Close to Novotel in pleasant location. About 10 minutes to centre by car.

Vadvirág
II. Nagybányai utca 18. T.: 176-4292. Eight rooms, garage, sauna, drink bar.

Camping sites

Camping is only permitted in Hungary on prepared sites. (Margitsziget is especially well-patrolled to enforce this regulation.) For information on camping in Hungary, apply to

MAGYAR CAMPING AND CARAVANNING CLUB
IX. Kálvin tér 9. T.: 118-5259.
KEMPINFORM: 117-7208

Expo Camping
Open 1 July to 31 August. X. Albertirsai út 10. Holds 750. Information: 133-6536. In the International Fair grounds.

Hárshegyi Camping
Open Easter to 20 October. III. Hárshegyi út 5—7. T.: 115-1482. Holds 580. Beside Európa Hotel.

Római fürdő Camping
Open 1 May to 15 October (all year round for caravans). III. Szentendrei út 189. T.: 168-6260. Holds 2,500. Take HÉV to Szentendre and get off at stop of this name. About 25 minutes from centre.

Tündérhegyi (Feeberg) Camping
Open all year. XII. Szilassy út 8. No phone. 50 pitches. Beautiful location, surrounded by nature reserve. About 25 minutes from centre by car.

Tenisz Camping
Open 1 May to 30 September (all year round for caravans). XVI. Csömöri út 222. T.: 163-8505. 50 pitches. Northern limit of Pest, 30 minutes by car to centre.

Zugligeti Niche Camping
Open 1 May to 30 September. XII. Zugligeti út 101. Holds 200. Deep in the Buda hills but 20 minutes to centre by car. Office in old tram.

Bungalows

These are detached chalets in which a family or a maximum of four adults can be housed. Toilet and bathroom either inside or out, depending on the category.

Hárshegyi Bungalows
See above under Camping Sites. 1st Class: 35 units, 2nd Class: 35 units and 3rd Class: 37 units. Bookings through Budapest Tourist, V. Roosevelt tér 5. T.: 117-3555.

Haladás motel Bungalows
Open 1 May to 30 September. IV. Üdülősor 8. T.: 189-1114. 2nd Class: 44 units.
On the Danube in northern Pest. 30 minutes from centre by car.

Római fürdő Camping
See above under Camping Sites. 2nd Class: 9 units, 3rd Class: 50 units. Bookings
can be made through Budapest Tourist. See Hárshegyi above.

Csillaghegyi strand
Open 15 April to 15 October. III. Pusztakúti út 3. T.: 167-1999. 2nd Class: 21
units, 3rd Class: 20 units. On Danube in northern Buda in large wooded strand
whose upper end permits topless bathing.

Youth Hostels

One of the major agencies that handle Youth Hostels is the Express agency.
EXPRESSZ KÖZPONTI IRODA (Main Office). V. Szabadság tér 16.
Second (Red) Metro to Kossuth Lajos tér. T.: 131-7777. Advance booking,
which is strongly recommended, should be made through the above office,
and not through the individual hostels. To book groups — at least 20 weeks
in advance — apply to EXPRESSZ AGENCY H-1395 Budapest, Szabadság tér 16.

There is also a round the clock EXPRESSZ OFFICE in Keleti (Eastern)
Station.

A hosteller arriving without a reservation should go to the above offices,
where, if space is available, a booking will be made.

A WORD OF WARNING: Lots of changes are to be expected on the youth
hostel scene. Always call ahead.

ALL YEAR ROUND:

Hotel Expressz
XII. Beethoven utca 7—9. T.: 175-2528. 120 beds. Equivalent of $6 per night. 20
minutes from centre by bus and metro.

Hotel Ifjúság
II. Zivatar utca 1—3. T.: 115-4260. 380 beds. Equivalent of $10 per night. 15
minutes to centre by bus. Fine view of the Danube.

Csepel Oktatási Központ
XXI. Erdőalja út 12. T.: 134-2522. 80 beds. Equivalent of $3 per night. Near
stadium in industrial quarter and 30 minutes from centre by tram and HÉV.

SUMMER ONLY:

ELTE Kollégium Hostel
XI. Budaörsi út 95—101. T.: 166-7788. Open: 10 July to 22 August. 180 beds.
Equivalent of $5. 20 minutes from centre by bus.

Kandó Kálmán Hostel
III. Bécsi út 104—108. T.: 168-2036. Open: July to 31 August. 400 beds. Equivalent of $4 per night. 20 minutes by bus to centre.

Kertészeti Kollégium Hostel
XI. Szüret utca 2—18. T.: 185-2369. Open: 15 July to 22 August. 180 beds. Equivalent of $4 per night. 20 minutes to centre by bus or tram.

Gyógypedagógiai Hostel
VII. Damjanich utca 41—43. T.: 121-3526. Open: 2 July to 25 August. 400 beds.
Equivalent of $4 per night. 10 minutes by trolley to centre.

Paying guest service

Travel agencies handle bookings for the paying guest service. (Look for **fizetővendég** counter in the office.) The room will be separate from the rest of the flat. Use of bathroom and kitchen is included — though not breakfast. For a stay of less than four days an extra 30% is charged. Usually the arriving guest can only gain entry on the first day after 5 p.m. since the hosts will normally be at work until that time. During the season there is less of a choice available of rooms for paying guests.

Budapest Tourist

V. Roosevelt tér 5. T.: 118-1453; VII Erzsébet körút 41. T.: 142-6521. VIII. Baross tér 3. T.: 133-6587; XII. Déli pályaudvar (Southern Station) T.: 155-7057. Approximately 5,000 rooms on their books.

IBUSZ Hotel Service

V. Petőfi tér 3. T.: 118-5776. (Open 24 hours); IBUSZ in Keleti (Eastern) Station. T.: 142-9572; IBUSZ in Nyugati (Western) Station. T.: 149-1770; IBUSZ Service, V. Felszabadulás tér 5. T.: 118-1120. About 3,000 rooms on their books.

Cooptourist

XI. Bartók Béla út 4. T.: 186-8240; I. Attila utca 107. T.: 175-2937; VI. Bajcsy-Zsilinszky út 17. T.: 131-0992; V. Kossuth Lajos tér 13. T.: 112-1007; Skála Metro Department Store VI. Marx tér 1—2. T.: 112-3621. About 2,500 rooms on their books.

Volántourist

VI. Teréz körút 38. T.: 153-2555. Approximately 1,300 rooms on their books.

Smaller offices also handle rooms but the choice is also much narrower. It is advisable to enquire about the landlord.

Rented apartments

The above agencies also handle holiday and short lettings of apartments, as do a large number of small agencies. However there have been some court rulings which have put the contractual responsibilities of these latter under a cloud.

For visitors on a longer stay and who can speak some Hungarian, the newspaper of classified ads, **Expressz**, should be consulted for its rental columns (**albérlet** in Hungarian).

Weekends and Nights

Food round the clock — Petrol stations at night — Nightlifing — Night transport — Night pharmacies

Budapest empties every Friday evening for the weekend between Spring and Autumn. Families rush off to "Balcsi" — Lake Balaton — or to their "plots". Their summer places are somewhere along the 180 kilometres of the shore of the lake. The more desirable places are on the hills of the northern shore of the lake, which shelves more steeply on this side. Family "plots" are usually somewhere around Budapest and are, quite simply, a small piece of land with a small house built of stone or wood usually with a lovingly cared-for lawn and vegetable garden. For many years, the very high number of "summer houses" has been due to the narrowness of the housing market; people simply have not been able to afford to buy their own home in the greenbelt or on the fringe of Budapest but have wanted to have a sense of space, a garden of their own. Indicatively, the first motorway built here links Budapest not with Austria or Yugoslavia, but with Lake Balaton. During the Sunday evening jam the number of lanes could be doubled without having any noticeable effect. At the weekends then, the tempo of Budapest becomes more relaxing. Buses and trams run less often, far fewer cars take to the streets. Shops are open between 9 a.m. and 1 p.m. on Saturdays, food shops generally until 2 and the larger stores until 3.

Until about three years ago there were no night shops in the town at all. Now there are well over a hundred. There is one in every neighbourhood. Some of the better known ones:

Food round the clock

Montázs
V. Október 6. utca 5.

Éjjel-nappal
II. Szilágyi Erzsébet fasor 13—15.

Metro Centre Supermarket
VII. Dohány utca 22.

Éjjel-nappal
VIII. József körút 26.

Nonstop bolt
V. Irányi utca 5.

Mozaik
V. Múzeum körút 27.
(Closed from Sunday 6 a.m.—Tuesday 6 a.m.).

Ínyenc éjjel-nappal
(only fruit and vegetable)
VI. Oktogon 3.

Delicatesse
VI. Podmaniczky utca 20.

ABC
XII. Orbán tér 17/a.

Éjjel-nappal bolt
XIII. Csanády utca 5.

Éjjel-Nappal Salátabár
XIV. Thököly út 122.

FOOD MARKET ON SUNDAY

XIII. Lehel út, corner of Váci út, at the Lehel tér stop on the Blue (No. 3) Metro. Not packed. A spectacle in itself. From 7 to 11 a.m.

Petrol stations at night

I. Alkotás utca 20—24.
II. Szilágyi Erzsébet fasor 53.
III. Szentendrei út 373.
V. Martinelli tér 8.
VIII. Keleti Railway Station

IX. Könyves Kálmán körút 24.
X. Kőbányai út 55.
XI. Műegyetem rakpart
XIII. Kárpát utca 21.

Nightlifing

Budapest's night-life is not much to write home about. The small number of cabarets almost all advertise in **Pesti Műsor**. (*See ENTERTAIN-MENT/Sources of Information.*) In night clubs someone trying to order a table in Hungarian is often told that there are no tables. Some of the better hotels are reputed to have strikingly attractive unaccompanied young women who are willing to strike up an expensive acquaintanceship with strangers. For hard currency.

The infamous centre of street walkers is around Rákóczi tér.

THE BEST KNOWN NIGHTCLUBS:

Béke Orfeum

In the Béke Hotel, VI. Teréz körút 43. T.: 132-3300. Dinner served between 9 p.m. and 4 a.m. Show starts at 10.45 p.m. Closed Sundays.

Casanova Piano bar

I. Batthyány tér 4. T.: 135-1113. Open 6 p.m. to 4 a.m.
Visited during the Second Walk. Expert barman with a thousand cocktails up his sleeve. Casanova himself is supposed to have stayed at this inn.

Thermal Star Nightclub

In the Thermal Hotel, XIII. Margitsziget. T.: 111-1000. Open: 10 p.m. to 3 a.m.
No more Cuban dancers and Hungarian disco champions.

Horoszkóp

In Hotel Buda Penta, I. Krisztina körút 41—43. T.: 156-6333. Open 10 p.m. to 4 a.m. Show starts at 11 p.m.
Popular with the moneyed young.

Maxim varieté

In Hotel Emke, VII. Akácfa utca 3. T.: 122-7858. Open 8 p.m. to 1 a.m. Shows start at 8 and 11 p.m.
A well designed, modern place. International show. Closed on Sunday.

Moulin Rouge

VI. Nagymező utca 17. T.: 112-4492. Open 8 p.m. to 5 a.m. Show starts at 8.30 p.m. and 11.30 p.m.
Long established, aspires to comparison with its Parisian namesake but has far less money.

Casinos

Budapest Casino

I. Hess András tér 1—3., in the tower of the Hilton Hotel. T.: 175-1001. Open 5 p.m. to 2 a.m. American and French Roulette, Black Jack, video games. The minimum stake is 2 DM, the maximum 1000 DM. You can ask to be banned for a certain period. You can't change your mind next day.

Imperial Casino

V. Szabadsajtó út 5. T.: 118-2374. Open 12 a.m to 5 a.m. The former Belvárosi Café, with recently redesigned neo-art-nouveau décor has been turned into a very ritzy, spacious place. At the Pest side of the Erzsébet-híd (Elizabeth bridge). American and French roulette, Black Jack, Poker, Red Dog. Four cocktail bars, restaurant. You can eat and drink for forints. Admission 10 DM, which is worth two tokens. Minimum stake 2 DM, maximum stake 1000 DM.

Schönbrunn Casino
On a boat anchored at the Pest side of the Chain Bridge (Lánchíd). T.: 138-2016. From April to October. Open 5 p.m. to 2 a.m. American and French roulette, Black Jack and video games. Stakes as above.

Night transport

There is a sign on every stop indicating when the last run commences — generally sometime between 11 p.m. and midnight. Principal routes are serviced by buses and trams even after midnight — the letter "É" after the number of the bus or the tram indicates night service (Éjszaka — Night). See the list of night buses and trams below. The figure in brackets indicates in minutes how often they come.

BUSES
3 Móricz Zsigmond körtér—Nagytétény, Landler Jenő utca. (30-40)
6 Móricz Zsigmond körtér—Moszkva tér. (15)
42 Batthyány tér—Békásmegyer, HÉV terminus. (60)
45 Baross tér—Cinkota, Szabadföld út. (60)
78 Örs vezér tere—Erzsébet híd, Buda side. (10-15)
111 Margit híd, Buda side—Bécsi út. (30)
144 Örs vezér tere—Rákosszentmihály, Csömöri út. (60)
173 Baross tér, Keleti Railway Station—Újpalota, Erdőkerülő utca. (30)
175 Népliget—Jászai Mari tér. (20)
179 Boráros tér—Csepel, HÉV terminus. (40-60)
182 Kőbánya-Kispest, Railway Station—Újpest, Rózsa utca. (20)
C Marx tér, Nyugati (Western) Station—Margitsziget, Zenélő kút. ("The Music Well") (30)

TRAMS
14 Lehel tér—Káposztásmegyer. (20-60)
28 József körút, Népszínház utca—Új köztemető, Kozma utca. (40)
31 Ferenc körút, Mester utca—Pesterzsébet, Pacsirta telep. (40)
49 Moszkva tér—Etele tér, Kelenföld Railway Station. (20)
50 Kispest, Határ út—Pestlőrinc, Béke tér. (20)

Night pharmacies

Pharmacies close at 8 p.m. at the latest but those below provide a night service. When you ring the bell, the duty pharmacist gets up, opens a small window and dispenses the required medicine. All pharmacies display the address of the nearest night pharmacies in the window. ("A legközelebbi éjszakai ügyeletet tartó gyógyszertár".) The list here, therefore, is not complete.

II. Frankel Leó út 22. T.: 115-8290
VI. Teréz körút 41. (On the corner of Szondi utca) T.: 111-4439
VII. Rákóczi út 86. (At Baross tér) T.: 122-9613
XI. Kosztolányi Dezső tér 11. T.: 166-6494
XII. Alkotás utca 1/B. (At Déli Railway Station) T.: 155-4691
XIV. Bosnyák utca 1/A. T.: 183-0391

In Trouble

As in so many other places in this book, your attention is drawn to the number **117-9800, the Tourinform** number, which is in operation between 8 a.m. and 8 p.m. They will be able to understand the problem you are trying to communicate and will be able to give you accurate advice on where you can turn to for help.

Ambulance: 04

If for any reason you cannot get through to this number, ring 111-1666. They can usually handle calls made in English and German. However they recommend that you get someone on the spot to report the incident and its location in Hungarian and only as a last resort try to make the call yourself.

To use this and any other emergency number, you still have to insert a coin into a call-phone. This will be returned to you after the call.

Fire brigade: 05

The alternative number if 05 is unobtainable is 121-6216.

Calls can be dealt with in Russian, speakers of other languages should contact the police. (See below.)

Under Hungarian law, even fires that have been extinguished have to be reported. Otherwise you can't claim on your insurance policies.

Call-boxes return your coin after an 05 call.

Police: 07

If you cannot get through, call 118-0800 or 111-8668.

These numbers are for emergencies only, not for enquiries or for routine police business. Calls can be handled in English, French, German, Polish, Russian and Spanish. For calls in other languages an interpreter can be obtained.

For other police affairs, see *General Information* for a list of the Budapest District Police Stations.

Lost and found

When documents are lost, we can hope that the finder will hand them in. Apply to the Central Lost and Found Office, the
TALÁLT TÁRGYAK KÖZPONTI HIVATALA V. Erzsébet tér 5. T.: 117-4961 (Hungarian only).

For articles lost on public transport, turn to BKV TALÁLT TÁRGYAK OSZTÁLYA VII. Akácfa u. 18. T.: 122-6613 (Hungarian only).

Lost documents should be reported to your embassy, which has a procedure for replacing them. For a list of embassies, consult the one volume, thinner telephone directory — the official and commercial one — under the heading Külképviseletek (foreign representations). Bear in mind that Germany is under Német Szövetségi Köztársaság, Greece under Görög, Italy under Olasz, Poland under Lengyel, USA under Amerikai and Britain under Nagy-Britannia.

Accidents

All cars driven on Hungarian roads must have valid insurance. Those without must obtain it at the frontier.

Any accident involving personal injury must be reported to the police. The ambulance service must also be called: no matter how well the injured person may claim to be, he should not be allowed to leave the scene as this could later lead to complications. **Hungária Biztosító** is the company which handles international business and reciprocal insurance with foreign companies. Information can be obtained from **252-6333** in English, German and some other languages occasionally. The damaged car and its papers must be brought to XIV. Gvadányi utca 69. Claims forms set out in foreign languages are to be filled in here. If you are responsible for a Hungarian motorist's vehicle, you must sign his **betétlap**. This is a special insurance form and your signature on it is legal acknowledgement of responsibility. (Without it no claim can be paid.) This is what you should show to the motorist in question: **Én voltam a hibás. Aláírom a betétlapját.** (It was my fault. I will sign the document.) This procedure might change in the near future. As everything these days.

Help for drivers

If your car breaks down or you are not able to start it, you should call in a "YELLOW ANGEL". Your call will bring help in the form of a yellow Trabant or VW Golf at an agreed time interval. This breakdown service of the AUTÓKLUB is on **169-1831** or **169-3714**. Calls can be understood in English and German and the service is available round the clock. You should state the model, nationality, colour, plate number and the exact location of your car. The dispatcher will give you a time — usually within 30 to 60 minutes — for you to be at your car to await the arrival of the service team.

The Autóklub has reciprocal arrangements with many other European clubs. Foreign motorists belonging to these associations pay exactly the same as Hungarians. A charge is made for any parts that are supplied.

If repairs cannot be made, the car is removed. The Autóklub will assist in finding a garage, which may not be easy. Tourinform has been known to be able to locate a mechanic to do the work on the following day.

Another, private service is BUDASEGÉLY, which, according to some of my friends, is much quicker in answering calls. T.: **188-6201.** (In English, too.) It is somewhat more expensive.

There are an inadequate number of garages servicing Budapest and there can be hiccups in the availability of spare parts. Many motorists would prefer to make use of the state-run garages but you have to phone in to get onto a waiting list and the date you are assigned to bring the car in on may be well into the future. If the Autóklub arranges the repairs for foreign motorists, the wait will be shorter. A large garage may involve you in language communication problems too. It may be better to turn to a smaller service facility.

The **Association of Small Traders** (Kisiparosok Országos Szövetsége) keeps a register of their members and they will gladly pass on the names of reliable and expert mechanics with experience of the marque and, where possible, who can speak a language in common with you. Telephone them at **131-0109** for information (in Hungarian only).

The larger Western makes have their appointed service agents in Budapest. The Yellow Angel numbers can supply information.

"I can't find my car!"

This may not mean that it has been stolen. The police remove cars which ignore no-parking zones and block traffic. Cars are initially taken to Szent

István park and can be taken out further to the suburbs later. The number to contact is **157-2811**, the ÉRDEKLŐDÉS ELSZÁLLÍTOTT JÁRMŰVEK IRÁNT, a formidable name which translates as "INFORMATION ON CARS REMOVED".

Since the Budapest preference is to steal and break into expensive cars rather than cheap ones, care should be taken to lock them and ensure that no articles are left in sight in the interior. Thefts should be reported to the police.

"I don't feel well!"

There are far fewer doctors in private practice than in any other countries in Western Europe or in the US. The **Szakmai útmutató** (professional register) at the end of the two volume grey telephone directory can be consulted but much of the information there is out of date. Many of the embassies hold a list of doctors and dentists speaking the language of their nationals. And the privatization of healthcare is on the immediate agenda. Very soon there will be lots of English-speaking private doctors available.

For cases not requiring urgent treatment, turning to a klinika can be recommended. The word in Hungarian signifies a specialised hospital, where medical students engage in their clinical training and where the senior staff is also engaged in teaching and research. Everyone there can speak at least some English and German. (The Hungarian equivalent of the English clinic is *szakorvosi rendelő*.) Below are listed some *klinikas* a visitor may have need of.

1. Számú Belgyógyászati Klinika (Internist Unit) VIII. Korányi Sándor utca 2/a. T.: 133-0360
II. Számú Belgyógyászati Klinika (Internist Unit) VIII. Szentkirályi utca 46. T.: 113-8688
III. Számú Belgyógyászati Klinika (Internist Unit) XII. Eötvös út 12. T.: 175-4533
I. Számú Sebészeti Klinika (Surgical Unit) VIII. Üllői út 78. T.: 113-5216
I. Számú Gyermekgyógyászati Klinika (Pediatrics Unit) VIII. Bókay János utca 53. T.: 134-3186
II. Számú Gyermekgyógyászati Klinika (Pediatrics Unit) IX. Tűzoltó utca 7—9. T.: 133-1380
Fogpótlástani Klinika (Dental Unit) VIII. Mikszáth Kálmán tér 5. T.: 113-1639
Nőgyógyászati Klinika (Gynecology Unit) VIII. Baross utca 27. T.:133-1130.

Pharmacies

The Hungarian word for a pharmacy, **gyógyszertár**, has little resemblance to its name in other European languages. The loanword from Latin is **patika**. They are listed under this heading on pages 247-248 of the thin telephone directory (companies, services book, in every booth). In town there are some fine old pharmacies wich are highly regarded; simply looking into them seems to have a curative effect. In most chemists, the pharmacists are able to speak English and German. Most of our medicaments bear unknown names to a foreigner but the active agent can often be identified from the name. For headaches, the best known branded drugs are **Algopyrin** and **Quarelin**. For toothache **Demalgon** is given. By an old custom, a jug of water and glasses are laid out on a table in the pharmacy so that medicines can be taken on the spot. Hungarian pharmaceuticals are of good quality and very cheap. Chemists also sell medicinal mineral waters and various cosmetics; although the latter are badly packaged, they are first rate. All types of herbal teas are kept too.

Here too can be had a spray called **Irix**, which is very effective against burns and sunburns — and is used for this purpose in hospitals. It is the concoction of an old man with no background in chemistry whatsoever. He had a long battle with jealous professionals to have his spray registered.

BEAUTIFUL PHARMACIES MENTIONED ABOVE:

Pázmány Péter Patika
V. Egyetem tér 5. T.: 117-5306. Open 8 a.m. to 5 p.m. Closed Saturday and Sunday.

Kígyó Patika
V. Kossuth Lajos utca 2/a. T.: 118-5679. Under the arcade. Open: 8 a.m. to 8 p.m., Saturday closing at 2 p.m., closed Sundays. Advice given in English and German.

Belvárosi Gyógyszertár
V. Martinelli tér 5. T.: 118-2986. Open: 8 a.m. to 5 p.m., Saturday closing at 2 p.m., closed Sundays.

Opera Patika
VI. Andrássy út 26. T.: 153-1753. Open: 8 a.m. to 8 p.m. Closed Saturdays and Sundays.

BUDAPEST BESTS :: BUDAPEST BESTS

Ferenc Bodor, gallery director, coloumnist, a fine judge of pubs

My favourite outings in the city. The strangest and most engaging panorama of the town is to be had by taking the Cogwheel Railway up to the Széchenyi Hill stop and by walking from there along Melinda út to the former Majestic Hotel. From behind the building an unknown metropolis lies before us. And we can marvel at those buildings constructed between the wars, in the functionalist vein, now little run-down and used as housing. It's well worth going in to see the staircases.

The discreet pleasures of the proletariat. From the Pest abuttment of Margit bridge we cross by ferry to the Kék Duna landing stage in Római part, watching the city shrink to the size of a picture postcard. Going across the bulky iron bridge — classified as a monument — keeping an eye on the city to the right, we reach Népsziget ("the people's island") which, in the people's language is also known as Szúnyogsziget — Mosquito Island. From one of the few restaurants with gardens comes the sound of a duo playing 1960s hit tunes; here we whirl one of the locals around the dance area. In another garden it's time to indulge in eating fish from greasy paper with greasy fingers, washing it down with beer from the bottle. At the city end of the island a concrete bridge leads us to the metro station. An outing only recommended for those who enjoy the simple, proletarian pleasures of summer.

A Stroll through Socialist Realist Past. "Socreal" architecture is, in our days, ripe. The finest example of a housing estate in the style is that in the XIVth district, between Nagy Lajos király útja and Kerepesi út. The reliefs over the entry doors and the whispering trees give it the appearance of a film set. The strange, enclosed spaces, the passages and deserted playgrounds are lit by ancient striplight advertisments. Coming out towards Fehér út metro station, brings us to the Mimóza Eszpresszó, where the lonely piano player caters for those who want to dance. Recommended for lovers of *couleur locale* at weekends.

The Most Difficult of Strolls. This is to find the white-haired Chicago-style saxophonist who features at a club that is always changing its name and venue. Latest news is that he is to be found in the Hauer on Rákóczi út.

A Stroll for Men. To the late-closing restaurant beside Divatcsarnok department store, and try to bump into Olga, queen of waitresses, spending one of her numerous days off, and smiling at each other.

A CITY
INHERITED

The Walks

The following five walks try to show visitors all the important sights of the city. My intention is to orient the visitors during the walks and to provide an image in depth of the city.

For short-stay visitors: the first walk

The magnificent view of Gellért Hill and the Parliament is worth adding to this route. The route itself can hardly be made quicker by car: most of it takes us into pedestrian precincts.

For three or four days: the first four walks

These routes include all the important sights. Completing them all, you will have a clear idea of the structure of the city. It is possible to follow part of the routes by car to save time.

An introduction to everyday life: the fifth walk

There are hardly any tourist attractions included in the fifth walk. It helps the visitor to glimpse the life of the districts along the Nagykörút. This walk is, in a way, halfway between the first four walks and the chapter "For the Second Time". It makes no sense to follow this route by car.

The Beginning and the End: Vörösmarty tér

It was not difficult to choose Vörösmarty tér as the starting and finishing point of all our walks. It is right in the heart of the city, near the river, close to the big hotels and to the junction of the three underground lines. The middle of the square has a statue, erected by donations, to the memory of Mihály Vörösmarty (1800—1855), a major figure of romantic poetry. Carved from Carrara marble, it has to be covered in ugly canvas from late autumn until early spring to protect it from cracking. In winter the middle of the square looks as if Christo the land artist had been there.

The poet himself is the centre of the composition, the figures around him are reciting his famous patriotic poem, whose opening line is carved into the pedestal of the statue. ("Be faithful to your land forever, O Hungarians") Below this line the black, round spot contains the most precious of all the donations. A beggar offered the lucky coin he inherited from his mother towards the erecting of the statue. Now you have to peer to find it among all the graffiti.

The dominant building of the square today is, unfortunately, a hideous modern office building. It used to be a German theatre, housing 3,500 people, and later a department store. A photograph of these buildings can be seen on the thick poster-pillar behind the statue (the building with the pediment is the theatre, the department store was the Haas Palace). The present "Palace of Musical Art" was finished in 1971 and reflects the bleak modernism of the 1960s. This building is the home of a symphony orchestra, a record company, a number of editorial offices, the Hungarian PEN Club, etc. It also contains the service area of the Vigadó concert hall which backs onto it. To be fair, it has a good selfservice restaurant for the staff on the second floor. The big window, displaying posters for various concerts, that looks onto the square belongs to the ticket office, which can be entered through the main entrance to the building. It sells tickets for musical events. At least twice a year a long queue of patiently waiting people is formed outside the front door. This is when the office starts selling tickets for various subscription concerts in spring or autumn.

To the right of the ticket office there is a gallery which handles contemporary Hungarian paintings; this is the **Csontváry Terem**, specializing in the more traditional trends.

The shop beside it is the largest record shop in the city, the "Hungaroton Szalon". On the left is the classical music department, on the right everything else. Opposite the classical music counter there are some booths where you can listen to the records you want to buy. The Hungarian classical music catalogue is also available here.

Opposite this modern building there is a Victorian one. Its ground floor is occupied by the **Luxus** department store, which, thanks to the liberalization of imports, begins to regain its primacy in the quality clothing scene, maybe without that posh bias that used to be characteristic of it before the revival of the retail trade (1982—1983). It used to be naff to buy something here. Not anymore.

However, the greatest attraction of the square is the confectioner's **Gerbeaud**, which has been in this building since 1870. Apart from a terrace, the café has three separate shops. The one on the left (entrance from Dorottya utca) is a modern café which does not have too much in common with this long-lasting institution. The main shop opens from the square itself and is always full of tourists.

It is worthwhile walking through all the rooms as the 19th century decoration and furniture is quite remarkable and very varied.

The confectioner's occupies the ground floor of two neighbouring buildings, which is why the rooms are so different. In the vaulted part, if you can find a table near the window, you can hear the trains of the old underground line thundering underneath. In one of the high rooms, with a richly decorated ceiling, there is the portrait of Émile Gerbeaud, the Swiss confectioner who bought the shop in 1884. He started selling his cakes at reduced prices; until that time only the very well-to-do could afford cakes here. He was the one to invent **konyakos meggy**, this Hungarian bonbon speciality which is dark chocolate with a sour cherry inside, matured in cognac. The story goes that he himself smashed the punch cakes whose colour was not what he had prescribed. The service in Gerbeaud is still very polite, although a little impersonal and strikingly slow. The waitresses are too busy and they have no time to chat about the guests in the code-language their old-time counterparts did. The choice, however, is first class, unlike the layout of the menu. Apart from Hungarian specialities, all the classics of Viennese confectionery are available.

Kis-Gerbeaud, the little shop in the right wing of the building, used to be a world apart: an eminent meeting place for the "Gerbeaud-ladies", i.e. old ladies who used to live better lives, wearing a lot of jewellery and waiting for their friends with a cup of coffee with whipped cream on the table. This place has been converted into a cake-shop. You can't sit down any more. You can't even drink a cup of coffee.

The terrace is a good meeting-point, there is always a free table to sit down at. And now: off we go.

Walk one
THE CASTLE AREA AND VÁCI UTCA

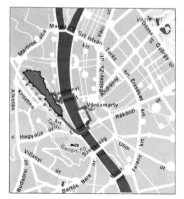

takes us across the river to Buda, looks at some houses from the Middle Ages and at a very old church, which King Mátyás would not recognize, even though he was married there twice. We shall visit the Royal Castle, which, finally, has a proper dome. We cross back to Pest by a modern bridge and plunge in the busy life of the city centre. We shall even visit a charming flowershop.

Time: 7-8 hours

The Promenade — Dunakorzó

When viewed from the river in the second half of the last century, Classicist Pest was hidden behind huge hotels. Here, on the river bank stood the Carlton, the Bristol, the Hungária and the Ritz; they were of the same height as the only building remaining from that period, the one on the corner of Vigadó tér. (Only one of these hotels survived the war.) The space in front of these hotels, the Korzó, became the area popular for promenading when tram tracks were laid along the old walk.

*This row of hotels contained no less than nine cafés, all overlooking the river, all of whose terraces merged into one another. People from everywhere in Budapest, of all walks of life used to stroll here from spring to autumn. This was a tradition that had survived from the time when Pest was a small town, when there was always a place to go to meet friends and to socialize. Pest once had three such promenades but this was the most important and the busiest — having no less than four rows of benches. (The other two were **Váci utca** and **Bástyasétány**, which will be visited later during this walk.) Dunakorzó relaxed the stricter rules: near strangers walked together or even talked to each other. There is a story of a famous bohemian writer who was once accompanied by a young man on the Promenade. They strolled along together chatting. Suddenly the writer was greeted by a passerby. The young man asked who it was. "How on earth should I know?" replied the writer. "I do not even know who you are!"*

Evenings were especially beautiful here with the cafés illuminated. There was music in all of them: the best gipsy and jazz bands played here. At a safe distance from the bright terraces, sat people who used to come here all the way in from the suburbs to listen to the music but who could not afford to sit in a café.

Now that a new row of hotels has been built, the promenade is beginning to come to life again after its apparent death. Although it is mainly tourists who stroll here, slowly the locals seem to be returning as well, especially the older generation. At night, however, sleaze dominates at the lower (Erzsébet-híd) end, with all three sexes offering themselves for sale.

Copies have been made of the old-time 'Buchwald-chairs', although now you do not have to pay 20 fillérs to the 'Buchwald-lady' with the big leather bag when you want to sit down. Hopefully the money will be found to keep the chairs free of rust somehow!

Hotel Forum, Hotel Hyatt 1E, 1F
At the Pest end of Lánchíd

Both hotels were built in the early 1980s, almost at the same time, bringing the Danube bank back to life. They are far too big, they have spoiled the inherent scale of the riverbank. They do not fit here. The austere postmodernism that the Prince of Wales preaches, would have fitted much

1 **A** Luxus Department Store, **B** Gerbeaud confectioner's,
C Vigadó Concert Hall, **D** Thonet House, **E** Hotel Forum,
F Hotel Hyatt, **G** Statue of Ferenc Deák, **H** Lánchíd — Chain Bridge.

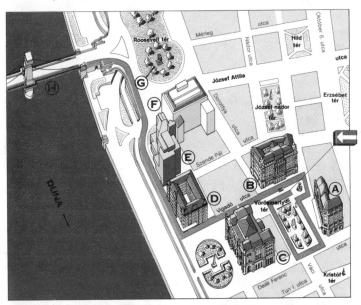

better here. They do not even match the Intercontinental Hotel south of
them. It was built 15 years earlier — a long time, especially for hotel architecture. Not that they were unsuccessful buildings as such. I do not
hold the common Budapest opinion that the Forum, which has 408
rooms, looks like a tape recorder standing on its side; it reflects the afternoon sun in too many angles for that (József Finta, 1981). In the
Forum Hotel the salads of the Grill Bar and, especially, the cakes of the
Viennese Patisserie on the first floor have gained the highest reputation.
The Hyatt, or more correctly, the Atrium Hyatt Hotel has 356 rooms. The
hive-like building reveals its true self from the inside. All its rooms open
onto a circular gallery around a central courtyard, hence the name Atrium
(Lajos Zalaváry, 1982). Over the atrium hangs a replica of the first
Hungarian airplane. The café underneath is one of the most pleasant,
coolest spots in Budapest.
At the entrance of the Forum Hotel is a statue of József Eötvös, a 19th
century writer and politician. The inscription says: "Erected by the Nation"
and the small tablet was added by Hungarian secondary school pupils
and teachers on the occasion of his 100th birthday.

*There was a pontoon bridge over the Danube between springtime and autumn
from the Middle Ages onwards. In winter the river froze up and even carts could
pass across the thick ice. Of course, there were times when a large number of citizens got stuck in Buda when the thaw set in. In the winter of 1800 the entire magis-
tracy of Pest went over to Buda for the wedding of the Austrian governor and were
not able to return to their own city for weeks.*
*It was impossible to build a bridge of wood and stone over a river of this width. In
1820, a young captain of hussars, Count István Széchenyi, had to wait at the bank
of the river for a week while travelling to the funeral of his father. He decided to
found a society for building a bridge. He brought over from England an architect,
William Clark, and a masterbuilder, Adam Clark, who in spite of their names, were
not related to each other. Even the iron was imported from England. After pro-
tracted and fiery debates, Parliament passed the law that even the aristocracy
should pay the toll on the bridge. Some members of the Upper House declared
that they would rather make a two-day detour to the south and cross the river by
ferry, so intent were they on maintaining the noblemen's exemption from tax.*

Lánchíd 1H—2A
Linking Roosevelt tér (Pest) and Clark Ádám tér (Buda)

The bridge was built between 1842—49. The span between the two pillars is 202 metres. The weight of the original structure was 2,000 tons. It was not quite finished when Austrian troops withdrawing to Buda towards the end of the Hungarian War of Independence tried to demolish it. The charges, however, had not been laid properly and no damage was done to the bridge; however the colonel who gave the order to set off the explosive charges was blown to pieces.

"When the bridge was ready, its English creator was so proud of it that he declared he would drown himself if anyone could find any faults in his masterpiece", begins an old anecdote. "So the people came and examined every little part of it, but in vain. They could not find anything wrong with the bridge. Then one day an apprentice cobbler discovered that the lions at the end of the bridge had no tongues. And Clark committed suicide..."

In fact the lions were made later than the bridge itself, and the sculptor gave his word that the lions do have tongues; you can't see them unless you stand directly opposite them. In January 1945 German soldiers were, unfortunately, rather better at preparing demolition charges for bridges. They also pushed the button and dropped the central span into the Danube.

The Tunnel *under Castle Hill was built in 1857; the contemporary Budapest joke was that it was built to have a place which the bridge could be pushed into when it rained.*

Cable Car — Sikló 2F—2G

The almost 100 metre long track, with a slope of 4.8 in 10, was opened for passengers in 1870. The idea was to provide cheap transport for clerks working in the Castle District. It used to be operated with a steam engine. Its successor, completed in 1986, is powered by electricity, although it still uses a cable; with the down car counter-balancing the up car. It runs from 7.30 a.m. to 10 p.m. Closed every other Monday. At the lower terminus there is a long queue in daytime even outside the tourist season, so if you get off the bus here, try the steps of ***Király lépcső***. Castle Hill rises only 50-60 metres above the riverbank, so you can walk to the top in 5 to 10 minutes. If you make a little detour to the left at the first point where paths cross, you can admire the fine proportions of Lánchíd from above the Tunnel and you can also see the cable car from a little bridge over the tracks.

Castle Hill, *this 1.5 kilometre long, flat rock, packed with houses, could be compared to a floating stone galley. At first sight the district may look poor and provin-*

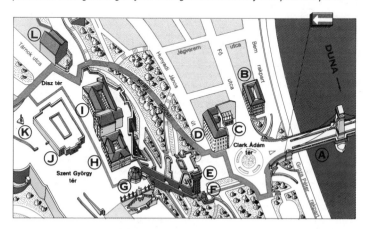

2   **A** Lánchíd — Chain Bridge, **B** 1. Fő utca **C** A café in the remaining part of a block destroyed during the war, **D** Hunyadi János út 1., **E** The entrance of the Tunnel, **F** The lower end of the Cable Car, **G** The upper end of the Cable Car, **H** Sándor Palace, **I** Várszínház — Castle Theatre **J** Ruins of the former Ministry of Defence **K** Statue of a Hussar **L** Batthyány Palace.

cial compared to some old city areas which have remained substantially intact since the Middle Ages in Western Europe. Apart from some stately town houses, most of the buildings are simple plastered burghers' houses. The streets, all of which lead towards the old gates, follow the shape of the hill. It was after an unexpected, devastating Tartar attack in the middle of the 13th century that the first citizens of Buda moved up the hill. Later the Royal Court was established on the southern end of the hill, and with this began the quite lengthy golden age of the district. Buda became one of the most important cities in Europe in the 15th century. The number of its inhabitants is estimated to have been about 8,000. Buda was a melting pot of different nations: "Pontiffs of Italian culture live in the neighbourhood of noblemen used to the rough life of soldiers... Swiss civil ambassadors open their doors to Turkish aristocrats", writes a historian. Buda started to decline under Turkish rule (1541—1686) but the siege and bombardment of 75 days before its liberation of 1686 left it in ruins. Austrian authorities counted 300 inhabitants in the city. Reconstruction began, retaining the outlines of the old streets but building only two-storey houses instead of the three-storey houses of before. A Baroque city came into being, hiding the old ruins behind its thick walls. The Castle became a district of government. It was besieged again in 1849, followed by another reconstruction; later the Hungarian Ministries moved here. Again, after a long period of peace, it was battered into ruin in January 1945, before the eyes of the anguished civilian population. A completely surrounded German force held out here for almost a month. This was the 31st (!) siege of the city.

The last reconstruction lasted for a long time — too long for the Ministries, which moved out allowing museums and student hostels to take their place. The dwelling houses are still used as flats, some of them have just recently been modernized. Cars have recently been banned from the area and now it is only the people who live or work in the area and guests of the Hilton Hotel and taxis that are allowed to drive here. The Castle has become quiet again. According to an architect-writer, the spirit of the city retired here. There is a peacefulness up here that cannot be found anywhere else in Budapest. The Venice Charter, regulating the reconstruction of historic buildings says, "If a building has more architectural layers one over the other, the reconstruction of the remains of some earlier state can be permitted only on condition that by doing so only parts of lesser value should be demolished while the reconstructed part should be of a great historical, archaeologic or aesthetic value..." The whole city of Buda is a good example for such reconstructions. While the rubble was being cleared away after the war, many remains dating from the Middle Ages came to light and these were not walled up afterwards. From what we have left it seems to be certain that the walls were painted in different colours everywhere, with black, white and green patterns. Even the doorways of the ruined houses held surprises. Dozens of niches were discovered among the ruins whose function is still not clear to archaeologists. Some think they were resting places for nightwatchmen, others say they were used as stalls by broadcloth traders. In total, 63 such niches can now be seen in the Castle area. Apart from some other Hungarian towns, they cannot be found anywhere else in Europe. The oldest ones from the 13th century are rounded off a simple round arch, later they were more and more richly decorated. It might have been a kind of competition between the old residents of Buda to have the most beautiful niche.

The great attraction of the Castle district lies so much in the unity of the place and discovering it alone that I was very reluctant to choose a route with the most interesting sights. The tablets on the walls of the buildings give information about them as to the century they were built in (SZ. = century, after a Roman number), or any previous buildings on the site (HELYÉN = on the site of).

The wall of the castle is well preserved almost everywhere. Except for some short sections, you can walk around on the wall. Let's start our walk here and see the part overlooking Buda. If we walk from the gate called Fehérvári kapu to the round bastion nicknamed the Sour Soup Bastion (Savanyúleves Rondella) we are walking where once the promenade of the Buda side was. Nowadays it is fairly quiet.

The Statue of András Hadik 3E

"The most hussar of the Hussars": that was the nickname of this daredevil general of humble origin (1710—1790), the commander of Buda Castle, a favourite of the Empress Maria Theresa. In the pediment there is a glass case with the names of the heroes of the Imperial and Royal 3rd Hussar Regiment. The statue (by György Vastagh Jr.) was unveiled in 1937. Experts say that it is a perfect image of the ideal, effortless, elegant cooperation between horse and rider. If you go very close, you can see that the testicles of the horse are shiny yellow. Generations of students of engineering have come and touched the parts on the morning of difficult exams. It allegedly brings luck.

Úri utca 31.

A three-storey building, its façade is almost completely Gothic. In its present form it was possibly built in the second half of the 15th century, under the reign of King Mátyás, using an even older house. The façade, which had been rebuilt several times, collapsed during World War II, and some medieval remains became visible. This building is the only proof that there used to be three-storey houses in Buda. There was enough of the wallpainting left to reconstruct the original. The function of the five windows in the arched protrusion is unknown. There are niches in the doorway, the staircase was restored in Baroque.

Országház utca 18—20—22.

These three houses, built in the 14th and in the 15th century, can show most of what the Castle district might originally have looked like in the

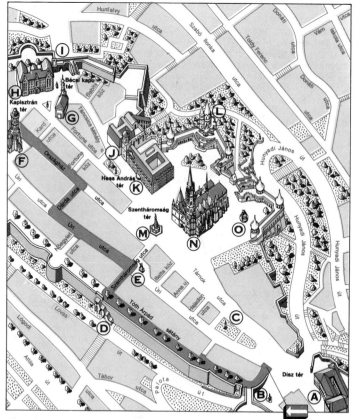

3 A Várszínház — The Castle Theatre, **B** Statue of a Hussar, **C** Memorial to the soldiers of 1848, **D** Way up to Castle Hill, **E** Statue of András Hadik, general of the Hussars, **F** Maria Magdalena Tower, **G** Lutheran Church, **H** National Archives, **I** Vienna Gate, **J** Statue of Pope Innocent XI, **K** Hilton Hotel, **L** Fishermen's Bastion, **M** Holy Trinity Column, **N** Matthias Church, **O** Statue of St Stephen, First King of Hungary.

Middle Ages, and explain why it used to be called **Olasz utca** (Italian Street). On the gate of the house in the middle the initials stand for the name of Johann Nickl, the butcher who had the house rebuilt in 1771. The present tenant does not want to lean out of the window, as was customary in the Middle Ages when the doorbell rang, so he put a rearview mirror on his window and keeps his house locked.

Maria Magdalena Tower — Mária Magdolna torony 3F
On the corner of Országház utca and Kapisztrán tér
This 13th century Franciscan church was the church of worshippers whose mother tongue was Hungarian in the Middle Ages. Under Turkish rule this was the only church which was allowed to remain as a Christian church, all the others being converted into Moslem mosques. The chancel was used by Catholics whereas the nave was Protestant; in the end, it too was converted into a mosque.
The chancel was destroyed in World War II and has not been rebuilt except for one stone window, as a memento.

"The Flying Nun"
On the corner of Országház utca and Petermann bíró utca
Quite a few street names have become protected by the city. Recognized artists were commissioned to make allegorical figures to illustrate them. This one was by Miklós Melocco in 1977.
According to the memorial plate next to the figure the convent of the Order of the Poor Clares was nearby (Országház utca 28.), in which later the Parliament held sessions. The building is now used by the Academy of Sciences. Some more protected street signs are at Dísz tér 8. and at Fortuna utca 4.

Military History Museum — Hadtörténeti Múzeum 4B
I. Tóth Árpád sétány 40.
It was built as an army barracks in the 1830s, with remarkable twin windows. On both sides of the gate some cannonballs can be seen in the wall; these have not been removed, out of respect for the Hungarian army which liberated the castle in the spring of 1849. On the round bastion, cannons from the Turkish era are exhibited, some of which have richly ornamented handles with imitations of a bird's head. On the ground floor of the museum there is an exhibition on the history of small arms with about 2,000 items displayed. On the first-floor level of the staircase there are two large paintings of famous cavalry battles and it is on this floor that the rest of the exhibitions are situated, documenting 19th and 20th century wars. In spite of the photographs, which may be horrifying, the uniforms and the shining armour arouse patriotic feelings.

Tomb of a Turkish Governor
Near the left wing of the museum there is a small tomb with the following inscription in Hungarian and in Turkish: IT WAS NEAR THIS SITE THAT THE LAST GOVERNOR OF THE 143 YEAR LONG TURKISH RULE IN BUDA FELL IN A BATTLE, AT THE AGE OF 70. HE WAS A HEROIC ENEMY. LET HIM REST IN PEACE.

Let's walk back into the centre of the Castle district past a modern building which is in ideal harmony with its surroundings (designed by Csaba Virág, 1979). The giant switches of the sectionalizing centre of the National Electric Supply Board needed the hard rock of the hill — that's why it had to be located here. The next building, the National Archives, does not give rise to such a question. The only question here is why it should be so big (designed by Samu Pecz, 1913—20). Quite a few medieval houses had to be demolished to clear the site.

Vienna Gate — Bécsi Kapu 4D
Bécsi kapu tér was called the "Saturday Market" in the Middle Ages. This was the market at which non-Jewish merchants bought and sold. This is the northern gate of the Castle District on which all the four streets that run the length of the hill converge. From this square it takes only a few

4 **A** Maria Magdalena Tower,
B Military History Museum,
C National Archives, **D** Vienna
Gate, **E** Lutheran Church.

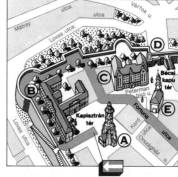

minutes to walk to the busy centre of Buda, Moszkva tér. If a child answers his parents back, they usually scold him by saying "Your mouth is as big as the Vienna Gate".

You can walk up to the top of the gate. Enjoy the panorama of Buda and the view of the relatively new Lutheran church in the square, built at the end of the last century. Parliament can be seen from an unusual angle. To the right of the Gate, next to the bastion wall there is a small grove. This is called the Europe-Grove because the mayors of cities all over in Europe brought and planted rare trees here in 1972. There are 16 types of trees planted here, among them a Turkish hazel, a Japanese cherry and a cherry laurel.

Bécsi kapu tér 7.

The building, which is standing on the site of a medieval house, received its present form in 1807, when a priest and teacher who lived here had it rebuilt. He also commissioned the portraits of Virgil, Cicero, Socrates, Livy, Quintilian and Seneca. There are beautiful gratings on the windows and on the door of a staircase in the gateway. In the first half of this century this was the house of Count Lajos Hatvany, an erudite patron of arts, who spent the major part of the profit of his sugar factory on art patronage. In 1935—36 Thomas Mann was his guest here no less than three times.

Museum of Commerce and Catering Trade — Kereskedelmi és Vendéglátóipari Múzeum

I. Fortuna utca 4.

The present building was built on the foundations of three medieval houses at the very beginning of the 1700s. It later became a hotel and later still an office building.

On the left there are the three rooms used by the Museum of Catering Trades. There is always a strong vanilla smell in these rooms, where all the confectionery instruments of old and recent times can be seen. Among the exhibits is a 40 centimetre long Easter rabbit shaped mould, an icebox with marble inside its lid and the entire furniture and equipment of a small confectioner's in Buda. One of the old attendants still remembers the old shop. "There were not more then five tables in it. At Sunday noon we streamed out of the church and dropped in for cake. Two ladies served the customers. They made their cream cakes in front of our own eyes. All these are gone now", she says. I remarked that small confectioners' are now opening again one after the other but she demurred. "I'm a merchant's daughter myself and my father always told us that you need a whole life to establish yourself. These new ones want to buy a house and a car within four or five years. It is not the same..." On the right you can see the exhibition of the Museum of Commerce; your ticket is valid here as well. Illuminated poster-pillars, whole shopwindows with their displays, and old shares can be seen here. A merchant's desk with piles of documents on it and his open safe are also exhibited.

Red Hedgehog House — Vörös Sün-ház

Hess András tér 3.

This is one of the oldest buildings of the district, its history can be traced back as far as 1390. The red hedgehog above the gate presumably comes from the coat-of-arms of its noble owner. After the Turks were driven out, the house was converted into an inn, where even theatrical performances and balls were held. In the small bookshop to the left an unbelievable amount of books can be found in an artistic mess. Apart from novelties there are some older ones as well, such as foreign language books published several years ago. The enthusiastic manageress does not seem to worry about the extra tax on books kept in the store-room.

Hotel Hilton 5B
Hess András tér 4.

This, the most elegant hotel in Budapest, was completed in 1976 and was given a warm welcome by both architects and experts on historic buildings. (It was designed by Béla Pintér.) At the opening ceremony the President of the Hilton chain called this hotel the most beautiful pearl in the whole string. One side of the hotel is the wall of the old Jesuit cloister built in late rococo style decorated with plaits. The Gothic remains of a Dominican church are enclosed by the modern hotel in such a way that it can be visited. There are open-air opera performances in the Dominican Courtyard in the summer.

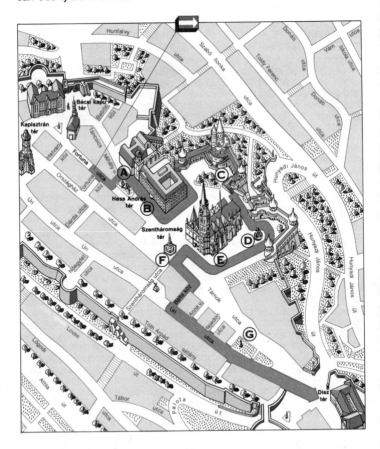

5 A Statue of Pope Innocent XI. B Hilton Hotel, C Fishermen's Bastion, D Statue of Stephen, First King of Hungary, E Matthias Church, F Holy Trinity Column, G Memorial to the Soldiers of 1848/49.

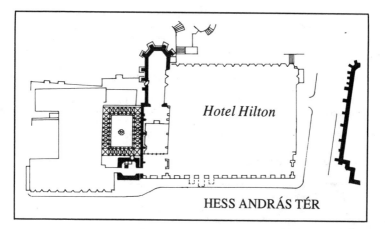

HESS ANDRÁS TÉR

The heavy bulk of the huge building is cleverly broken up. There is a water tower between the two wings of different height (4 and 6 floors) which is built on top of the medieval Miklós Tower. (Inside there is a Casino.) The large glass surfaces reflect the surrounding old buildings. The whole hotel is a non-assertive and functional building.

Fishermen's Bastion — Halászbástya 5C
A look-out terrace, totally unfit for defence purposes, with five round towers and a main tower with several floors. It was built between 1890 and 1905. In the Middle Ages the fishmarket was nearby and this part of the wall was traditionally defended by the Guild of Fishermen, hence the name. We have just seen its replica at the confectionery exhibition, only slightly more sugary than the original. While the tourists are at the dinner table, Halászbástya is visited by teenage couples intent on their first kiss when the musicians have left.

Matthias Church — Mátyás templom 5E
I. Szentháromság tér
The real name of the church is the Church of the Blessed Virgin in Buda, but it is universally known as the Mátyás (or Matthias) Church. Its popular name derives from the fact that the legendary Hungarian king, Mátyás, held both of his weddings here. Originally it was the church of the German burghers. The main eastern gate and the long apse are from the 13th century, the latter built after the French pattern and ends in the 7 sides of a regular polygon. The central part of the church was built around 1400. In Turkish times all the furnishings were removed, all the decorated walls whitewashed. Later it was converted into a Baroque church and the rose window was walled in. As a result of all this, the church in the middle of the last century looked rather miserable. Between 1873 and 1896 Frigyes Schulek restored the church seeking all its original elements when pulling down the walls. His dream was a new building retaining the inherited elements. He added a row of chapels along the north wall. The 80 metre high spire has a ground floor and first floor in rectangular form, above that there is an octagon. Up to the third floor Schulek kept the original tower intact but from there he finished it according to his own plan. It was also at the end of the last century that the walls were repainted on the basis of the fragments found at the time of the restoration.

There is a clash of opinion on the artistic value of the church. Some regard it as a masterpiece of European eclecticism, others that it is no more than overdecorated stage scenery. Both may be true. The building is evidence of all the knowledge the hardworking 19th century had of the Gothic period, but at the same time it is able to arouse emotions immediately, rather like the scenery in a film seen only momentarily. Anyway, the man in the street likes this church a lot.

Holy Trinity Column — Szentháromság szobor 5F
In the middle of Szentháromság tér
The square is at the highest point of Castle Hill. The 14 metre tall monument was erected between 1710 and 1713 by the inhabitants of Buda to fend off another plague epidemic. There was no square in this place in the Middle Ages, only a street less than 10 metres wide.

The Old Town Hall of Buda
I. Szentháromság utca 2.
The first session of the Council was held here in 1710. The statue on the corner of the building represents Pallas Athena, the guardian of towns; it has been there since the end of the 18th century and was made by an Italian immigrant sculptor. (This is a copy.) The various alterations on the building were carried out by half a dozen builders ranging from the masters of Buda to internationally known builders. The prison was in the yard, a place with such a low ceiling that even the shortest could not stand upright.
In 1873, the year of the union of Buda and Pest, the building lost its function. Today it houses the Linguistic Institute of the Academy of Sciences. The tower clock used to strike the quarters. The building is much admired for the fine proportions of its windows and for its inner, forked staircase.

Modern Cornerhouse
I. Szentháromság utca 1—3.
On the site of the buildings destroyed in the war some "neutral" buildings were built after the Italian pattern. Fortunately, before these could grow into an independent group, this trend was abandoned and today only "nonpolluting-modern" buildings, which harmonize with their environment, are permitted. The planning rules are strict: in the case of this corner house, the bulk, the height and even the roof structure were strictly prescribed (György Jánossy, László Laczkovics, 1981). The traditional Hungarian aspect of towns favours vertical directions, lines running upwards. This explains why the architects omitted the third horizontal line under the roof. Thus the pillars in a way repeat the vertical directions of the church opposite, only on a smaller scale. The broken façade follows the medieval site.
(More successful modern buildings in the Castle district: Úri utca 4., 10., 32.; Országház utca 6.; Fortuna utca 16.; Tóth Árpád sétány 30.)

Tárnok utca was the site of the weekly market of the German burghers on Wednesdays. Ordinary bread was sold from tables, black loaves from mats. Until the middle of the 15th century, bread was made without leaven. There was a wide choice of game and fruit. Only live fish were sold, on the second day their tails had to be cut off to show they were not quite fresh. Peaches and grapes could be sold only by special permission from the Council, as these could be used to make alcohol.

The House of a Medieval Warlord
I. Úri utca 19.
The house presumably belonged to an infamous Italian aristocrat of the 15th century. It is here that the only street-bridge has survived, although various documents mention quite a few such bridges. It was rebuilt in its present form in the 1830s. In Turkish times it was occupied by monks. In the courtyard a tomb and a sundial can be seen.

Entrance to the Catacombs — Waxwork Exhibition
I. Úri utca 9.
There is an underground labyrinth, about 10 kilometres in length, under Castle Hill. The caves were joined to one another by the Turks for military

purpose. Today a section of about 1.5 kilometres can be visited. It has recently been occupied by a fancy waxwork exhibition — a memorial of Hungarian history which is both funny and serious. It is a completely private initiative which required a large bank loan; this is why entrance fees are considerably higher than in any museum subsidised by the state.

Guided tours in four languages start out every 10-20 minutes, visitors are not allowed in on their own because of the high risk of getting lost. While waiting for enough people to form a group, you can have a snack in the cave bar. The bustling manager comes from Milan and speaks broken Hungarian; if the group starts out earlier than expected, he follows it to bring the coffee to his guests.

Water always drips in limestone caves and this one is no exception. After heavy rain the dripping resembles a shower in some places. The temperature is 14 Centigrade, the humidity is about 90, so making the figures of wax was out of the question. Instead of wax a plastic mixture was used, but even the textile clothes become mouldy very easily. The show takes the visitor a long way back into the past of Hungary. It starts with the mythological beginnings and finishes in the flourishing Renaissance court of King Mátyás. Nothing of more recent but less glorious times is shown. Only a street sign on the wall reminds us of the time of World War II, when thousands of people lived through the siege in here, and some say that even the postman came down here to deliver their letters for a while.

(The Waxwork Exhibition is closed on Monday.)

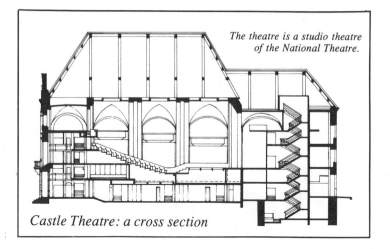

The theatre is a studio theatre of the National Theatre.

Castle Theatre: a cross section

Castle Theatre — Várszínház 6C
I. Színház utca 1—3.

The building itself was completed in 1736, as the church of the Order of Our Lady of Mount Carmel in late Baroque style. In 1784 Joseph II dissolved this order, just as he did all other orders. The monastery was converted into a casino, the church gave place to a theatre. The latter was designed by Farkas Kempelen, the inventor of the famous chess automaton. The theatre had a wooden structure and housed 1,200 people for the performances which were in German. But it was also here that the first play in Hungarian was performed in 1790. The theatre was rebuilt several times but the wooden structure remained until, in 1924, a part of the gallery collapsed. The next performance was not until 1978, when the new theatre, of marble and concrete, but housing only 264 (!) people, was opened. Unfortunately, the dress circle and the foyer are not separated so even the slightest sounds can be heard from outside. And there are always some sounds from outside.

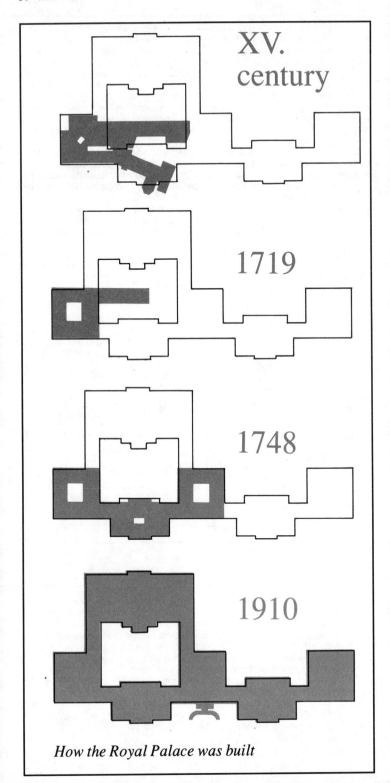

XV. century

1719

1748

1910

How the Royal Palace was built

Opposite Várszínház, there is the last ruin left from the war, the torso of the building that once used to be the four-storey Ministry of Defence. Restoration work on the last but one ruin, the old-time Sándor Palace, is already nearing completion. Before the war, this building used to be the office of the Prime Minister. The latest news is that it is going to house a hotel. Even later news: a museum of modern arts.

Royal Palace — Várpalota 6G—6M

The history of the palace is very much like that of the Mátyás-templom since this is also a mock-historic building with many original parts. However it is even younger than the church: a Royal Palace whose royals have never been residents, only visiting guests.

The first Gothic Palace, which was built and added to for 300 years, has been totally demolished. It was ruined by the Christian army which liberated Buda from the Turkish occupation in 1686. In 1715 work started on a completely new, much smaller Baroque palace. Its ground area was increased by 1779. After some minor reconstruction, the Palace was almost doubled in length at the end of the 19th century (now it is 304 metres long) and a huge wing was added at the back. All the halls on the ground floor could be opened into one another. The neo-Baroque palace, which also had some art-nouveau elements, had a false dome, with an attic underneath. Reconstruction finished in 1904 (by Miklós Ybl and Alajos Hauszmann). At the end of World War II, it was the last redoubt of the besieged German troops. The roof fell in all around and most of the furniture was destroyed. At the end of the 1940s, the experts on historic buildings decided that the palace should not be restored in its original form although it was still possible using the remains and some of the plans. They declared that they wanted to return to an earlier, 18th century form of the palace, but at the same time they wanted to retain the dimensions of the 1904 version. So finally they built a Baroque façade which had never existed before and added a newly designed, though pleasing, real dome to the building. The idea behind all this was that architects of the time saw no value in eclectic architecture, even though this is now considered to be the most valuable feature in the buildings of Budapest.

The inhabitants of the city knew nothing of this dilemma, they were just happy to take possession of the castle step by step again. Nowadays the building houses three large museums and the National Széchényi Library.

The National Széchényi Library in Wing F of the Royal Palace, overlooking Buda.

The Main Reading Room

The Statue of Eugene of Savoy 6K

Opposite the front entrance overlooking the Danube is the bronze equestrian statue of the famous general (József Róna, 1900). It was he who led armies that liberated Buda and began the expulsion of the Turks from Hungary. The commission for the statue was originally given by the town of Zenta; the town however went bankrupt and could not pay the artist. Hauszmann, the architect who directed the final work on the enlargement of the palace, discovered the statue in the artist's studio. He persuaded the Prime Minister to raise funds and buy the statue with the help of the King-Emperor. Franz Joseph was willing to supply the money and, what is more, he ordered this statue should be erected in Buda instead of his own equestrian statue, as had previously been planned. After the restoration of the Palace it was doubtful for a while if a statue of the "Austrian general" could be set up in Buda at all: it was rumoured that he could not abide Hungarians.

National Gallery — Nemzeti Galéria 6H—6J—6L
Royal Palace Wings B—C—D

The art of a small country is always a private affair and this is especially true of the art of the past. Still, those who spend half an hour strolling around the exhibition of **Hungarian Painting in the 19th Century** will not regard it a waste of time. They should not bother about the names with strange spellings and historic figures unknown to them. The paintings in this exhibition, which takes up one floor of the gallery, breathe a definite awareness of life. There is a Hungarian word, *honfibú,* for this feeling but such a word seems to be missing from other languages. It can be best glossed as "patriotic sorrow". There is the grief of generations behind this word, the grief common to all for their ill-fated country. This short Hungarian word is one most frequently used in patriotic poetry. Hungarian painting developed its unique character during the Romantic era. It is a deeply sentimental way of painting, even elements of horror are not foreign to it.

The painting of the late 19th century may seem familiar. Impressionism and other developments became popular in the rapidly developing Budapest, which, like Vienna, was a flourishing intellectual centre. Hungarian painting has one mysterious, lonely genius, three of whose major paintings can be seen on the staircase, on the landing between the second and the third floor in dim, protective light. Kosztka Tivadar Csontváry (1853—1919) first took a pencil in his hand when he was 27. Outside a village chemist's shop, where he was working, an oxcart stopped and he made a sketch of the dozing oxen on the back of a prescription-form. It was then that he started to draw and paint. He sent his first drawings to a famous art-teacher in Budapest and later studied in Rome, Paris and in Munich. During these years he also opened his own chemist's shop to cover his expenses. He was already a well-known artist at the beginning of our century, although he was frequently attacked for his style. He had four exhibitions in his lifetime. After his death, his family had already agreed with some carriers to sell his large canvases for tarpaulin. When suddenly a 24-year-old architect turned up and invested all his inherited money in the paintings.

In 1949 the Hungarian Embassy in Paris exhibited some of his work. When Picasso saw the paintings he asked to be left alone in the room with the doors locked for an hour. At a later exhibition he told Chagall, "There you are, you old master, I bet even you could not paint something like this". Most of Csontváry's paintings can be seen in a museum in the city of Pécs, about 200 kilometres south-west of Budapest.

Mátyás Well — Mátyás-kút 6I

A bronze statue of King Mátyás (Alajos Stróbl, 1904) as a huntsman, in the company of his shield-bearer, his chief huntsman and his Italian chronicler. On the right at the bottom, the beautiful Szép Ilonka can be seen, a girl of low birth who fell in love with the king while he was hunting, not knowing who he was.

6 **A** Batthyány Palace, **B** Ruins of the former Ministry of Defence, **C** Várszínház — Castle Theatre, **D** Sándor Palace, former residence of the Prime Minister, **E** The upper end of the Cable Car, **F** Statue of the legendary Turul bird, **G** Modern History Museum (Royal Palace Wing A), **H** National Gallery (Royal Palace Wing B), **I** Matthias Fountain, **J** National Gallery (Royal Palace Wing C), **K** Statue of Eugene of Savoy, **L** National Gallery (Royal Palace, Wing D), **M** Lions, **N** National Széchényi Library (Royal Palace Wing F), **O** Budapest History Museum (Royal Palace Wing E), **P** Gothic Great Hall, **Q** Palace Gardens, **R** "War Hammer" Tower, **S** Southern Round Bastion, **T** Tower of the "Gate of Sighs".

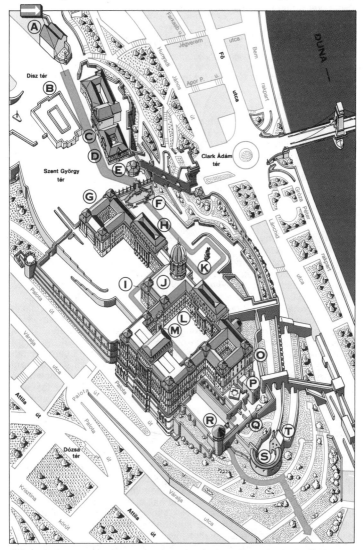

Modern History Museum of the National Museum — Legújabbkori Történeti Múzeum 6G *Royal Palace Wing A*

The Museum used to be called "The Museum of the Working Class Movement" — a singularly fitting function in the Royal Palace. However, its exhibitions always focused on the history of Hungarian civilization. Last year there was a very succesful show on Hungarian Stalinism.

When the totalitarian regime started crumbling, the museologists were busy collecting the leaflets that called for demonstrations. When the small, primitive stencilling machine was solemnly given back to the samizdatniks, the museum wanted to buy it. (It was not for sale.)

This museum is situated in the northern wing of the Palace, so visitors can enjoy the view of Buda and Pest in three different directions. On the ground floor there is a quiet little bookshop, run by an elderly couple, where there is an unbelievable range of books; you may even find some foreign language curiosities, published years ago. The museum also owns one of the largest photo collections in Hungary.

Looking down from the western side of the Palace to the foot of the castle wall, you can see that archaeological excavations are still going on. It was, in a way, made possible by the devastation of the war and by the slow pace of reconstruction work afterwards. Although archaeologists have not found the very first 13th century palace, some very remarkable finds have been made from the Anjou dynasty (14th century). The stripes in the pavement of the courtyard mark the place of previous walls.

Lions

guard the entrance of Oroszlános udvar (The Lion Courtyard — designed by János Fadrusz, 1904). Two of them are trying to discourage visitors with their grim looks; the other two, inside the gate, roar angrily at those brave enough to enter. The huge door in the gateway between the lions leads to a lift which will take you down to the bottom of the wing overlooking Buda, to the stop for the 16 bus.

The entrances to the National Library, the Budapest History Museum and the National Gallery can be found in the courtyard, visitors can get to some of the exhibitions from here as well.

National Széchenyi Library
Royal Palace, Wing F

The inside of the building was restored only in the 1970s. The building itself has two floors above the level of the courtyard, but the ground floor is really the fifth floor of the library. This is the so-called Ybl-wing (added in 1890—1902), which extends over the edge of Castle Hill.

The library has about 2 million books and even more manuscripts, musical scores and newspapers. Among these are the few codices which have not been dispersed from King Mátyás' celebrated library. (These codices are called Corvinas, referring to the Latin name of the King.) There are 70,000 books shelved in the reading rooms. The Large Reading Room, which consists of several smaller rooms, is not very elegant but very spacious, creating ideal working conditions with the view from the windows. It takes natural light from above. The books are taken to and fro by small carriages which run between the glass roof and the mock-ceiling. They are rather noisy if they happen to be working.

Budapest History Museum — Budapesti Történeti Múzeum 6O
Royal Palace, Wing E

A most carefully arranged intimate exhibiton, the 2,000 years of Budapest can be seen here, presenting clear maps and the result of the 40 years of hard work to reconstruct the medieval Gothic palace. After World War II excavations began around and under the ruined Baroque palace on an area of 30 acres. In the basement front hall of the History Museum there is a good plaster model of Castle Hill, shown as if the Palace had been removed from the top. On the surface there are several numbered ditches along which the excavations were led and, in the ditches, copies of what was found there. Above this model there is a graphic realisation, a white drawing on a black ground of the Gothic Palace, as research believes it to have been. Its largest hall was 70 x 17 metres, where even tournaments took place.

Compared to this, the ten or so surviving rooms seem to be humble, but nevertheless fascinating. These are the rooms which were restored from the wonderful palace, once famous all over Europe, praised in the writings of more than 80 travellers and ambassadors. (In the second half of the 15th century, King Mátyás had a larger income than either the English or the French kings.) Almost all of the restored rooms were outside the main building: a cellar, an ice-pit, a cistern, corridors. Only two major sights can be found here: the Gothic Hall, which presumably belonged to the Queen's apartment, and the Crypt. It is in these parts that the "Gothic statues" are exhibited, which, after a very unquiet life, were found in 1974.

Sometime at the beginning of the 15th century, because of some hurriedly started construction work, about 50 stone statues were thrown out into the yard, which was later filled in. The statues probably portrayed the courtiers of the previous king, all dressed in clothes after the French fashion. (They were the playboys of the trecento, as the archaeologist who led the excavations called them.) So it is only these "dumped" statues that remain to us; most of those which were held in high esteem did not survive Turkish rule. The secular statues are in the Gothic Hall (Room 11), the ones on a religious subject are exhibited in the Crypt (Room 16).

From spring until autumn visitors may go out to a small garden which is arranged in a medieval pattern and from there they may also climb the

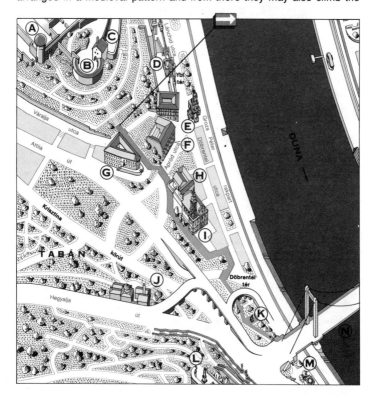

7 **A** "War Hammer" Tower, **B** Southern Round Bastion, **C** Tower of the "Gate of Gasps", **D** Castle Bazaar, **E** Castle Garden Kiosk, a former restaurant, **F** Semmelweis House, Medical History Museum, **G** Deer House, **H** The House of Benedek Virág, an 18th century poet, **I** Tabán Parish Church, **J** Rácz Baths, **K** Statue of Queen Elizabeth, wife of Emperor Francis Joseph I, **L** Statue of St Gellért, **M** Rudas Baths, **N** Elizabeth Bridge.

castle walls. The Southern Courtyard of the Castle may be reached by going through the front hall of the History Museum. From there we leave the courtyard through Ferdinánd Gate.

Deer House — Szarvas-ház 7G
I. Szarvas tér 1.
This triangular café was built at the beginning of the 18th century in late-Rococo style. The signboard can be seen above the gate even today. It houses the Aranyszarvas Restaurant, famous for its game dishes. Until the 1930s the northern slope of Gellért Hill was packed with small, old houses with wine-cellars, later with pubs. This was Tabán, a popular place of entertainment, the "Budapest Grinzing". All of these houses were demolished for hygienic reasons. Szarvas-ház and the yellow building opposite have preserved the atmosphere of the old district.

The Statue of Queen Elizabeth 7K
The whole nation mourned the death of Elizabeth, wife of Franz Joseph, when she was assassinated in 1898. She was a great friend of Hungarians and even spoke our language. This statue originally stood on the other side of the Danube. The people waited for forty years until it was set up again in 1986. Before the war there was another statue on this place; the statue of the ultra-right wing politician whose policies directly led Hungary to allying herself with Nazi Germany. This statue was blown up by communist resistance fighters at the time of the German invasion. A tablet in the ground near the statue of Queen Elizabeth commemorates this.

Elizabeth Bridge — Erzsébet híd 7N—8A
Linking Március 15 tér (Pest) and Döbrentei tér (Buda)
The predecessor of the present bridge was called so in honour of Queen Elizabeth. 53 (!) designs were entered for the competition, which was won by three German engineers. The plan, however, was rejected by the builders as it was a suspension-bridge and Hungarian industry could not produce cable of the required quality. Instead, a chain bridge was built between 1897 and 1903 using huge scaffolding all across the riverbed; but it followed the elegant arch of the prize-winning design. The old bridge reflecting the late eclectic centre of Pest was demolished by the Germans in January 1945. The damage was more serious than that to the other bridges and reconstruction would have cost too much. Its successor is a suspension bridge, designed by a Hungarian engineer (Pál Sávoly, 1964). The two towers were built on the old piers and connected them with the suspension cables, each with 61 separate cables making up the bundle. The new bridge imitates the arch of the old one, which is perhaps why the people of Budapest like it so much. The opening of the bridge was on the afternoon of 21st November 1964 and turned into an impromptu festival despite the drizzle. (Even my piano lesson was cancelled — I could go to see the new bridge, with my teacher.) The new Erzsébet híd has virtually become the symbol of the capital, the first modern yet beautiful attraction of the city. (See *For the Second Time* for some remarkable modern buildings.)

Inner City Parish Church — Belvárosi Plébániatemplom 8B
V. Március 15. tér
Walking across the bridge from Buda, you would not imagine that there is a centaur-church behind the nondescript Baroque façade. From the waist down the church continues in a Gothic chancel.
This is the building with the most eventful history on the Pest side. There are remains here even from the end of the 12th century, and each century has left its mark on the building (it was a mosque in the Turkish times); at the end of the last century, when the original Erzsébet híd was built, there were even plans to demolish it, as it was in the way of construction. Until the 1930s it was surrounded by small shops.

1. *Romanesque Basilica (XIIIth century)*

2. *Gothic "hall church" (XVth century)*

3. *In Turkish times the chancel served as a mosque (XVIIth century)*

4. *Today — one-naved baroque church, since the early (XVIIIth century)* ◗

Phases of building the Inner City Parish Church

Váci utca stretches from Vörösmarty tér to Vámház körút, that is, as far as Szabadság híd, to the south. In the Middle Ages this was the length of Pest. The two parts of the street, to the north and to the south of Erzsébet híd, are very different from one another. The northern part is a pedestrian district, the southern end is traffic-jam prone and busy. According to a monograph on local history, the two parts of the street resemble each other just as little as a famous over-adorned prima donna and her sober, humble housewife sister. When the inhabitants of the city say "Váci utca", they only mean the "over-adorned" part and regard it as a legend. This place had developed into a most fashionable shopping street at the end of the 18th century and was becoming more handsome and richer until World War I. Ten of the present-day buildings witnessed the days when in the mornings the loud gossiping of maidservants, waiting for the horse-pulled rubbish-cart, woke up the tenants in the houses, and reliable "civil servants" in uniform caps, that is, porters, were waiting for orders, standing on the corner all day long. The shops often changed managers, as owners were continuously putting up leasing fees.

Today the same is done by the Municipal Council: the idea behind the ever increasing fees is that only quality shops should be found here. At the beginning of the 1970s, the steam-roller of modernization hit the street: all the shops were given uniform "modern" shopwindow frames, regardless of the style the building itself was built in.

Recent features of the street include the ethnic Hungarian peddlars from Transyl-vania, dubious money-changers and even the wandering Chinese who will write your name in ideograph — the latter has been a great hit with school kids.

Second-hand Bookshop — Antikvárium
V. Váci utca 28.
The plans for this building were made by the architect of the Parliament in 1877. There has been a bookshop in here for about a hundred years. György Lukács, the philosopher who lived nearby, went into the shop every day in the last years of his life to see if they had anything interest-ing for him. He used to have a chat with the manageress who wore spec-tacles and had curly hair that was just beginning to turn grey. She has recently been forced to retire. My friends and I demonstrated against this — in vain.

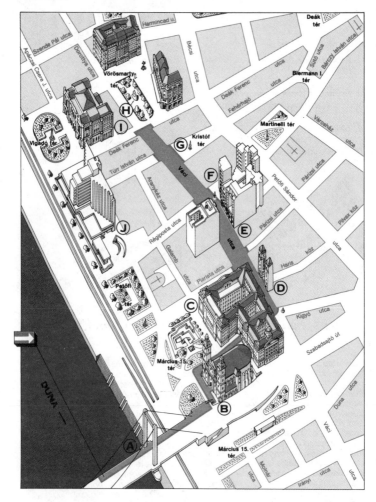

8   **A** Elizabeth Bridge, **B** Inner City Parish Church, **C** Faculty of Arts, Eötvös University, **D** Entrance to Haris köz, **E** Hotel Taverna, **F** Fontana Department Store, **G** Statue of Fischer Rézi, symbol of the fisher-men's guild, **H** Statue of Mihály Vörösmarty, romantic poet, **I** Vigadó concert hall, **J** Hotel Intercontinental.

Haris köz 8D
At the beginning of the century the owner of a piece of land in the neigh-bourhood of Váci utca had the idea of building a street on the site of his old bazaar. So as not to lose his ownership, he closed his street every year for one single day. The last such occasion was in 1949. In that very year the piece of land was nationalised, together with the street.

The Queue at the Adidas Shop
V. Váci utca 24.
Earlier if there was a queue in Budapest it was either bananas sold in wintertime or a famous novelist was dedicating his/her new book. Adidas is an Austrian sportware brand, coined from the name of the owner, Herr Adi Dassler. The permanent interest is due to somewhat lower prices - the wholesale firm acts as a retailer here. But why not open another shop, and another and another - until there is no queue?
Because Adidas (here) operates on a barter basis. And the company could not find more merchandise it is interested in. The moment the forint is convertible, there will be more shops. Until then: the queue. Somewhat shorter than last year. No more East Germans.
Stop press: a second Adidas shop opened in Váci út, in the XIII. district (what a difference!). Will the queue last? Hold the front page! No queue.

Hotel Taverna and Trade Center 8E
V. Váci utca 20. and 19.
It took a long time for post-modernism in architecture to arrive in Hun-gary, although it fits into the eclectic townscape very well. On the small area where the hotel is situated the architect (József Finta, 1985) man-aged to find place for 224 rooms and catering for 600 guests. There is a fast food restaurant, a beer cellar, a confectioner's, a champagne bar, a sweetshop, a bowling club and a sauna. The façade gives the impression of permeable material. According to an architectural magazine "it is exte-rior and interior at the same time". Opposite the hotel the International Trade Centre (József Finta, Gyula Csizmár, 1985) was built on two neigh-bouring lots. The border was where the pillar of the façade can be seen. The passage is open to the public, from which you can look into the pleasant, intimate hall of the building. The figure on the pillar of the fa-çade (Tibor Borbás) waves the flag of trade in his hands.

Taverna Grill Bar
On the ground floor of the hotel
When this fast food restaurant was opened in 1985 it immediately be-came a favourite café and meeting place for teenagers. They spend hours sitting at a table over a hamburger. If any of them has something to do, he leaves — for his chair is well guarded by the others, who say "Sorry, it's taken" to any stranger who tries to sit there. The opening of the McDonald's nearby was a shock to the place. Recovery is somewhat slow.

Philanthia Flower Shop
V. Váci utca 9.
The art nouveau decoration of the shop, although it does not suit the classic façade of the building at all, has miraculously survived various hard times. Its name is the Greek for "the love for flowers".
Maybe one day the chandeliers will go.

The site of Vác Gate
Next to the corner of Váci utca and Türr István utca
The white line on the pavement marks the site where the medieval city wall once stood with its northern gate, Váci kapu. According to contem-porary sources, there used to be a "deadly hustle" around the gates. In 1789 it was quietly pulled down.

This has been a long walk. If you do not want to go back to Gerbeaud again, you can sit in Anna presszó (V. Váci utca 7.) or Muskátli (Váci utca 11/a.). The latter used to be the haunt of young artists who wanted to redeem the world at the very beginning of the 1960s, before the Hungarian beat-movement. They either do not come here any more or have become so conventional that you would not recognize them. The former seems to be haunted by dubious businessmen.

BUDAPEST BESTS :: BUDAPEST BESTS

Peter Doherty, Dubliner, translator, teacher, vistuoso of English

The riverscape, the finest in Europe. The Danube scurries through Vienna, avoiding eye-contact, like an elderly aunt who lives with relatives who are ashamed of her. But she parades through the heart of Budapest in grace and beauty, boldly returning the admiring looks she draws.

There are many vantage points to admire her from. In autumn one of the best is from the Pest side of the Margaret Bridge: Parliament rises from the curve of the river, the Castle lies aslant opposite and Gellért Hill looms over all the gray stillness.

The Budapest markets, better than any calendar. Budapest people, so many still with their roots in the country, have the countryman's appreciation of fresh produce. And follow the progress of the year through their tables.

Fő utca, stories in stone. The history of a city is encompassed in this one street, every building a talkative witness of what is past, passing and to come.

The Katona József Theatre Company, the play's the thing. In particular their productions of the Russian classics in recent seasons.

Jókai Bean Soup, a Hungarian variation on a Central European theme. A supper for a winter evening, to dispel the cold outside, to warm the heart. Like almost all the delights of home cooking, ignored by the luxury restaurants — but can be savoured in those scruffy, over-heated, cheerful places that the locals know and treasure.

The Opera House, comforting grace. Ybl's maginificent building, so lovingly restored, always seems at its best for the Sunday matinées laid on for school children, when it gently calms and comforts its young — and future — audiences.

The Holocaust Memorial by Imre Varga, the poetry of pity. Varga is the creator of some of Budapest's finest modern public sculptures. When near any of them, there are many who steer themselves so as to pass by. This, in the courtyard of the Great Synagogue, thunders in quiet remembrance of Hungarian Jews murdered by Nazism.

Hungarian folk music. An atavistic experience, especially when the solo voice is that of a woman.

Walk two

THE CITY AND THE VÍZIVÁROS AREA

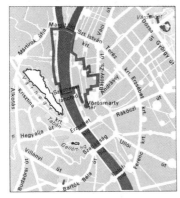

takes us all around the city of Pest, passes at the back of the Parliament. As you can see the whole of the building only from a distance, we shall walk over to Buda, visit a Turkish bath and walk under the chestnut trees lining the river. We shall also look in through some gateways.

Time: about 6 hours, refreshments included.

József nádor tér used to be one of the most attractive squares of the City before the advent of the motor car. It takes its name from Archduke Joseph, the seventh son of Emperor Leopold, who was the governor or palatine (nádor in Hungarian) of Hungary from 1796 for over fifty years. His statue is in the middle of the square. The original plan was that he should face in the opposite direction but, because of the great construction work he originated, it was decided that he should look towards the City. After so much reconstruction some now think he should look the other way.

Gross House
V. József nádor tér 7.
A typical neo-classical block of flats (János Hild, 1824). At the beginning of the last century it housed the famous Blumenstöckl pub where guests could choose from three set meals. The most expensive was 2 Forints, and for that price you could eat as much as you wanted to. (That was a different forint, of course. The present one was introduced in 1946, and currently it loses about 30-35 % of its value a year.)
Anyone who told a bad joke or argued loudly had to pay a fine into the Saracen head money-box.

Derra House 9G
V. József Attila utca 16.
This used to be a beer-merchant's house (József Hild, 1838—39), the second three-storey house in Pest. In the courtyard you can still see the entrance to the stables. Like many of the front gates in the City, this one also has a stone ball on each side to prevent carts from bumping into the building. (In the suburbs of Pest you can occasionally see horses even today. By law they cannot come further into town than the outer ring road.) The expression "to beat somebody like the sodamerchant beats his horse" is still used, even in the inner city area.

Október 6. utca 3. 9H
The house with the passage-way was built in 1844—45 and has recently been restored. Together with the two small spiral staircases hidden at the sides, it has four staircases. The statue in the garden honours Béla Czóbel, an impressionist painter.

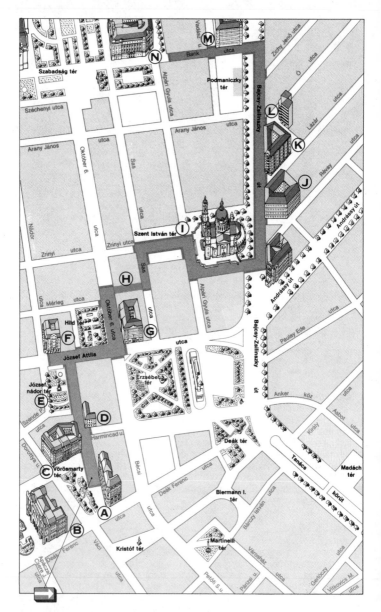

9 **A** Luxus Department Store, **B** Vigadó Concert Hall, **C** Gerbeaud, **D** József nádor tér 7., **E** Statue of József nádor, Hapsburg Regent, **F** József Attila utca 16., **G** Derra House, **H** Október 6. utca 3., **I** St Stephen's Church, the "Basilica", **J** Bajcsy-Zsilinszky út 17., **K** Bajcsy-Zsilinszky út 19/a, 19/b, **L** Bajcsy-Zsilinszky út 19/c, **M** Bajcsy-Zsilinszky út 34., **N** Hungarian National Bank.

The "Basilica" 9l
V. Szent István tér

The largest church in the city, holding 8,500 people. The dome is 96 metres high. The name may be misleading since, strictly speaking, basilica means a church of a totally different shape. (It has the rank of "basilica minor", hence the name.) It took so long to build it that it is remembered even in the saying "I'll settle up when the Basilica is finished."

The work on the building started in 1851, when Pest was still a small town. The designer, József Hild, died soon afterwards, then Miklós Ybl, the architect who later designed the Opera House, directed the construction. On examining the original plan, he was astonished to find cracks in the walls. Ybl had a fence built around the half-ready church and set watchmen to guard it. Eight days later, in January 1868, the dome fell in. You can imagine the lack of traffic, since the disaster, which happened in broad daylight, had only one eye-witness: a baker's apprentice. In the newspapers, he gave an eloquent account of what he had seen: "I can see that small clumps of stone start rolling down from the tip of the dome. As they are falling slowly downwards, tumbling in the air, a kind of groan-like sigh permeates the air, and the whole dome is starting to tilt. First in

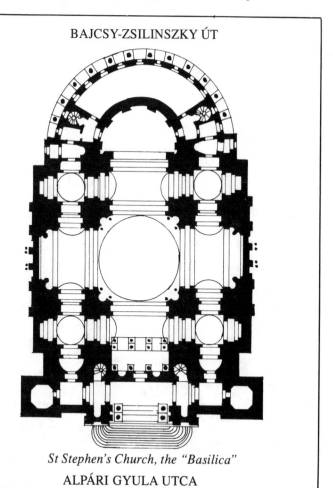

BAJCSY-ZSILINSZKY ÚT

St Stephen's Church, the "Basilica"

ALPÁRI GYULA UTCA

absolute silence, then with a horrible roar." More than 300 windows were broken in the area. Inferior building materials were reported to have been used.

Then Ybl made new plans and work started again, almost from the beginnings. But he did not live to see the church finished, dying in 1891.

The Basilica was finished by József Kauser in 1906. Franz Joseph gave a speech at the opening ceremony and, it was rumoured, cast suspicious glances at the dome, which is 22 metres in diameter.

The general opinion is that the Basilica has insufficient light. Only mysterious patches and beams of light bring some life into the statues and ornaments at some lucky times of the day. Behind the main altar the statue of King St Stephen I can be seen (Alajos Stróbl), who is the patron saint of the church. There is another statue of him above the main entrance. The mosaics were designed by Hungarian painters and made in Venice. The ground plan of the neo-Renaissance basilica shows a Greek cross. The main façade is not on the busy Bajcsy-Zsilinszky út; it is on the opposite side. The Basilica is a rare example in city planning in the sense that during the time it was built the structure of the city around it changed. When the second plan was made there was already a need for a "second façade" and Ybl cleverly solved this problem. The walls outside the chancel are richly decorated with an elegant Ionic colonnade and with statues of the 12 apostles.

The Holy Right Hand (Szent Jobb) the alleged right hand of (St) Stephen I (1000-1038). This is the most revered relic of the Hungarian Catholic Church. Though there is a gap in the story of the relic, between the death of the king and the first time the relic was claimed, it is relatively short. Historians don't say it's altogether impossible. It can be visited in a chapel to the left of the main altar. You drop a 20 forint coin in the slot and the relic is lit up. If not right away, the guard knocks at the case, and behold, it does.

Under the church there is a large cellar, it was here that many of the important documents of the city and some valuable art treasures survived the last war. The windows of the church overlook Bajcsy-Zsilinszky út. In the second half of the 1960s some unknown elements painted here with large letters: LENIN, MAO, CHE. Since they did not have paint sprays, they must have had to carry buckets of paint to the spot. You can still see the fading graffiti on the wall. (After he read these lines, a friend of mine, a well-known aesthetician called me and claimed responsibility.)

The chancel is worth looking at from the other side of the road as well, for example from the pastry shop. These few metres do make a difference. Or you can look at the Basilica again from an unusual angle, sitting on the terrace of Dóm presszó.

A Nice Block of Flats 9J—K—L

Bajcsy-Zsilinszky út 19/a, 19/b, 19/c.

In the 1930s modern architecture made a breakthrough in Hungary and much building started everywhere in the city. The optimum use of space was combined with plans for healthy, cleverly arranged flats. This block is an example of how well this style could be fitted into the 50-100 years older surroundings (Jenő Schmitterer, 1940). All three gateways have their own surprises. The 19/a building has lead glass windows on the ground floor and interesting lamps on the capitals of the columns. The gateway of the 19/b block has pleasant proportions, and, what is more, on the ceiling behind the entrance the present tenants have managed to solve the problem of squaring the circle. The third block is in the best state at the moment. This one has the best preserved lighting, and even the mosaic glass has survived, reflecting the atmosphere of old times. All the tranquility and elegance of this style is summarized in the stone giant, resting on the edge of the roof of the 19/b block. It can only be seen from a distance so do not forget to look back!

Podmaniczky tér *was once occupied by houses but cleared by the war. The square, housing a station on the Third (Blue) Metro Line, is becoming a new gate* to the City It was named after Baron Frigyes Podmaniczky, who was a leading figure in city planning in Budapest. The City Protection Association requested that the square be named in his honour.

Hungarian National Bank 10B
V. Szabadság tér 8—9.
The stately bulk of the National Bank shows an eclecticism already being made lighter by the art nouveau style (Ignác Alpár, 1901). Between the first-floor windows a fine relief shows people working; from peasants through mint workers to a tycoon just signing a bill. The inside of the building can no longer be visited.

Szabadság tér (Liberty Square) is a hidden treasure of Budapest — it is not along any major streets or boulevards. You just bump into it, as if by chance. Out of the eclectic palaces one art nouveau block sticks out: the American Embassy. That's where Cardinal Mindszenthy spent the years from 1956 to 1975. The archbishop was imprisoned in the fifties (needless to say, under false charges). In 1956 he was liberated, but when Budapest was invaded, he couldn't leave for the West. There is the statue of a stocky man in front of the building: that of the US General Harry Hill Bandholtz. As an officer of the entente peace-keeping force in 1919, he saved the treasures of the National Museum. He went to the building and "sealed" the doors — with the only (paper) seals he had at hand: censorship seals. These had the US coat of arms, so they kept Rumanian soldiers from looting the building.

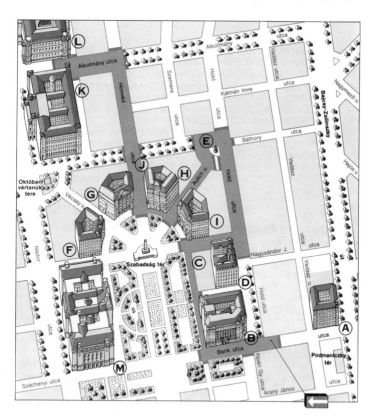

10 A Bajcsy-Zsilinszky út 34., **B** Hungarian National Bank, **C** American Embassy, **D** Post Office Savings Bank, **E** Batthyány Eternal Flame, **F—G—H—I** Office Blocks, **J** Honvéd utca 3., **K** Ministry of Agriculture, **L** Ethnographical Museum, **M** Hungarian Television (former Stock Exchange).

Post-Office Savings Bank — Postatakarék 10D
V. Hold utca 4.
"Hungarian style has not a past but it does have a future", said Ödön Lechner, one of the most influential architects of Hungarian art nouveau (1845—1914). When he finished this building (1901) it got a warm welcome from his contemporaries, who saw the synthesis of a simple way of handling space and Hungarian folk ornamentation. The beautiful simplicity of the main walls give no indication how restlessly alive the building is inside and at the roof. You can walk into the main hall, where the cashiers work, in office hours, between 8 a.m. and 1 p.m. on weekdays. Torn banknotes are exchanged here for new ones. (By tradition you get back the same percentage of the value of the percentage of its undamaged surface.) Photographs may be taken only with special permission in the whole building. Although you cannot go in, it is worth looking into one of the staircases.
The greatest attraction of the building is undoubtedly its roof of green, yellow, blue and brown hexagonal tiles, hidden behind the yellow majolica waves, which crown the top of the main walls. The roof is full of flowers familiar from folk embroidery, angel-wings, Turkish turbans and scaly dragon-tails. This, however, can only be suspected, even from further down in Nagy-Sándor utca or opposite the market.
At the time of the burial of the architect, all organized building workers stopped work for five minutes.

Batthyány Eternal Flame — Batthyány örökmécses 10E
At the convergence of V. Báthory utca, Aulich utca and Hold utca
On 6th October 1849, shortly after the defeat of the Hungarian insurrection against Hapsburg rule, 13 Hungarian generals were executed in a country town and the Prime Minister of the Revolutionary Government, Count Lajos Batthyány himself, was shot on this site. The present square was then the courtyard of a huge army barracks.
Batthyány is remembered by the permanent flame inside a red cup. (Móric Pogány, 1926.) Some years ago people living nearby were shocked to see that the flame had gone out and wrote indignant letters to a newspaper. The permanent flame has quietly been lit again.
In the dying years of the old régime, police broke up commemorations here with force.

An Art Nouveau Block of Flats 10J
V. Honvéd utca 3.
There is a bus stop outside the building but nobody is tempted to look up while waiting for the bus, as the ground floor is so unattractive, totally spoilt by reconstruction. The building has four floors, the long open corridor on the "fifth floor" opens directly from the loft. Above that starts the two-storey high, steep roof. From the other side of the street you can see all the majolica ornaments intact, only the plasterwork has been damaged. Here it is not enough to look into the gateway, you have to climb up at least as far as the first floor. Notice the tiles on the floor, the ear-shaped painted windows, the doorframes and the brass peepholes in the doors (Emil Vidor, 1904).
The family of the one-time owner of the block still lives on the first floor, the "piano nobile". Though in 1949 no compensation was paid, the family has just been offered the possibility to buy the flat from the state...

*This part of the Fifth District, called **Lipótváros** (after Leopold, an Austrian Archduke) in daytime swarms with people; in the evenings it is completely dead. Its main street, the broad, elegant Alkotmány utca, does not really lead anywhere and so has little traffic. But this is the route taken by all important guests when visiting the Parliament.*

11   **A** Ministry of Agriculture, **B** Ethnographical Museum, **C** Statue of Lajos Kossuth, **D** Statue of Ferenc Rákóczi II, **E** Houses of Parliament, **F** Kossuth Lajos tér 13—15., **G** Statue of Mihály Károlyi, **H** Szalai Confectioner's, **I** A block inhabited by American diplomats, **J** Playground, **K** "White House"

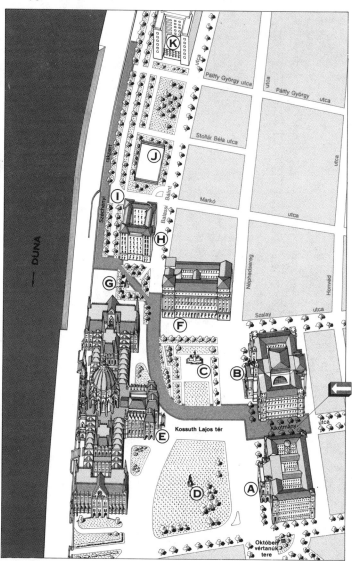

Houses of Parliament — Országház 11E
V. Kossuth Lajos tér
"No more than a Turkish bath crossed with a Gothic chapel", ridiculed Gyula Illyés, a recently deceased poet. Work on the Parliament started in 1885 and an average of a thousand people worked on it for 17 years. Its designer, Imre Steindl (1839—1902), was originally an apprentice stone-carver, then studied architecture in Vienna and Budapest. He was

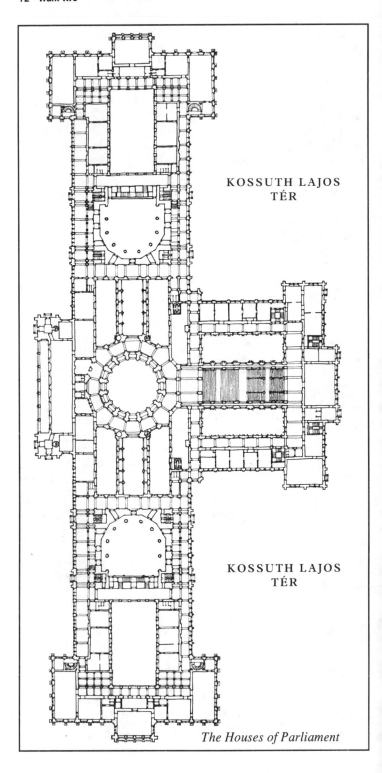

KOSSUTH LAJOS
TÉR

KOSSUTH LAJOS
TÉR

The Houses of Parliament

44 when this work started. When the building was nearing completion he was already so ill that he could direct the work only from a chair carried to the spot. He died just some weeks before the building was put into use. Parliament is 268 metres long and 118 metres wide. The spire is 96 meters above ground.

There are 691 rooms in the building, the length of all the stairs together is about 20 kilometres. It readily reveals its structure, especially if seen from the river. To the right and to the left of the central hall under the dome, the council chambers of what were formerly the Commons and the Lords are situated. "I did not want to establish a new style with the new Parliament because I could not build such a monumental building, which should be in use for centuries, with ephemeral details. My desire was to combine this splendid medieval style with national and personal features, humbly and carefully as is required by arts...", the architect said in his inaugural address at the Academy of Sciences. He must have meant Gothic when speaking of "style" even though the ground plan of the building shows Renaissance features and the way space is organized inside is very often Baroque in character. It is thus a summary of Hungarian eclecticism.

Kálmán Mikszáth the novelist (See *For the Second Time / Twelve streets and squares*), who went to the first session in the building as an MP, summarized his impressions by declaring "True, it's dazzling, still gaudy". The writer said this about the inside of the building, the outside was covered with white, Hungarian limestone. As it turned out, the stone was not hard enough. Renovations began as early as 1925 and have not finished yet.

There are guided tours of the Parliament for an entrance fee. Only for groups — whenever there is no plenary session. Groups have to register with an agency called Budapest Tourist, V. Roosevelt tér 5. T.: 137-3493. Visitors are allowed in through Gate XII, the first gate to the left from the Main Entrance with the Lions.

Since the first edition of this book, much has happened to this building. The red star (not part of the original design) has been removed from the spire. Strangely, it seems somewhat bare. But more importantly, since the last elections there is real work being done inside — Italian style politicking. As there is only one chamber, only one of the big rooms is used. There are six parlamentary parties which achieved more than 4% of the votes, the percentage required to secure seats on the national list under our electoral system.

Ethnographical Museum — Néprajzi Múzeum 11B
V. Kossuth Lajos tér 12.

Showing a strong resemblance to the Reichstag in Berlin, although much more elegant than its German counterpart, this neo-Renaissance palace was built to house the Supreme Court and the Chief Public Prosecutor's Office (Alajos Hauszmann, 1893—96). Building another dome opposite the Parliament seemed out of the question. From the Ticket Office you get into an astoundingly huge and richly decorated hall where it is well worth looking around and up. In the back there are some chairs around a big table where you can sit down. From here you can admire the ceiling of the first floor, the large painted windows and the splendour of the staircase. The fresco on the ceiling shows Justitia, the Goddess of Justice, sitting on her throne among the clouds. By her side the groups represent various qualities; on the right Justice and Peace, while on the left Sin and Revenge. Károly Lotz worked on this fresco for ten months.

The museum is a very pleasant place, and has recently attracted much attention with daring, unusual exhibitions, such as a collection of objects and photos presenting life during the 40 years after World War II. Among the exhibits there was a shabby housing estate room and even a Trabant, the car you meet so very often in the street.

*There are four statues in Kossuth Lajos tér, the Kossuth and the Rákóczi statues are in front of Parliament and those of Attila József and Mihály Károlyi near the river on the right and on the left of the Parliament. (See **Who was Who**.)*

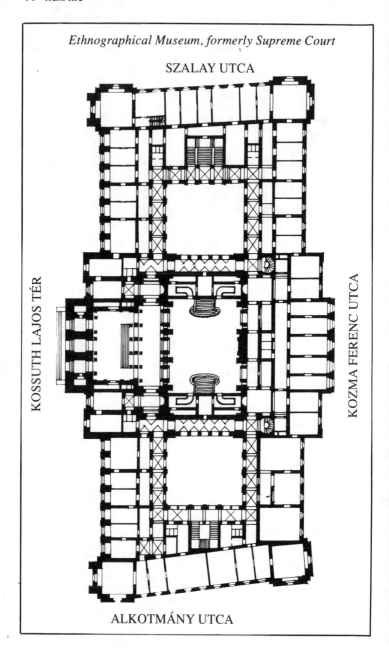

Ethnographical Museum, formerly Supreme Court

SZALAY UTCA

KOSSUTH LAJOS TÉR

KOZMA FERENC UTCA

ALKOTMÁNY UTCA

An Elegant Block of Flats 11F

V. Kossuth Lajos tér 13—15.

This was vacant land for a long time; the city authorities gave permission for a building with thousands of restrictions. All the measurements of the building, even the number of the windows, were prescribed to preserve the unity of the square. The building is a rare example of successful planning (Béla Málnai, 1929). The general conservatism of the 1920s changed the direction of the development of architecture: neo-Baroque became once again the most popular style.

The gateway is worth seeing even if this means climbing upstairs and looking down from above. The staircase is especially attractive from the bottom. The details of the doors to the flats are also quite remarkable. There used to be a row of cafés at the front of the building and all the flats used to have a dumb waiter.

A Private Confectioner's 11H

V. Balassi Bálint utca 7.

Even during the time of the catch-all nationalisation after the last war there were some confectioner's in the city which remained in private hands. In time they earned a legendary reputation, even though all their proprietors did was to continue their trade like masters of the old school, wholeheartedly filling the pastry with custard and stirring the ice-cream. "He spares nothing from it", the older generation used to say. They used to know their customers personally and the staff did not change much either, most often family relatives took over. The furniture also remained the same, all these shops look movingly obsolete in spite of some efforts to modernize them. You would not think that this strict, tall, bald man, Master Szalai, is a living legend. Perhaps the legend is not really about him though, but his cakes.

Until 1949 he had a bigger, more elegant shop nearby (V. Szent István körút 7). Will he get it back?

A Playground 11J

Between Balassi Bálint utca and the river

In the grim 1950s there were only two things in a playground, swings and a sandpit. Swings were always painted red. Parents were always arguing with their kids to get them to fasten the safety chain and not to stand up on the swings. There were usually some see-saws as well, which gave a chance for social activities. You could "send your partner on a summer holiday", (which meant that you kept him in the air for a long time) or let him go down fast and so "make him jump".

But the real socializing area was the sandpit. Unfortunately the old park-keeper would not allow us to bring water. "Watering again, are you!" he used to shout, waving his stick with the nail at one end for collecting dry leaves and litter. At that time there was much less for kids to do. And there was not even a single slide in town.

(See *For Children* for information on good playgrounds.)

White House 11K

V. Széchenyi rakpart 19.

No more lines of black Mercedes any more; the once dreaded power-centre, from where the country was governed nominally by the Central Commitee of the Hungarian Socialist Workers' Party, in point of fact by János Kádár, for 32 years, now contains office facilities for MPs. Nobody wants to move in the former Kádár suite.

In 1971 was erected the statue to Marx and Engels (György Segesdi). Will it stay here? Or will it go to the proposed theme park, with all the Lenins?

You cannot imagine how good the feeling was to take a right turn coming off the bridge from Buda — a privilege once reserved for higher party functionaries.

Margaret Bridge — Margit híd 12C—13A

Linking Jászai Mari tér (Pest) and Germanus Gyula tér (Buda)

This was the second permanent bridge over the Danube, built between 1872 and 1876, designed by the Frenchman Ernest Gouin and built by a Parisian building firm. At the middle, the bridge turns at a 150° angle, partly so that all the piers should be at a right angle to the stream, partly so that the bridge should continue the line of the Nagykörút. The bridge has a branch that leads to Margitsziget (Margaret Island) starting out

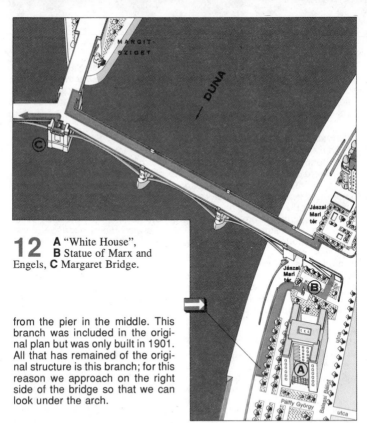

12 **A** "White House",
B Statue of Marx and
Engels, **C** Margaret Bridge.

from the pier in the middle. This branch was included in the original plan but was only built in 1901. All that has remained of the original structure is this branch; for this reason we approach on the right side of the bridge so that we can look under the arch.

Margaret Island — Margitsziget
Between Margit híd and Árpád híd

The island, now one of Europe's finest parks, was formed in the Danube over the last million years. With a length of 2.5 kilometres and a width of 500 metres at the widest point, it can be strolled through in about 2 hours at a leisurely pace. However, it is well worth spending half a day here.

A bridge connected the island with the Buda bank even in Roman times. In the Middle Ages it was called the "Island of Rabbits" and was a Royal hunting reserve. The present name was given in honour of Princess Margit, daughter of King Béla IV; she lived in the nunnery on the island. During the Turkish occupation the whole island functioned as a harem.

There are more than 10 thousand trees on the island, most of them plane-trees, carefully planted by various Hapsburg gardeners to counteract the ravage of floods. János Arany (1817—1882), one of the greatest poets of the last century, wrote his touching poems in old age, "Under the Oak Trees" here. In fact, although there are some oaks on the island as well, gardeners say that the poet's favourite oaks were probably plane-trees. Up to the end of the Second World War the island was the property of a private company and maintenance was financed from the entrance fees paid by the public. Now there is no entrance fee and the park is still well cared for. You can walk on the grass everywhere, something still unusual for the citizens of Budapest. There are various amenities on the island: a swimming pool, a strand, a tennis stadium, an open air cinema and an open air theatre, a game reserve, a rose garden, a Japanese garden and a statue garden.

On the northern end there is the famous old Grand Hotel, which is now the Ramada Grand Hotel. The terrace is a pleasant place to sit around and enjoy the shady trees, the tranquil and the elegant ambiance — everything which makes the island worth visiting.

Access: bus 26 and 26A, terminus at Nyugati Railway Station in Marx tér. On Margit híd the trams, on Árpád híd the buses stop at the access road to the island. Cars are allowed access only from Árpád híd and only as far as the car parks around the hotel. On Saturdays and Sundays from 10 a.m. to 6 p.m. "micro buses" take visitors on a sightseeing tour. (Only 1 May to 30 September.) Two private enterprises hire out special vehicles converted from bicycles, called "sétacikli" and "bringóhintó". Hirers have to deposit a personal document and sign to acknowledge that their bikes were in good condition when hired. Leaving the island, we go through the slightly urine-smelling underpass which has been modernized without any sense of style, we get to the "elbow" of the bridge. It is worth pausing here for some minutes. There are so many gulls flying above the boils at the piers that they sometimes get entangled in the lines of the anglers. From here the views of Buda and Pest merge into one another, with the Danube curving gently in the middle, embracing the City.

On this bridge occured the greatest disaster in the history of the city. In November 1944, in the broad daylight of the afternoon rush hour, when hundreds of people were crossing the bridge on foot and by tram, the charges placed by the Germans on the section of the bridge between the island and Pest went off, presumably by accident. The number of casualities will never be known, but it ran into hundreds.

The Przemysl Memorial 13B

Left of the Buda side of Margit híd

This, one of the most masculine lions in Budapest, symbolizes the Hungarian defenders of Przemysl, the fortress in southern Poland. A Hungarian soldier modelled it in 1932. Memorials of the Hungarian victims of World War I have been set up at various places of the city, most of them erected from donations.

Margit híd continues to Mártírok útja (Avenue of the Martyrs), whose name recalls a demolished prison, where a large number of left-wing political prisoners used to be kept. After about 200 metres the road takes a sharp turn to the left, still further it turns right and finally runs into busy Moszkva tér, the centre of Buda, which epitomises the traffic problems of the city. The winding Mártírok útja follows the line of a hill, Rózsadomb, on which first summer houses and later elegant villas were built. In the 1960s and 70s hundreds of cube-like blocks were built next to the old, low buildings. The eastern slope of the hill is practically full. The other sides are also the scenes of busy construction work (Endrődi Sándor utca, Gárdonyi Géza utca, Törökvész út). For Budapest residents, 'Rózsadomb' is now a social category. If someone builds a house or buys his own home in this expensive area, people just say "he has moved up to the hill". In this area there are very few low-rent council flats. It is the hill which the folks live on.

*We walk on in Frankel Leó utca, a street which could just as well be on the Pest side. You can see a notice in one of the ground-floor windows of No 9: which translates as TROTTING ALL YEAR ROUND, FLAT-RACING FROM SPRING TO AUTUMN. It is one of the 13 betting offices in the city. The two types of racing have two separate race-courses and two separate sets of followers. (See **Entertainment** for more information on horse-racing.) At No 1 there is a small shop of a skate-grinder. The old fashioned notice in the window says: "Skates for grinding or assembling are welcome." Opposite on the ground floor of No 2 is the Bambi confectioner's just as it was in the 1960s: the curtains, the uncomfortable chairs covered with red plastic, the trapezium-shaped cash desk and the figure of the (Disney) deer that inspired the name. The notice above the fridge containing soft drinks is seen in lots of other such places: DRUNK ELEMENTS WILL NOT BE SERVED. The other one above the cash desk reflects the spirit of the place better: ONLY FOOD SERVED TO THE TABLE MAY BE CONSUMED THERE. Which must mean that things sometimes happen differently here. Perhaps the old-age pensioners passing time in the Bambi may be offering each other the home made cookies they have brought with them; I wonder.*

Statue of József Bem 13C

II. Bem József tér

Of Polish nationality, Bem was one of the most successful generals on the Hungarian side during the 1848—49 Hungarian Revolution and was especially revered by ordinary Hungarian soldiers. He was called "Father Bem" (Bem apó) by them. The statue (János Istók, 1934) depicts the small figure of the general, wounded, his arm in a sling, commanding his troops into attack at the bridge of Piski. The inscription says: THE BATTLE OF PISKI 1849. And underneath: I SHALL RECAPTURE THE BRIDGE OR SHALL DIE / FORWARD, HUNGARIANS / IF WE DO NOT HAVE THE BRIDGE, WE DO NOT HAVE THE COUNTRY.

13 **A** Margaret Bridge, **B** Przemysl Memorial, **C** Statue of General Bem, **D** Flórián Chapel, **E** Király Baths, **F** Military Tribunal, **G** "Point House".

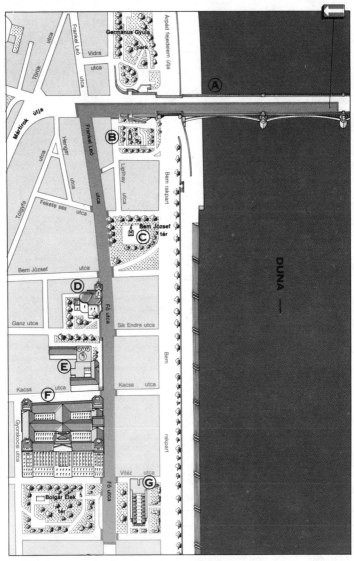

The bridge was recaptured. As the saying goes: "We won this battle as well, it was only the war we lost."

After the crushing defeat of the revolution by the combined forces of the Tsar and the Hapsburgs, Bem escaped to Turkey. He adopted Islam, became governor of Aleppo under the name of Murad Pasha. The statue has always had an important role in anti-government demonstrations.

Flórián Chapel — Flórián kápolna 13D
II. Fő utca 90.

We are now entering Fő utca, which includes almost the entire history of the country. It was a baker who had the chapel built in the middle of the

18th century. Before the quay was built there was flooding by the Danube several times. Then the area was filled up with earth. All the older buildings are considerably below street level because of this. The church was lifted by 140 centimetres in 1938. A modern painter, Jenő Medveczky painted the frescos in the same year. Now it is the parish church of the Greek Catholic community in Buda.

I saw a touching scene here, an old lady dusting the ceiling of the chapel with immense affection and thoroughness. She was using a long pole made up of several shorter ones joined together.

Király Bath — Király fürdő 13E
II. Fő utca 84.

The part built by the Turks, called the Bath of the Cock Tower, was built around 1570 inside the Víziváros town wall, so that the garrison could enjoy the benefits of a bath even during a siege. It was a smaller copy of the famous baths in Buda. The classicist wings were added between 1717—27. It took its present name (Király = King) not from some ruler but from the König family which owned the place for a time. The steam bath is a fine spectacle. After buying the ticket, go up in the spiral staircase and follow the sign GŐZFÜRDŐ (steam bath). In the dressing room the attendant hands over a cotton apron which you take with you into one of the free boxes. After undressing, you lock the door of the box with the key you find inside and tie it on a string on the apron. Memorize the number of your box and you can go straight into the bath. Taking a shower is compulsory, the sauna is not. You get to the actual Turkish bath, to a pool under an octagonal roof, which can be seen also from the outside, through a low door. There are mysterious beams of light of different colours coming through the hexagonal openings in the dome, illuminating the steam. Once you have been in and out of the steam of different temperatures and waters of 26-40 Centigrade enough times, the next stop is the towel room. You leave your apron at the entrance, take a towel and dry yourself. You dump the wet towel take a dry one and go up to the first floor **Pihenő** to have a rest. There are notices here on the wall saying "Silence, please" and "Time of Rest: 15 mins"; the latter is never taken seriously. From here you go back to your box, but you cannot open it with your key alone; like a safe it needs two keys to open and the attendant has the other one. It is customary to leave a tip for him.

The bath is open for men on Mondays, Wednesdays and Fridays, and for women on Tuesdays, Thursdays and Saturdays from 6.30 a.m. to 7 p.m. (on Saturdays to 12 p.m.). It is closed for maintenance on every first Thursday of the month. Apart from a steam bath, you can use the bath tubs, the sauna and several other facilities. On one of the corridors there is a red scale, the sort that used to be everywhere in the streets of Budapest. In the beginning you had to drop in 20 fillér, then two 20 fillér coins. Not long after that, the scales disappeared.

Fő utca is the main street of the district called Víziváros (literally 'Watertown'). Looking up the streets to the right, for example, up Kacsa utca, you can enjoy a magnificent view of the slope of Castle Hill and you can get an idea of the poetic disorder of the district in the past. Bolgár Elek tér, however, could well be a museum of modern architecture. In Fő utca 70—72 the severe block of the Military Court of Justice (13F) is situated, an excellent example of the primary aim of such buildings: to serve as a deterrent (1915). During the rebuilding of the façade it was perhaps felt that three revolving doors in the façade were two too many and iron bars were placed on the ones at the sides; the one in the middle was replaced with a simple narrow door, which is not in the least in proportion with the large building. It truly seems impossible to slip out of this place unobserved.

The building opposite (Fő utca 69.) is a typical block of flats of the 1930s, while the red brick building opposite the side wall of the Court, on the other side of the square, was the first building in Budapest which was built in winter — in 1941-42. After the last war, it was planned to build on the Danube bank, using tall buildings. All that was realized of the plan was the famous high-rise block, "pointhouse" (Fő utca 61., 1948) which is called that because all the flats open from one single staircase in the middle of the building. But the rumour went around that the origin of the name is that there was no point in building it, as it cost twice the price of a traditional block. (14A).

We have arrived at one of the finest spots of this walk, at Batthyány tér. Apart from its own buildings, its attraction lies in the fact that it is opposite the main façade of Parliament. (A quite unusual view of the Parliament can be enjoyed from the first floor of the Market Hall, from the windows of the stalls hidden on the left.) The quietly stretching huge building seems to be quite a long way away. You can imagine the size of the explosion when a German ammunition store went up here on 2nd January 1945, if all the windows of Parliament broke, even on the other side of the building.

The sleepy little square suddenly came to life in 1972, when this section of the Second (Red) Metro Line was opened. The terminus of the green suburban train (HÉV) is also here, under the square.

You can make a shortcut here to finish this walk; if you take the underground in the direction of Örs vezér tér, the second stop is Deák tér, which is just 3 minutes walk from Vörösmarty tér.

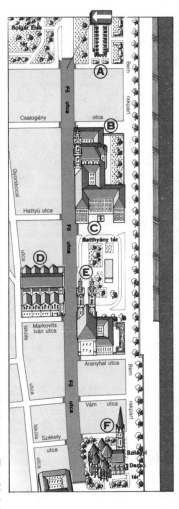

A World famous Lavatory — Nyilvános vécé
In the subway, Batthyány tér

"A little money takes away every smell", to vary the Emperor Vespasian's famous dictum. This institution, which was always a busy but scruffy place, was leased out to a private entrepreneur some years ago, who brought here the atmosphere of tropical countries, soft music and two chairs. He has been interviewed by journalists from almost every leading newspaper in the world. However, according to a letter in a Hungarian paper, there was somebody who almost got beaten up because he could not pay.

Hikisch House
I. Batthyány tér 3.

The residence of an architect who lived at the end of the 18th century (the house was built in 1795). It is below the level of the square, as is every other old building here. There is a relief with four cherubs on the façade. They symbolise the four seasons.

The Former "White Cross" Inn
I. Batthyány tér 4.

The Ballroom used to be in the prominent middle part, which also saw theatrical performances. The ironwork on the balcony on the left is Baroque, on the right it is Rococo. Joseph II (1780—90), called the 'King with a Hat' since he was never crowned, stayed here twice, to emphasize his puritanical character. You will be surprised at the large and wonderful courtyard hiding behind the gate. The Casanova Piano Bar entices those who like that kind of thing. They say Casanova himself put up at this inn.

To the left of the back gate of the building, there is the tradesman's entrance of the Market Hall.

14 A "Point House", B Church of the Elizabeth Order, C Statue of Ferenc Kölcsey, Romantic Poet, D Market hall, E Saint Anne Church, F Calvinist Church.

The Church of Saint Anna 14E
I. Batthyány tér

A building with fine proportions in every detail, to my mind, one of the finest. (Kristóf Hamon, Máté Nepauer, 1740—1762). Inside there is an Italianate elongated, octagonal nave. One of the builders was Kristóf Hikisch, who used to live in this square, and whose house we have already seen. Since the church was built, it has been attacked by earthquakes, floods and wars.

On the ground floor of the vicarage one of the most pleasant cafés in Buda, the Angelika, opened at the beginning of the 1970s. Under the vaulted ceiling, the traditional middle-class of Buda make up most of the regulars, due to the slightly snobbish decoration and the pleasant staff. A place where ladies wear their hats as they take their coffee — and where the wayward boss takes the secretary.

If we walk further down Fő utca, we shall pass a neo-Gothic Calvinist church with an extremely complex ground plan on the left (Samu Pecz, 1896), then soon arrive at Corvin tér. It is surrounded by a concert hall (the so-called Vigadó of Buda), some charming Baroque blocks of flats (Corvin tér 2., 3., 4. and 5.), a church of medieval origin, rebuilt in Romantic style, and the hillside. We turn left into Halász utca and leave the Víziváros district for the chestnut trees on the Danube bank. It is worth looking into the side streets on the right. On the corner of Pala utca and Fő utca there is a late Baroque building which used to belong to a Greek merchant; a modern office building can also be seen which the majority of Hungarian children believe is the headquarters of the homicide squad because this is where the popular Hungarian television thriller series, "Linda" is usually shot. Linda is a slight, 47 kilogram, karate expert policewoman, who is always ordered to investigate petty crimes but still manages to solve all the major crimes that are committed. And she has never been promoted.

From here you can see, and this is the only place you can see it well from, Roosevelt tér at the Pest end of Lánchíd. The square is enclosed by the Hungarian Academy of Sciences, the "Spinach-palace", Gresham Palace, the Ministry of Home Affairs and the Hyatt Hotel. Naturally the Roosevelt memorial tablet on the wall of a building in the square cannot be seen from here. The inscription on the tablet says: "FDR, 1887—1945, who, in the last war between the peoples of the world, fought for the freedom of the oppressed and for the victory of human rights. He helped democracy to win a final victory".

Chain Bridge — Lánchíd 15I—16A
We have already crossed this bridge on the First Walk. In its present form, this is the third bridge. During the renovation in 1987, sixty tons of paint was used and most of the 100,000 rivets were changed.

Gresham Palace 16C
V. Roosevelt tér 5.

The plan accepted in London for the centre of the English insurance company (Zsigmond Quittner, 1904—6) did not harmonize at all with the style of Lánchíd. In spite of the art nouveau style its proportions are surprisingly peaceful, and, as one would expect, its surface is richly decorated. The banker who once founded the London Stock Exchange is in a gold setting so dominant that it can be seen even from the other end of the Tunnel. At sunset the portrait and the golden tiles of the façade, which are at other times of the day so pale, seem to glow. It makes a difficult but striking photograph if you can set up for it from the Buda side of the bridge. The figures above the windows of the first floor illustrate a working life and a carefree life, the latter undoubtedly being the result of buying a good insurance policy.

Hungarian Academy of Letters and Sciences — Magyar Tudományos Akadémia 16B
V. Roosevelt tér 9.

This institution, together with so many others, was founded in the second quarter of the last century, in what is called the Reform-Age. On the wall facing Akadémia utca the large relief immortalizes the moment when Count Széchenyi, in 1825, offered one year's income for the foundation of the Academy (Barnabás Holló, 1893). To the question of what he would live on, he answered: "My friends are going to support me..."

This was the first neo-Renaissance building in the city and was built between 1862 and 1864, to the plans of Friedrich Stüler, an architect from Berlin. On the second floor there are six allegorical statues on the façade, symbolizing the sciences which were studied in Hungary at the time. On the same level there are six statues also at the corners; near Roosevelt tér, the statues of Galileo and Miklós Révai (a 18th century Hungarian linguist), near the river Newton and Lomonosov, and towards Akadémia utca Descartes and Leibniz. Today the Academy has ten departments. By the charter of the Academy, the number of members who are younger than 75, can be a maximum of 200. Members get a monthly salary, receive all the journals of the Academy and have their taxi fares paid as well.

The richly decorated interior of the building is unfortunately not open to visitors and the armed guard politely but firmly warns them off. The name

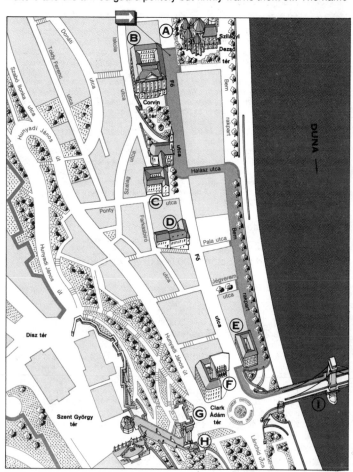

15 **A** Calvinist Church, **B** Buda Vigadó, **C** Church of the Capuchin Order, former monastery, **D** Fő utca 20., **E** Fő utca 1., **F** Café in the remaining part of a block destroyed during the war, **G** The entrance to the Tunnel, **H** The lower end of the Cable Car, **I** Lánchíd — Chain Bridge.

of the institution stands modestly between the second and the third floors with golden letters. I remember that in my childhood there used to be a full stop at the end. Then this last-century full stop disappeared because according to the orthographical rules published by the Academy "there is no full stop after a title".

The Academy used to dominate the square but lost its primacy at the beginning of this century when the headquarters of the two financial institutions were built. It fell back even further when the "Spinach-palace" was built, the office building so nick-named because of its colour (Miklós Hofer, Tibor Hübner, 1979). Two foreign trading companies started the expensive construction (the weight is carried by steel balls), but ran out of finance. The building was finished by the state and finally three ministerial institutions moved in. There is also a canteen on the top floor for the staff.

The Gresham Palace *was built from a durable material; its façade has resisted the ravages of time. The T-shaped passageway, however, has given up the struggle. The glass ceiling, which was once painted, was replaced by plain glass after the war. Only some fragments remained at the bottom. Relics of old decencies, as they say in Dublin.*

16 **A** Lánchíd — Chain Bridge, **B** Hungarian Academy of Letters and Sciences, **C** Gresham Palace, **D** Statue of István Széchenyi, "the greatest Hungarian", **E** Statue of Ferenc Deák, **F** Hotel Hyatt, **G** Gerbeaud, **H** Vigadó, **I** Luxus department store.

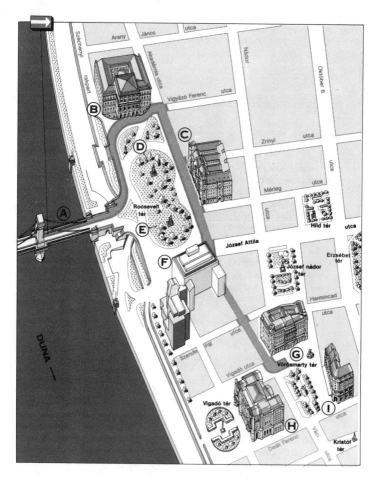

Here we suddenly seem to arrive into a rundown district. From the passageway you can see the backdoor to the Gresham Casino, all sorts of office windows, where the lights are always on and an old-fashioned hairdresser's. Here is the entrance to an office whose plate has changed frequently. It has been a lonely hearts agency, an agency for the building industry and a shoeshop; a modest, hidden reminder of our age of entrepreneurs. There are offices, as here, in many residential blocks in the City area, often in the most inappropriate premises. Their staff, especially the women, do their very best to decorate these offices, keeping postcards sent to each other over the years on the wall or under the glass sheet on their desks.

The staircases have their own names (Gresham, Kossuth and Andrássy stairs). At some places here some of the old glass windows have been preserved. The walls of the inner courtyards are white or covered with light blue tiles.

Everyone agrees that the decline should be stopped some way or other. There seems to be no other way but to turn the block into a hotel. But the tenants - with the leadership of the grande dame of the Hungarian stage - protest. They want to stay. (And pay the low rent — of course).

By the way. The Roosevelt tablet disappeared during the recent renovation. A shame.

Ten minutes away from here is the **Megálló Restaurant**, which is rather stark but has a magnificent kitchen; there is never a free table during office lunch hours (VII. Károly körút 23.).

Beside the kitchen, there is a conspicuous "diploma" hanging on the wall. It is written in Hungarian couplets: "If the lady with you is not your wedded wife / We won't give you away, you can live your own life / We won't breathe a word, man, this just wouldn't be fair / And you won't know either about your wife's affair."

So at least you don't have to worry about that.

BUDAPEST BESTS :: BUDAPEST BESTS

Péter Molnár Gál, aka MGP, a wit and a theatre critic; the wickedest pen

There is a small restaurant in the old Józsefváros, the **Gólya** (in Bókay János utca). Its regulars include the local shopkeepers and tradesmen, folk musicians and the occasional off-duty whore. Outside in the courtyard in summer a curtain of trained vines almost reaches your soup plate. Inside it's all wood-panelling, the old white of the hall cupboard has been given a fashionable brown coat. The menu card has four or five simple dishes, always a delight. Your conversation scintillates at the Gólya's tables. (Provided I cut the band's amplifier lead with a pair of pliers.) I have checked it out recently, this tiny throwback to the turn of the century Józsefváros. And it's been taken over by a standard type of restaurants. Their pre-fabricated menu is just like all the others.

Wherever you eat well, eat plenty. For the next time you got there you won't find again what you so enjoyed before. In Budapest you can't dunk your bread in the same sauce twice.

The city is going through a time of transition. As it has been doing for five hundred years.

Before you set out to eat in the evening, toss a coin. And put your trust in blind fortune.

One of my favourite places was in Dohány utca, opposite the old Tolnai printers. It was a place that couldn't make up its mind whether it was a scruffy pub or a family *kifőzés*. It closed. It was rebuilt. Now there's a Korean restaurant in its place. I've eaten well there three times in a row. But I still don't dare to recommend it — it can have changed by the time the guide comes out.

There is still a **tobacconist's** at number 2 Nádor utca. A white-haired, smiling, elderly lady stands behind the counter. I'm always in a good mood for a few hours after dropping in there.

Don't eat! Smoke! It makes you slim.

Walk Three

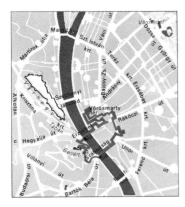

leads through the City area built at the end of the last century. We shall go over to Buda and climb a 141 metre high hill, then come back across another bridge to Pest to have a look at some buildings which were built at the beginning of the last century. Perhaps we shall have some sausages on the way.

Time: about 6 hours

Vigadó 17C
V. Vigadó tér

This single word is the full name of this romantic concert hall and ball-room. It means something like 'merrymaking', a place for entertainments. When it was opened, a Hungarianized Italian word was planned for it, as were several other suggestions, ranging from Gondilla to Búfúdda. It was intended as a concert hall and a ballroom and took seven years to build, beginning in 1859. It took so long partly because the builders needed several attempts to cope with the unusual task. The demanding designer, Frigyes Feszl, stuck to his guns and planned even the smallest sections.

When the building was finished in 1865, it was received with unanimous obtuseness. Some found it to be too unusual, some others to be too Hungarian. Still others criticized the lack of uniformity and also said that the main façade was "bare" and the height of the main hall was monstrous (22 metres). An architect from abroad said, and perhaps not quite in mockery, that the building was "auskristallisiert Tschardasch".

In its present form, rebuilt after the war, it was re-opened in the winter of 1980. Music lovers could hardly wait for the Large Hall accomodating 640 people. To make the once infamously bad acoustics better, the ceiling was lowered 3 metres and awkward-looking white plaster pyramids were placed on it. The musicians were disappointed in spite of all that, but the audience was flattered by the amazing variety of colours. Restoration work has been done very carefully, for the colouring the original plans have been used and photographs have been consulted for other parts.

Unfortunately, the Large Hall and the equally luxurious staircase can only be seen when a concert is on and the foyer is open only after 12 p.m. when the ticket office opens. (The show-cases on each side of the main entrance were thought at first to be a bad practical joke, but later it turned out that they were meant to be set up there, so they stayed.) The Söröző Restaurant and the Gallery, which does not sell its paintings, are in a style different from the rest of the building. The Vigadó can be rented for balls or receptions. (Information on events in the Vigadó and on costs can be obtained in English and in German. T.: 118-9903.)

The building is anything but uniform, the façade almost explodes from the lively ornaments. The façades at the side are much simpler, and they cleverly hide the fact that the building is not straight but follows the line of the site which slightly breaks at an angle.

Vigadó tér used to be the busiest square in Pest. Before the permanent bridges were built, this was where the pontoon bridge was moored. Once Lánchíd was opened, calm fell on the square.

Hotel Duna Intercontinental 17D

V. Apáczai Csere János utca 4.

The hotel was opened in 1969 (designed by József Finta, László Kovácsy). All its 39 suites and 349 rooms overlook the Danube. About a hundred years after the scandal that broke out about the Vigadó, a new one started over this hotel. It is generally held that it is too high, its proportions are different from those of the city; what is more, it turns its back on the capital, looks like a fortress and at least the back, windowless side is, quite simply, ugly. As the comment goes, if you stay in the Duna, you can't see it.

Beneath the row of small shops at its entrance is one which has a name for being elegant, selling industrial products and cosmetics for hard currency. The lovers of the Duna-korzó would like to drive the noisy No 2 tram underground and have the promenade widened. As this plan would be expensive, there is no sign of it being adopted.

Greek Orthodox Church — Orthodox templom 17E

V. Petőfi tér 2.

There used to be a large group of Greek merchants in Budapest who initiated much development. They commissioned an architect to build this baroque church (József Jung, 1791—94). Its southern spire was demolished in World War II. Nowadays services are usually conducted in Hungarian, always accompanied by singing (at 6 p.m. on Saturdays; at 10 a.m. on Sundays and some other times as well on public holidays). The building is open to visitors from spring to autumn between 10 a.m. and 5 p.m.

Statue of Sándor Petőfi — Petőfi szobra 17F

V. Petőfi tér

The statue is a bit far from the taste of our times (Miklós Izsó, Adolf Huszár, 1882). It shows the poet at the age of 25, reciting his most famous patriotic poem, beginning "Talpra, magyar!" (Rise Hungarians!).

Petőfi (1823—49) started as a poor student and strolling player and soon became the most popular poet of his time, also praised by literary circles. A genius, he was a master of poetic form. He introduced the vernacular into Hungarian verse, acquiring inevitably the title of the Robert Burns of Hungary. His short life was the full life of a man whose love was returned, who had taken part in a victorious revolution and who had become a soldier to fight for his country. He was killed in one of the last battles of the Hungarian War of Independence. After his death the rumour that he was still alive circulated round the country for years and years. Most recently, the rumour was acted upon by a self-made millionaire, who sent a team to Siberia to dig up a grave. The corps they happened to unearth later proved to be that of a young lady.

He is the first poet Hungarian children study in detail at school. Despite various attempts at translation, he is virtually unknown abroad.

Eighteen different streets and squares are named after Petőfi in the Budapest of today. (The size of the number is due to the 1949 enclosing of a number of villages within Budapest.) There are lots of other things named after him: a museum, a bridge, an army camp, a radio channel, to mention just a few. His is the portrait on the 10 Forint banknote.

The Ruins of Contra Aquincum 17G

V. Március 15. tér

An open air museum, showing the remains of the old Roman fortress. The eastern border of the Roman Empire was the line of the Danube, which means that only the Buda side was within the province of Pan-

17 A Luxus Department Store, B Gerbeaud, C Vigadó, D Hotel Intercontinental, E Orthodox Church, F Statue of Sándor Petőfi, G Contra Aquincum, H Péterffy Palace, I Faculty of Arts, Eötvös University, J Inner City Parish Church, K Klotild Palaces, L Paris Arcade — Párisi Udvar.

nonia. From the end of the 3rd century an outpost was placed in this 84 x 86 metre fortress with walls of 3 metres. The name shows that it was situated opposite the nearby town, Aquincum. Documents mention that Emperor Julian and even Constantine the Great visited this place. There are other and more important Roman remains in a much better preserved environment in the Aquincum Museum, in the IIIrd district. From springtime to autumn Contra Aquincum is a popular place for the students of the Faculty of Arts, the building overlooking the square. They call the place the "concrete castrum", or at least they did in my time. Another place frequented by students is the steps by the river between Erzsébet híd and Lánchíd. The popularity is due to their being suntraps and ideal for sunbathing.

Faculty of Arts 17I

V. Pesti Barnabás utca 1.

The university moved into the building, which was originally a Catholic monastery and school (Dezső Hültl, 1915—18), in the early fifties. The university is named after Loránd Eötvös, the famous physicist. It also has a Faculty of Natural Sciences and a Faculty of Law. The real main entrance of the building is not in Pesti Barnabás utca, but through the famous "B Gate" in the narrow passageway between Váci utca and the Danube bank. This area is very busy during term time, from the middle of September to the beginning of December and from the beginning of February to the middle of May. The corridors on the ground floor and on the first floor are almost totally covered with posters advertising various meetings and amateur performances, university magazines and the university clubs. The most crowded place is the small, smoke-filled canteen on the first floor. It is raided by the students in the breaks during the lectures (usually between 9.30 and 10 or 11.30 and 12) for a cup of coffee or for the notes of a missed lecture. The current word is that the building will most probably be given back to the Piarists, whose *gimnázium* it originally housed. This is said to be likely since the Prime Minister is a former student — as were several luminaries of the old regime.

Péterffy Palace 17H
V. Pesti Barnabás utca 2.
The building of the University dwarfs the little house, which looks even smaller as it is below street level. In the old Pest which still had the city wall, all the houses had such measurements. (Probably designed by András Mayerhoffer, 1756.) The restaurant situated in the palace is actually much older than its name indicates; it is not 100 but at least 150 years old.

Párisi Udvar 17L
V. Felszabadulás tér 5.
This block was built in 1909 (designed by Henrik Schmal) and the bank which commissioned it opened its offices on the ground floor. (Now used by IBUSZ Travel Agency.) The arcade has recently been enlarged by a new passageway which branches off and opens into Haris köz. The block is worth exploring. If you take the lift between the bookshop and the leathershop and go up to the top floor you can walk over to the other staircase and down the stairs again. The lift used to be in the middle of the staircase. From the windows between the first and the second floor you can look down on the witty roof structure of the yard.

Jégbüfé Confectioner's
V. Felszabadulás tér 5.
Although a confectioner's needs custom, the bustle in this shop, however, is too much, even in winter, with people simply trampling all over each other. The blind lady sitting outside the shop, selling lottery tickets, is the complete antithesis. She is the secret centre of the square, with the people living nearby leaving messages with her or talking to her about the state of the world. She has been coming here for twenty-odd years from a village outside Pest.

Franciscan Church 18A
V. Ferenciek tere 2.
The church shows the influence of Italian Baroque and not that of the Austrian version, which resulted in yellow churches with the "radish helmet" towers. After the medieval Franciscan pattern, a separate tower was built near the church at the vestry. There was a Gothic church on the site in the 13th century. The present building was finished in 1758, in the honour of St Peter of Alcantara (1499—1562), who founded a branch of the Franciscan Order. His statue is in the niche in the middle, above the window of the choir. Above the front gate is the crest of the Order: two arms with stigmatic hands, of Jesus and of St Francis of Assisi. On the left-hand wall of the church a large memorial tablet can be seen. This commemorates the catastrophic flood of 1838, when the whole present-day inner city was under water. There were districts where 90 % of the buildings collapsed. Count Miklós Wesselényi, "the sailor of the flood", portrayed in action, was a hero of the rescue efforts.

Klotild Palaces 18C—18C
V. Szabadsajtó út 5. and 6.
These twin palaces were built at the same time as the original Erzsébet híd. They are almost mirror images of each other (Flóris Korb, Kálmán Giergl, 1902). In the building on the left there is the Imperial Casino, formerly Lido, previously the Belvárosi Kávéház. ("Café Downtown"). In the old days, this was one of the most conservative cafés of the city, where typists and messengers were at guests' disposal and which had its own post box, which meant that the regulars could have their letters

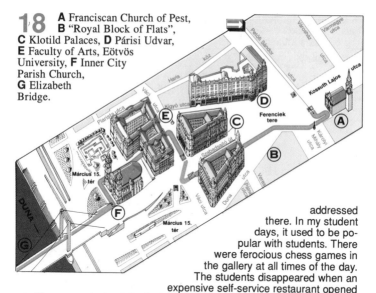

18 A Franciscan Church of Pest,
B "Royal Block of Flats",
C Klotild Palaces, D Párisi Udvar,
E Faculty of Arts, Eötvös
University, F Inner City
Parish Church,
G Elizabeth
Bridge.

addressed
there. In my student
days, it used to be po-
pular with students. There
were ferocious chess games in
the gallery at all times of the day.
The students disappeared when an
expensive self-service restaurant opened
up. Then a posh, tourist-oriented restaurant-cabaret. For details about
the Casino, see *Weekends and Nights / Nigtlifing.*
 On the other side of the building there is an expensive furniture and fittings shop. Several dozen such shops have opened in the last few years.
It is very difficult to find good modern furniture.

Photos by György Klösz
In the subway between the two parts of V. Váci utca
In the pedestrian subway under the Pest end of Erzsébet híd you can see
photos taken by a famous photographer who lived at the end of the last
century. The photos were originally taken on 18 x 24 cm glass negatives.
His studio used to be nearby, on the first floor of the first building after
the Franciscan church. The photos exhibited in the subway portray the
area around Erzsébet híd, before and after the reconstructions made
necessary by the building of the bridge. It is mostly Klösz's photos that
can be found in a recently published illustrated book (Budapest Anno...),
see the chapter *Reading.* The graffiti and the beggars show how far we
have come since.

Inner City Parish Church — Belvárosi Plébániatemplom 18F
You may remember this church from our *First Walk.* Then we did not
pause at the statue on the outer wall of the chancel. This is the statue of
St Florian, the saint who protects men from fires. It was erected in 1723,
after the great fires in Pest.

Elizabeth Bridge — Erzsébet híd 18G—19A
A suspension bridge, built between 1960 and 1964. (More thoroughly
covered in the First Walk.) The vertical suspenders of the bridge are not
fastened to the cables, only the weight of the bridge keeps them in place.

*The beautiful location of Budapest is largely due to a 140 metre high dolomite rock
which descends steeply into the riverbed. The underground part of this rock is
1,000 metres under the surface at Városliget. The western slope is much more
gentle. In area, together with its northern slope, the Tabán, it is almost 60 hec-
tares. Naturally, the city tries to protect every single one of the 5,766 trees here.
(Some fig trees were planted by the Turks.) According to the legend, the hill was
the dwelling-place of witches, who arrived every night riding on the back of a
human being, to get their daily wine. Nowadays there is no wine produced here —
yet it was once covered in vineyards.*

St Gellért Monument 19C
Facing the Buda end of Erzsébet híd
The bronze statue surrounded by a colonnade (Gyula Jankovits, 1904) is interesting not so much because of its own qualities but because of its location. St Gellért (or Gerald), the Bishop of Csanád, was pushed from the top of the hill by pagan Hungarians rebelling against Christianity, nailed into a barrel, as the legend goes (or, as most historians say, on a wheelbarrow) in 1046.

It takes 20-25 minutes to climb to the top of the hill. The trees mask the city on the way up so the panorama appears suddenly as you get to the top.

Citadel 19E
On top of Gellért Hill
The grim stronghold on the top of Gellért-hegy was built after the collapse of the Hungarians after the Revolution of 1848—1849; its military purpose was to control Castle Hill. It came into the possession of the capital in 1894, when it was symbolically demolished some places. There have been plans to set up a Hungarian Pantheon or to make the relief map of Hungary here. It has been a prison camp, temporary accommodation for the homeless, the site of an anti-aircraft battery and finally, since 1961, a tourist attraction.

It is worth walking this far, if for nothing else, than to hire a telescope to look down on the city. On 20th August, Gellért-hegy is the site of the great fireworks display, with the rockets released from various parts of the hill. The 14 metre tall statue of the woman holding a palm leaf in her hands is the Statue of Liberty, to commemorate liberation from Fascist rule. It has become the symbol of Budapest abroad so it is unlikely to be removed. Though perhaps not the Russian soldiers at the base... It was erected in 1947 and can be seen from all parts of the city (by Zsigmond Kisfaludi-Stróbl, allegedly originally designed to commemorate the death of the son of the ultra right inter-war Governor Horthy).

Instead of the usual path leading to the foot of the hill, let me recommend an even more pleasant route, through the villas of the hill. Find Verejték utca, then follow Kelenhegyi út down to the Gellért baths.

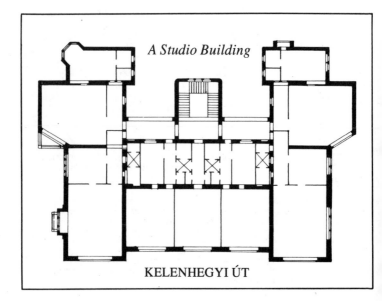

A Studio Building

KELENHEGYI ÚT

A Studio Building
XI. Kelenhegyi út 12—14.
An art nouveau building made of traditional materials in a bold, functional way (Gyula Kosztolányi Kann, 1903). Painters and sculptors live here even today. Its architect is also better known as a painter. Of all his many building designs, few were actually built.

Hotel Gellért and Gellért Baths 20C
XI. Kelenhegyi út 4.
If you follow the route I have recommended, you first see the open-air part of the baths which has recently been enlarged. The new part was uncommonly well made; the postmodern softness matches the heavy bulk of the art nouveau building which was completed in 1918 (Ármin Hegedüs, Artúr Sebestyén and Izidor Stark). The open-air swimming-pool stretches over to the other side of Kemenes utca and is connected to the main area through a subway.

"The Gellért Hotel looks like a huge white gem, which, unlike other buildings which get black with time, becomes whiter and whiter", claims a friend of mine, who is also the illustrator of this book. The hotel, together with the baths, was built by the city as part of a conscious policy to make Budapest into a city of baths. If you cannot spare the time to swim, at least walk into the hall through the entrance at the side of the building for the sake of the mosaic floor and the glass ceiling. From the back of the hall you can look into the roofed part of the swimming-pool. Try to slip in — you are supposed to have a swimming pool ticket. Hotel guests have a separate lift at their disposal to come down to the baths.

The main entrance of the hotel looks onto the Danube. The lobby was rebuilt at the beginning on the 1960s in the so-called 'old-modern' style. Now it is beginning to look elegant in the way that the 1965 Opel Rekord

19 **A** Elizabeth Bridge, **B** Rudas Baths, **C** Statue of St Gellért, **D** Statue of Liberty, **E** Citadel.

20   A Citadel, **B** Statue of Liberty, **C** Gellért Baths and the Hotel,
        D Former Pauline monastery, **E** Liberty Bridge.

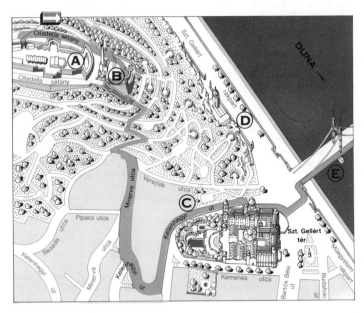

is, which fascinated me in front of this hotel on an autumn day, a long
time ago. For this was the hotel where we could see all the latest models;
for all I know Budapest schoolboys still go there car-spotting.

Pauline Monastery 20D
XI. Szt Gellért rakpart 1/a.
This is another pseudo-historic building which fits into the surroundings
wonderfully. No one would think that it was built as late as 1932 (!) (Károly
Weichinger). A grotto chapel belonged to it as well. For 40 years it was the student hostel of the Ballet Institution. I am not sure that the students felt at home
in here.
The grotto that opens from the balcony nearby has recently been recon-
sacrated.

Liberty Bridge — Szabadság-híd 20E—21A
Linking Gellért tér (Buda) and Fővám tér (Pest)
The third permanent bridge (originally Franz Joseph Bridge) was opened on
the occasion of the Millennium celebrations in 1896. It was Franz Joseph himself who hammered in the last silver rivet. Not by hand, naturally: he pushed a
button in a tent on the Pest side, which operated the 45 ton hammer. There are
very few things around which give a better example of how much the people
took pleasure in ornaments. It would be difficult to imagine what the bridge
would look like if the designer (Virgil Nagy) did not stick to the following principles: "When designing the bridge, I had to obey the requirements of beauty,
simplicity and economy". The bridge has a modular-structure, that is, if its
middle were removed, it would still stand firmly (János Feketeházy).
On top of each pillar, standing on a golden ball, is a "Turul bird", the mythical
bird of the Hungarians, stretching its wings, preparing to take off. Some would-
be suicides still climb up here — most of them are rescued by the fire brigade.
The famous silver rivet with the F. J. initials was stolen during World War I. So
was its replacement. Today the rivet can be seen under a glass sheet. This
one is not silver.

21 **A** Liberty Bridge, **B** University of Economic Sciences,
C Central Market Hall, **D** A part of the Medieval
City Walls, **E** Calvinist Church, **F** Former Two Lions Inn,
G Headquarters of an Insurance Company,
H National Museum.

University of Economic Sciences 21B
IX. Fővám tér 8.
The neo-Renaissance building, originally the Main Customs Building,
proved to be a trend-setter
(Miklós Ybl, 1870—74),
largely influencing
construction along
Andrássy út.

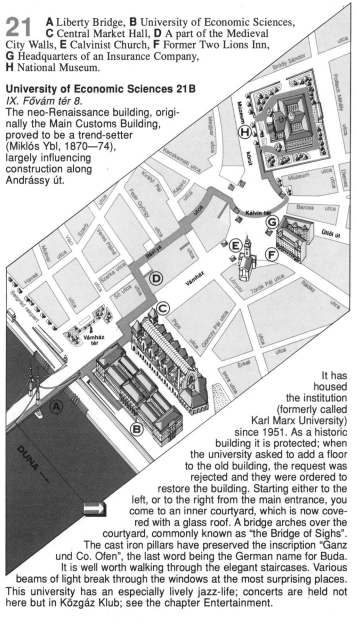

It has
housed
the institution
(formerly called
Karl Marx University)
since 1951. As a historic
building it is protected; when
the university asked to add a floor
to the old building, the request was
rejected and they were ordered to
restore the building. Starting either to the
left, or to the right from the main entrance, you
come to an inner courtyard, which is now covered with a glass roof. A bridge arches over the
courtyard, commonly known as "the Bridge of Sighs".
The cast iron pillars have preserved the inscription "Ganz
und Co. Ofen", the last word being the German name for Buda.
It is well worth walking through the elegant staircases. Various
beams of light break through the windows at the most surprising places.
This university has an especially lively jazz-life; concerts are held not
here but in Közgáz Klub; see the chapter Entertainment.

Central Market Hall — Központi Vásárcsarnok 21C
IX. Vámház körút 1—3.
At the end of the last century the city had five large, roofed markets all
of which were built in a very similar style. All five were opened on the
same day; the other four are in Rákóczi tér, Klauzál tér, Hunyadi tér and
in Hold utca. This is the largest of them (designed by Samu Pecz), along
the sides of the 150 metre-long hall are six aisles. The structure, the lighting and the coldstore were very modern in their time and work even
today. Formerly, laden barges sailed right into the Market Hall through a
canal under the ground. The canal still exists; above its opening a notice

says: "TUNNEL INTO THE CENTRAL MARKET HALL" (on the quay next to the ill-famed Matróz Csárda Restaurant).

The greatest attraction of the hall is the roof structure, which has resisted the ravages of time better than the plastered wall. Let's walk down from the main entrance to the end of the hall and go up to the gallery on the right. This is where florists reign. The large notices warn that they cannot serve retailers. It is amazing how large the space is under the roof. The market is changing. The old-fashioned market-women, dressed in black or pied clothes, and loudly bargaining with the customers, are slowly disappearing. Instead, the rowdy, 30-40-year-old small entrepreneur, with his well-dressed wife at the stall, and joking with the customers, are becoming the typical figures. There are still some, although fewer and fewer, peasant women in black skirts and wearing kerchieves on their heads, Transylvanian visitors selling clothes, or smallholders dressed in a provincial fashion; they all represent the old couleur locale. Newspapers now write a lot on the fruit and vegetable trade. The producers get only less than one third of the high price the goods are sold at. Authorities say that the trade is controlled by a "mafia" so in spite of the growing amount of produce and the growing number of sellers, prices still do not seem to be getting any lower.

An extensive facelift is on the way - you might find it closed. Come back later.

Former Hotel Nádor
V. Vámház körút 2.
The building took its present form in 1840 and is now a residential block. There are quite a few classicist buildings, even though the others may not have such fine proportions, in the quiet parts of the City, that is, in the area between the Danube, the inner boulevard and Kossuth Lajos utca. This area is more or less like the Reform-Age city used to be (before the 1848 Revolution).

On the ground floor, towards Vámház körút, there is a butcher's which has preserved its hundred-year-old, painted tiles. Here you can try the typical lunch of the simple clerks and old age pensioners in the area: have 100 grams of cooked sausage at the counter. Take some mustard or horse-radish and a slice of bread with it. If you want the crust, you have to tell the shop assistant.

A Part of the Medieval City Wall of Pest 21D
V. Bástya utca, corner of Veres Pálné utca
The wall stretched in a semicircle from about the present Vigadó tér to Fővám tér. It was almost 2 kilometres long and a little more than 8 metres high.

Kálvin tér and the Eastern City Gate
V. Kálvin tér
This square was the site of one of the medieval gates of the city until it was pulled down in 1796. During the war as many as five buildings suffered irreversible damage; luckily the two most valuable buildings, the Calvinist church (József Hofrichter, József Hild, 1813—51) and the old Two Lions Inn, open until 1881 (Kálvin tér 9.) survived. You can still see the two lions cowering above the main entrance.

The silhouette of the city gate is hidden by the much-debated new hotel. You can have a look at it in the New York-style café/salad bar/community space at the back of the left hand side part. The gate is also recalled by a marble statue suffocating in the subway, at the Kecskeméti utca end. The statue, some people feel, tries to symbolise the birth of the city, or rather a mother's lap. For others, it is an all too convenient public convenience.

National Museum — Nemzeti Múzeum 22A
VIII. Múzeum körút 14—16.
The largest museum in the country, built between 1837 and 1847, to the plans of Mihály Pollack. At that time this was so far from town that the weekly fair was held in Kálvin tér and some cattle sometimes wandered into the museum. It is almost 8,000 square metres in area, and it has five independent departments: the Archaeological Collection, the Medieval Collection, the Modern Collection, the Numismatics Collection and the Historical Portrait Collection.

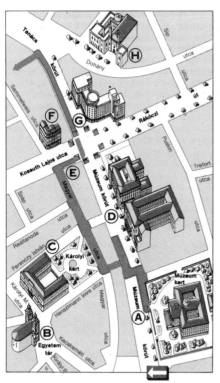

22 **A** National Museum, **B** University Church, **C** Károlyi Palace, now Museum of Literature, **D** Faculty of Sciences, Eötvös University, **E** Hotel Astoria, **F** House of Soviet Culture and Sciences, **G** Block of flats. **H** Synagogue.

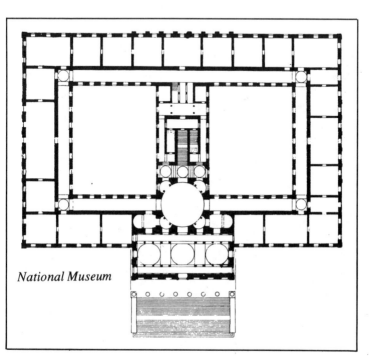

National Museum

The museum played an important role on the first day of the 1848 Revolution. On 15th March a huge crowd of demonstrators gathered here to listen to the speeches of "the Youth of March", their leaders. The speakers were standing on the wall left from the stairs while the crowd listened to them, clutching their umbrellas. Not everyone recognized the importance of the day; the director of the museum wrote the following into his diary on that day: "Some noisy mob had their hurlyburly outside which disturbed me in my work so I left for home". To the left on the ground floor are displayed the Hungarian crown jewels. They have a particularly spectacular history, having been lost, stolen or misappropriated at various times in history. The crown was made in the early Middle Ages, but is probably totally different from the one which was placed on the head of King St Stephen I, the founder of the Hungarian state, in the year 1000. The last king crowned with it was the last Hungarian king, Charles IV of the Hapsburgs in 1916.

After World War II it was taken out of the country by escaping Hungarian fascists. Then it was held in the United States for decades until President Carter decided to return the crown to the Hungarian state. Secretary of State Cyrus Vance brought it back to Budapest in 1978, escorted by a large American delegation.

There are more than ten statues in the Museum Garden. There is even a column straight from the Forum Romanum, a donation from Italy in 1930. The garden is locked at 9 p.m.

Around Museum Garden *are the most beautiful town houses built by the aristocrats of the last century. Some of them can be seen even today, like the one at Dienes utca 2., which is now the headquarters of the Association of Hungarian Architects, or another building on the corner of Múzeum utca and Pollack Mihály tér in line with the garden. Somewhat left of the latter there is a beautifully restored iron fence, which, however, hardly compensates for the sight of the glass blocks behind it. That is Hungarian Radio.*

At Múzeum körút 15. is the largest second-hand bookshop in Budapest. It has a wide range of antique books and foreign books. You may be lucky and find some surprising treasures, especially in German. Let's go back a couple of houses and go into No 21. It is a building with a passageway leading right through it and in the courtyard is the old city wall. On the other side there is a garden, Károlyi kert, where 15-20 years ago there used to be concerts in summer. People could hire cushions to put on the uncomfortable chairs. The garden used to belong to a palace which was under reconstruction for years, and when it was ready the tradition of the concerts was not revived. The streets around were already too noisy for music.

Behind Károlyi kert, Egyetemi templom (the University Church) stretches its chubby spires. Since it has been surrounded by larger buildings, its fine proportions cannot be enjoyed. The best place to look at it is perhaps exactly here, at the entrance to the building we have come through. The peculiarity of the church is that its chancel is not directed eastward.

Hotel Astoria 22E
V. Kossuth Lajos utca 19.
This busy crossroads of the city has taken its name from the hotel which was built with an old fashioned touch (Emil Ágoston, Artúr Hikisch, 1912—14). The lobby of the hotel is luxuriously elegant. Before reconstruction the Café looked the same.

Astoria *divides the inner boulevard road, Kiskörút, into two halves, which means that if you look towards the City, you will get to the Danube, no matter which direction you start walking, to the left, to the right or forward. The busy thoroughfare leading out of the city is Rákóczi út, which is a shopping street and ends where you can see the yellow façade of Keleti Railway Station in the distance. At Astoria, on one of the corners there used to be a large empty site: only one half of a large plan for a new complex has been completed (VII. Rákóczi út 4.: Béla Barát—Ede Novák, 1935; Rákóczi út 1.: Dezső Hültl, 1940). The war did not allow time and energy to finish the second half. The recent development doesn't really fit the environment — it's far too big and obtrusive, though it tries to echo the block opposite (Lajos Zalaváry, 1991).*
This is where the National Theatre was once located — pulled down in 1908.
The Astoria metro station on the Second (Red) Line is accessible from the subway although access is becoming more and more difficult. The way is often blocked by

vendors. The people wearing their folk costumes are from Transylvania, Hungarians now living in Romania, who sell things they have brought from their villages. The men can easily be recognized by their straw hats, blue broadcloth jackets and black boots.

Broadway Cinema
VII. Tanács körút 3.

This is the former cinema of the Institute of Cinematography, primarily showing old films and serious films, although sometimes box-office successes are not neglected. There are 6-8 films on at the same time, not only those which are advertised on the façade, in a complicated but logical order (see *Sources of Information* in the chapter *Entertainment*). Above the ticket office a display shows when and for which films you can get tickets. If the light is on, the tickets for that performance are still available. Unfortunately it does not compare with the Cinemathèque in Paris or the N.F.T. in London in range of programming.

The Great Synagogue 23C
VII. Dohány utca 2—8.

This is one of the largest synagogues in Europe (Ludwig Förster, 1844—59). The two onion-shaped domes are 43 metres high. Above the main

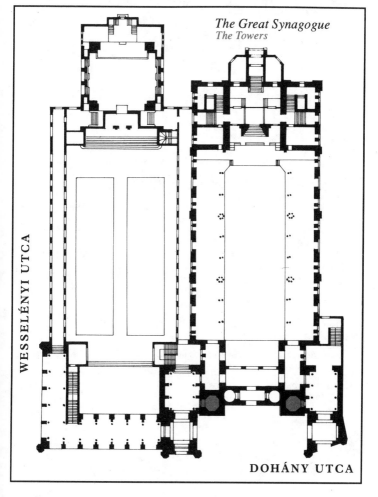

The Great Synagogue
The Towers

WESSELÉNYI UTCA

DOHÁNY UTCA

23 **A** House of Soviet Culture and Sciences, **B** Block of flats, **C** Great Synagogue, **D** Pest County Hall, **E** Former Design Center, **F** Budapest City Hall, former hospital for aged soldiers, **G** Main Post Office, **H** Servite Church, **I** Parking block, **J** Lutheran Church, **K** Block of flats, the beginning of a never completed avenue.

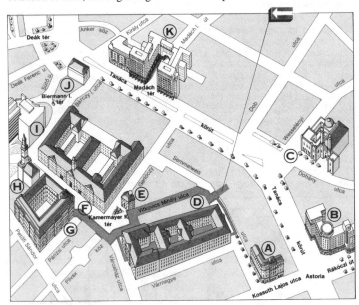

entrance the Hebrew line reads: "Make me a sanctuary and I will dwell among them" (Exodus 25,8).

The building which has three naves and a flat ceiling holds almost 3,000 worshippers: 1497 men on the ground floor and 1472 women in the gallery. The nave in the middle was built with a 12 metre cast iron piece spanning the distance. Ferenc Liszt and Saint-Saëns played the famous organ on several occasions.

The synagogue was originally built in an enclosed area. One of the buildings was the birthplace of Theodor Herzl, writer and journalist, who founded the Zionist movement (memorial tablet in the staircase of the corner building).

The arcade and the Heroes' Temple, which accommodates 250 people and is used for religious services on weekdays, were built when the building was enlarged (László Vágó, Ferenc Faragó, 1931). Outside hours of worship, the synagogue is open for visitors between 10 a.m. and 6 p.m. (3.30 p.m. in winter) on weekdays.

The Holocaust Memorial in the back garden (Imre Varga, 1989) is directly over the mass graves dug during the 1944—45 Hungarian Fascist period. On every leaf there is the name of a martyr.
In 1944, after the Nazi occupation of Hungary Budapest Jews were forced to move into a ghetto (they had never lived in one before) as a preparation to deportation. That finally — miraculously — didn't happen. But many died because of ill health, starvation and random murders. The pre-war percentage of 5% dwindled to 0.5% after the war. Practicallly all of them live in Budapest.

Röser Bazaar
V. Tanács körút 22.
In Farsi the word "bazaar" means marketplace, a broad street. In Budapest, it is usually a building with a passageway full of shops and workshops. They have recently begun to come to life again.

County Hall — Pest Megyei Közgyűlés 23D
V. Városház utca 7.
If you follow the route in this book, you can go into the County Hall from the back, between 6 a.m. and 5 p.m. on a workday. You should pretend that you belong here — then you are not stopped. The three-part building was completed in 1811, 1832 and 1841. In this surprising oasis was also the country prison and the prisoners' chapel. If you find the near gate locked, walk round the building from the right, via Vitkovics Mihály utca.

Budapest City Hall — Polgármesteri Hivatal 23F
V. Városház utca 9—11.
The construction of the building started in 1711 and it was intended to be a home for disabled soldiers and to have an area of 189 x 189 metres. In the end only the eastern wing was built by 1747 (by Anton Erhard Martinelli, Court Architect) and gave home to two thousand soldiers. Maria Theresa found it more beautiful than her own palace in Vienna. The rest of the building was never built, simply because permission was not given to break through the city wall. Later it became the Károly Army Barracks, and it has been the Town Hall since 1894. There are 47 windows in each row of the façade. The statues above the main entrance have been freshly sculpted.

Main Post Office 23G, 24A
V. Városház utca 13—15. Back door V. Városház utca 18.
This is the building which blocks the view of the Town Hall (Antal Skalniczky, 1875). Let's walk through the building on the ground floor. Right after I entered I could count four types of marble and six types of painted marble at the foot of the stairs. This is where the Poste Restante letters are held. Since the post office bought a Japanese lettersorting machine a few years ago, non-standard envelopes need stamps of double value.

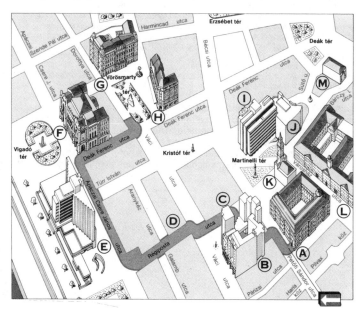

24 A Main Post Office, **B** Hotel Taverna, **C** Fontana Department Store, **D** McDonald's, **E** Hotel Intercontinental, **F** Vigadó, **G** Gerbeaud, **H** Luxus Department Store, **I** Office block, **J** Parking block, **K** Servite Church, **L** Budapest City Hall, **M** Lutheran Church.

A Block of Flats from the Early Forties
V. Párisi utca 6.
Only a few inhabitants of the city raise their heads to inspect the vivid, elegant façade of this building from Párisi utca. It was built in the middle of the war (Gedeon Gerlóczy, 1942—44). Council flats can be changed on a free market within certain limits; this means that if you move into a bigger or better flat, the law permits the former tenant to ask for a certain amount of money, as compensation, for the smaller flat he will have.

Hotel Taverna 24B
V. Váci utca 20.
We have seen its front façade on the First Walk. Now let's walk just as far as the crossing in the inner yard, and there, at the small clock tower, we turn right. On the four sides of the tower, four marvellously fusible small statues show the pleasures of relaxation (Géza Stremeny, 1985).

A Row of Lamps
V. Régiposta utca 10., between ground floor and first floor
Art nouveau neglected the cult of lions in Pest, these lamps are a rare exception. Rescue teams have been organised to save and repair the old lamps. In Váci utca there are a few too many of them — too much anti-quarianism is as bad as none.

Aranykéz utca 2.
The corner of V. Régiposta utca
The bold imagination of the design had the Vigadó in mind (Miklós and Ernő Román, 1930). The ground floor is occupied by offices, the lift starts from the level of one and a half floors. The City Protection Association has a separate group which specialize in lifts, attempting to save as many old lifts as possible.

Apáczai Csere János utca was on the river before the building of the quay; now it is overshadowed by the back of the Intercontinental Hotel. The street is homogeneous, all classicist buildings, all built with taste and all have their own surprises. At No 3 there is a half-naked beauty in marble, musing in the staircase, trying to hide one of her breasts behind a colourful and inadequate bunch of flowers. (Her name is Persephoneia.) At No 5 there are some exceptionally pretty iron gratings, wooden and stone ornaments protecting the corners of the building. Into No 7 a building company has moved in. Behind the gate the surprise is another door and some fine statuary.

This walk took me four and a half hours and that was without going into the National Museum. I collapsed on the terrace of Dunakorzó. This café existed at the time of old Promenade. Then I went to the Hyatt hotel to inspect the airplane. I would have liked to go to the top floor by lift, but this is now only usable by those staying at the hotel. The cheapest room is well over hundred dollars, which is rather expensive for a ride in a lift.

Walk Four

ANDRÁSSY ÚT AND VÁROSLIGET

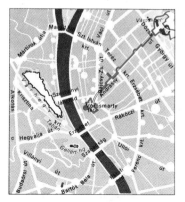

follows "Radial Avenue" at first. We shall look into two apartments here. We will take a bird's-eye view of Városliget and if you wish, you can row on the lake (or skate in wintertime). We shall visit a castle which is not part of the Amusement Park and we return by the underground built for the Great Exhibition.

Time: approximatchy 5 hours

"Merino" Textile Shop
V. Petőfi Sándor utca 20.
The older generation simply call it "Brammer's". Ödön Brammer, the textile merchant built the shop in 1924, when he had to move from a shop which he had been running successfully for years. His materials with their red, white and green labels were to be found in most large department stores in Western Europe at the beginning of the century. The English mahogany decoration of the shop is under a preservation order which means that not even a nail can be hammered into the walls. Now that the shop is owned by the state, the restorer wished to emphasize this by adding the state coat-of-arms in several dozen places on the old plaster decoration on the ceiling.

Former Török Bank Building
V. Martinelli tér 3.
The façade is an architectural battle-field between art nouveau and modernism (designed by Ármin Hegedüs, Henrik Bőhm, 1906). This building is typical of the City, the first two or three floors are occupied by offices and above these are flats. The title of the large glass mosaic is "The Apotheosis of Hungary". The modern elements seem to dominate now, perhaps because the astonishingly heavy Atlas statue, which used to crown the building, has been removed. Unfortunately the bank's owner was not a relative of mine.

Rózsavölgyi House
V. Martinelli tér 5.
The building was commissioned by a tailor's and it is only six years younger than the bank building (Béla Lajta, 1912). "In Hungary the buildings... speak French, German, Spanish, English but not Hungarian", wrote the designer of the building. Few were able to find such a modern way of speaking Hungarian! The building takes its name from the music shop which is still there, although the original interior was damaged by fire in 1955. They have a marvellous range of scores and old records.

The new buildings in the square unfortunately are out of place with the old. A government building and a multi-storey car-park, which criminally make the square smaller, and the telephone exchange, clashing with the church, were all built in the 1970s.

Café Quint
V. Bárczi István utca 1.
Behind the modest sign and the shopwindow a uniquely preserved interior used to be found. It was probably from the end of the 1950s, which did not differ largely from the style of pre-war Budapest. You could drink one of the best coffees in Pest here, which was made with the antique instruments displayed on the counter. Even the waitresses were conservative in their dress and manners. The caricatures on the wall commemorated the fencing victories of the proprietor. I can only hope that the facelift is not going to destroy the spirit of the place. (Closed for renovation at the time of going to press.)

There are not as many types of coffee in Budapest as in Vienna; people simply ask for "kávé", "fekete" or "dupla", which all refer to exactly the same: black espresso coffee. (The word "dupla" has survived from about twenty years ago, when "szimpla", a smaller portion, still existed.) For a cup of strong, Italian espresso-type coffee about 6 grams of pure ground coffee is used, and people drink it with or without sugar, milk, cream or whipped cream. In larger cafés you can order two different types of white coffee: one is made of real black coffee, the other from coffee substitute.

Lutheran Church and Museum 25I, 25H
V. Deák Ferenc tér 4.
A memorial tablet says "Sándor Petőfi, the romantic poet was educated here." The church attracts attention with its unornamented, spireless dignity. I remember there was a rather gigantic bust of Luther in the tiny courtyard, standing there as if it had grown out of the ground. It is not here any more. I went into the Lutheran Museum to ask about it. In the classrooms of the former school a touching exhibition has been arranged. Old clergymen, now pensioners, show visitors around and answer questions (in German as well). When examining one of the treasures of the collection, an altar-cloth from 1650, I had two questions put to me: Why do the disciples have red noses in the embroidered cloth and which of the disciples is missing?
The church (Mihály Pollack, 1799—1808), did have a spire originally but this had to be pulled down because the roof structure, which, out of necessity, had been built of cheap material, could no longer bear it. The inside of the church is amazingly simple, even by Lutheran standards. The choir was built only to diminish the echo. It is open only at times of religous services. The church is a vivid musical centre and the events are advertised on the front gate.
The Luther statue, I learned, had been left unfinished because of the war. Recently it was finished and set up in front of the Theological Academy, in the XIVth district.

Underground Railway Museum
In the subway at Deák tér
When building the Metro station, a short section of the first line became redundant. Some old carriages are exhibited here beside the old platform — and that is the whole museum. A tablet near the entrance in four languages gives a short history of the Franz Joseph Underground Railway, which was opened in 1896. There are more than the usual number of mistakes in the English version. If you walk to the end of the museum, it is there that the story really begins. The little museum has preserved the smell of the old line as well. Unfortunately, you cannot go into the old carriages. (I've seen rare exceptions made, however.) Entry into the museum is with a tram ticket.

After the museum, let's go one stop by the underground, which is now the First (Yellow) Metro Line (or, as people refer to it, the little Metro), in the direction of Mexikói út.

When you come up out of the station, you can see Andrássy út, originally Sugárút, or "Radial Avenue" in front of you, a masterpiece of the bold city planning of the

25 **A** Vigadó, **B** Gerbeaud, **C** Luxus Department Store, **D** Office
block, **E** Parking block, **F** Servite Church, **G** Budapest City Hall,
H Lutheran Museum, **I** Lutheran Church, **J** Block of flats, **K** Anker
palace, former Insurance Company, **L** Coach station, the youngest of Hungary's architectural monuments (1949), **M** Office block,
N St Stephen's Church.

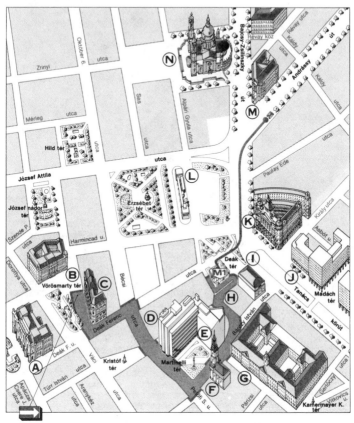

last century. It was finished in 1885 and took 14 years to build in the course of which 219 houses, mostly one-storey, had to be demolished. Although few of the individual buildings stand out from homogeneous impression, it is one of the finest streets in the eclectic style in Europe. Not that everyone shares this opinion: an American guidebook claims that the buildings of the road are "an architectural hodgepodge, although most of them are described as neo-classical". I would call it neo-Renaissance (or eclectic), and not neo-classic, which is called classicist in Hungary.

The city was so anxious to preserve the character of its beloved Sugárút that no form of public transport was allowed to ruin it. They did permit an underground line of 3 kilometres to be built underneath between 1894 and 1896. This was the second underground railway in Europe, after the London tube. The terminus at the far end was not where it is now: it was originally in Városliget, above ground. Long ago at the entrances to the stations there was a light on the street showing when a train was coming.

The name changes of Andrássy út are instructive: Sugár (Radial), Andrássy (after the 19th century statesman), Stalin (after the wise father of the world's proletariat), Hungarian Youth (in the days of the Revolution of 56), and Népköztársaság (People's Republic, 1957-89) and, now again Andrássy — the name that the real Budapesters never stopped using.

26 **A** Office block, former Insurance Company, **B** Drechsler Palace, **C** State Opera House, **D** The Goethe Institute, **E** Operetta Theatre, **F** Statue of Mór Jókai, novelist, **G** Statue of Endre Ady, poet.

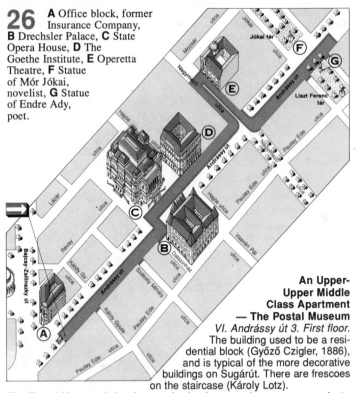

An Upper-Upper Middle Class Apartment — The Postal Museum
VI. Andrássy út 3. First floor.
The building used to be a residential block (Győző Czigler, 1886), and is typical of the more decorative buildings on Sugárút. There are frescoes on the staircase (Károly Lotz).

The Postal Museum is in what used to be the owner's seven-room private apartment. His initials: A.S., that stand for Andreas Saxlehner, can be seen all over the flat and the house. Apart from the portable furniture, everything is intact; the bath tub has only recently been sent to another museum.

The individual items of the collection can be put into operation by the attendants. You can see a section of a pneumatic dispatch, an old franking machine and even a model telephone exchange. From the window can be seen the dome of the Basilica from another angle.

Arany János Theatre
VI. Paulay Ede utca 35.
The fin-de-siècle cabaret has been modernized a couple of times since it opened in 1909. (Designed by Béla Lajta). During a recent facelift, the façade was restored in an exemplary way. (By Kőnig & Wagner Associates, Budapest, 1990). As the designer told a press conference, the restoration of the façade cost only 1/75 of the total budget. The foyer is somewhat controversial, reminding me of Trump Tower, New York. The auditorium is marvellous, though.

State Opera House 26C
VI. Andrássy út 22.
This is the most important building on this walk and, one of the most important buildings in the history of Hungarian architecture (Miklós Ybl, 1884). Work on the building lasted 9 years; the architect, who also directed the construction work, is said to have checked every cartload of bricks.

The huge building, perhaps because of the nature of its character, does not look that large at all, except perhaps when viewed from Gellérthegy. On the right there is the stage-door, on the left the carriage-way and entrance to the Royal Staircase. The auditorium sits 1,289 people. It is decorated by hundreds of statues and paintings both inside and out. It was lovingly restored in the 1980s.

In the niche to the right of the carriage-way a statue of Ferenc Liszt, to the left one of Ferenc Erkel, the father of Hungarian opera. In the niches at the corner of the building at the first floor level are statues of the muses of opera: Terpsichore, Erato, Thalia and Melpomene.

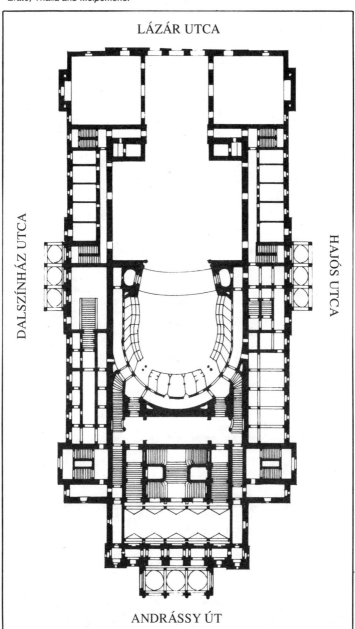

LÁZÁR UTCA

DALSZÍNHÁZ UTCA

HAJÓS UTCA

ANDRÁSSY ÚT

State Opera House — the façade

On the stone cornice of the terrace above the second floor level are the statues of (from left to right) Monteverdi, Alessandro Scarlatti, Gluck, Mozart, Beethoven (on the left); Rossini, Donizetti, Glinka, Wagner, Verdi, Gounod, Bizet (in the middle); Moussorgsky, Tchaikovsky, Moniuszko and Smetana (on the right).

The Opera House quickly became one of the leading musical centres of Europe. Gustav Mahler was the director here for three seasons and personally staged two Puccini operas. (After the first night of Madama Butterfly, the composer made drastic cuts in the score on his friends' advice.) After World War II, Otto Klemperer was director of the company for a short time. At present they have a repertoire of about 90 operas, a number unique in the world. The Erkel Theatre, seating 2,400 people, also belongs to the Opera.

The box-office is on the left-hand side of the building and is open between 10 a.m. and 7 p.m. from Tuesday to Saturday (lunchbreak between 2 and 2.30 p.m.) and between 10 a.m. and 1 p.m. on Sunday. The decoration around the office is in harmony with the building. The brass bars are intended to ensure civilized queuing. Some tickets are usually available on the day of the performance, although these are for the worst seats. When I last went to buy a ticket on a November morning I had no difficulty in getting one for the same evening. However stamped on the ticket was: "Warning! The stage cannot be seen from this seat".

Seats like that (all in the upper circle) are accessible from a separate staircase, through a side entrance. In fact I could not see anything of the stage although I could hear everything perfectly. I was sitting quite close to the fresco on the ceiling showing Olympus and all the Greek gods (by Károly Lotz) and closer still to the 3 ton bronze chandelier. From up there I could also see empty seats in the stalls. You can usually go down and take one of these seats in the interval.

There is an Opera Shop to the right of the main entrance, with very good books, collectibles & CDs. You can collect what you have bought after the performance.

Drechsler House 26B
VI. Andrássy út 25.
The apartment block opposite the Opera House took its name from a large café which used to occupy the ground floor (Ödön Lechner, Gyula Pártos, 1882). Six successive owners went bankrupt or committed sui-

cide; this is not necessarily the reason why the café disappeared. Now the building houses the State Ballet Institute, whose students are on the move in and out of the building at all times of the day. You can walk through the inner courtyard of the building which has an enchanting atmosphere (in wintertime only one of the gates is open). The graffiti indicates the time of the last renovation: BREAK.

Goethe Institute 26D
VI. Andrássy út 24.
The ground floor of this choice building — one of the most valuable spaces around town — has been conspicuously left empty. As a plaque at the gate commemorates, here, to the right of the gate used to be the Café Three Ravens (Három holló), where that genius of early twentieth century poetry, Endre Ady spent many a night.
The Hungarian government offered this premises, as a Romanian Cultural Centre to be opened on the same day when a Hungarian one opened in Bucharest. But all that was kept in secret. This did not happen for 15 years. Meanwhile, the Goethe Institute bought the space.

Művész Confectioner's
VI. Andrássy út 29.
It opens early in the morning, at 8 (10 on Saturday). This intimate middle-class place is rather noisy early on because of the staff but later their chatter is overcome by the hum of the customers. I like sitting in the inner room, left of the marble lady, who has an intense charm from the front. At around 9 a table would form of the old hands in show-business. At around 10 a very old, solitary man arrives and sits at his "törzsasztal" (doyen of customer's reserved table), in the right corner. He is the doyen of men of letters, a prolific author of dozens of historical novels. He has got an ancient, wooden coathanger in the self-service cloakroom, with the initials E. J. on it. Don't use it.
Fresh pastry arrives around half past eight. I usually order a white coffee, a French brioche and the chandelier. They are reluctant to turn on the chandelier in the middle. Closed on Sundays.

Andrássy út is cut in half by a market place, which used to be at Nagymező utca. The part which is now to the left of the road is nicknamed the Broadway of Pest. It has three theatres, a nightclub and the famous former Arizona nightclub, hence the name of the theatre next door. The short section to the right has a theatre, a cinema, an exhibition hall and a "little green house", an old public lavatory.
A con-man at the end of the century one morning started taking measurements at the upper end of Váci utca, attracting a great deal of attention. Finally a shop-keeper came out of his shop and asked him what he was doing. He replied that he was going to put up a "green house" there. The shopkeeper gave him some money to build it ten metres down the street, away from his door. There another shop-keeper came out as well and the whole story started all over again...

The Naffest of the Naff Interiors
VI. Andrássy út 37.
"Alles was gut und teuer": (everything that is good and expensive) as the ironic Budapest saying goes. Marble and mirrors all over the place, gilded plastic horn of plenty, Christ on the (plastic) cross over the Corinthian coloumns, a standard telephone and four monitors on the walls, with the MTV programme on three. Remarkably ostentatious: singular in Budapest.
The cakes are outstanding, despite the heavy hand with the sugar. Service is attentive and quick: not a state owned operation. For the sake of American readers: "naff" in British English means something like "tacky". In Hungarian: "ciki". A word that spread like prairie fire in the seventies.

Divatcsarnok Department Store
VI. Andrássy út 29.
This seven storey building, housing the old **Parisian Department Store**,

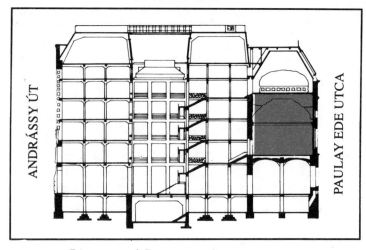

Divatcsarnok Department Store   Lotz Hall

opened its doors in 1911. Before there had been a casino on the site. The architect succeeded in persuading the commissioner to preserve the large ball room, which is now called "Lotz terem" (Lotz hall) and can be seen at the back of the department store between the first and the second floors. Sales and Christmas toy sales are held there. The roof garden, however, can no longer be visited, which is a pity since a splendid view is to be had from there. Now there is nothing to recall the slogan that appeared on handbills the year the department store was opened "The oldest European-standard department store in the country".

*At the crossing of Andrássy út and the Nagykörút, the buildings form an octagonal square, hence its name, **Oktogon**, used during all those 40-odd years when the signs showed "November 7 Square". There is an old café in the square, rebuilt in appalling taste (Abbázia), a shop where you buy various drinks, a Burger King shop (the biggest in the world) which is one of the most refreshimg modern spaces in town today — it would make a perfect Amsterdam-style "grand café".*
At this point the road widens and makes room for four rows of trees. Between the trees, where there is now a pavement, used to be a track for horse-riding. The road was paved with wooden cubes to absorb the noise of cartwheels and hooves. The trees were planted at that time and were undisturbed for about 90 years, until about ten years ago some men appeared with chainsaws one morning and removed the crown of most trees. This shocked the people of Budapest, who were somewhat comforted by the Parks and Gardens Department's explanation that it was a choice between pruning the trees back or watching them die.
But that didn't prove to be enough. Most of the trees had to be replaced since then. The new-old, recast lamps have recently been set up, entirely from donations. The big ones cost 150,000, the small ones 45,000 forints. (About 3000 and 900 dollars, respectively). A small plaque commemorates the donors' name — mostly corporate ones.

The Former Secret Police Building
VI. Andrássy út 60.
Now a state foreign trade operation called "Chemokomplex", this is where the secret police of the ultra-right wing inter-war regime operated. Many left-wing activists and Communists were detained, beaten and tortured here. After World War II, during the Communist "dark fifties", their secret police kept on using that headquarters. Many left-wing activists and communists were detained and tortured here. Some of those who had already been there. They were "persuaded" by the same equipment, inherited from the previous regime...
Some people would like to turn it into a museum of Stalinism.

27

A Statue of Mór Jókai,
B Statue of Endre Ady,
C An Unattractive Café,
D A Stamp Shop,
E Ferenc Liszt
Memorial Museum,
F Academy of
Fine Arts,
G Lukács
Confec-
tioner's.

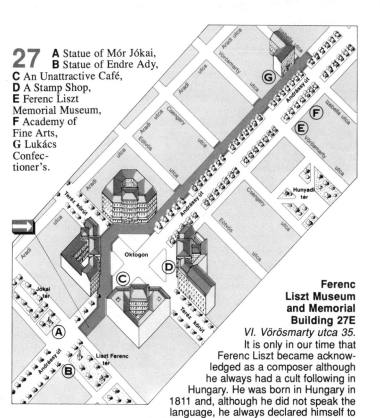

Ferenc Liszt Museum and Memorial Building 27E

VI. Vörösmarty utca 35.

It is only in our time that Ferenc Liszt became acknowledged as a composer although he always had a cult following in Hungary. He was born in Hungary in 1811 and, although he did not speak the language, he always declared himself to be Hungarian. His concerts at home were always great events. After his years in Paris, Weimar and Rome, he settled in Pest in 1875, partly because he wanted to found a Hungarian Royal Academy of Music in his own house. He moved into this building in 1879, into the first floor where the museum is situated. In the hall you can see the copper plate which was on the door of one of his apartments. The inscription says in Hungarian and in German: "Ferenc Liszt is at home between 3 and 4 p.m. on Tuesdays, Thursdays and Saturdays". Visiting hours are now longer: between 10 a.m. and 6 p.m. from Monday to Friday and between 9 a.m. and 5 p.m. on Saturdays. In the flat most of the furniture is original. The ground plans near the doors show the original pieces. There are many portraits, beautifully decorated rare musical instruments, even his travelling keyboard and his glass piano. Andrássy út can be viewed from the window.

At the entrance Liszt records and various editions related to the composer can be bought. There are several small concert and rehearsal halls in the building and the sound of rehearsals can usually be heard. The building resounds with music. Through a window on the ground floor you can peep into a wind instrument workshop where the instruments of music students are repaired.

The Old Exhibition Hall — Képzőművészeti Főiskola

VI. Andrássy út 69.

This building, which was erected by public subscription, tries to summarize all the architectural delicacies of the Italian Renaissance, and does so with considerable success (Adolf Lang, 1877). Now it houses the offices of the College of Fine Arts, and has recently started to organize exhibitions again. Everything inside, even the ceiling, is of painted and genuine marble. In the basement the State Puppet Theatre gives performances.

Lukács Confectioner's 27G
VI. Andrássy út 70.
The modest bill of fare may look familiar: it belongs to the Gerbeaud chain. You can choose between the Baroque splendour upstairs and the elegance of the 1930s on the ground floor. Service is considerably slower upstairs but you can admire the naked porcelain lady combing her hair on the marble fireplace. You can buy a copy in most large souvenir shops, in different sizes.

This confectioner's has long traditions and its décor is protected. Who permitted, then, that obnoxious "clock" over the counter, the bottom of a fake beer barrel? And the lit-up beer advertisements? And the primitive telephone set to the right of the entrance, while there is a notice on the original telephone booth to the right end of the shop, saying, out of work? It once belonged to the Lukács family. It was confiscated in 49 and closed to the public — it became the cafeteria of the secret police.

The maitre in the shop says that nowhere in town can you get two of his cakes (dobostorta and sarokház) as delicious as here. The shop is open every day from 9 a.m. to 8 p.m. (in summer to 9.30. p.m.).

Kodály körönd is one of the finest circuses of the city. It is enclosed by four town houses which used to be rented out and which by their shape form the circle that gives the circus (körönd) its name. Of the four, architectural experts usually prefer the one at No. 88—90; my favourite is No. 87—89, perhaps because of its rambling turret-rooms. In one of these rooms is the studio of Jenő Barcsay, the recently deceased master of modern Hungarian painting. In the same block, where the composer used to live, there is a Zoltán Kodály Museum now.
Further along from the Kodály Körönd, the road becomes even more airy. The houses are further apart, hiding behind front gardens. After a while a row of detached villas line the road. Unfortunately, after the last war, permission was given to build four modern buildings on this part of the road. Two of them are especially out of place and of strikingly inferior quality.

Former Pallavicini Palace 28D
VI. Andrássy út 98.
There are three courts inside and a rich neo-renaissance space (Gusztáv Petsacher, 1885). The ground floor copies the inner courtyard of the Palazzo Marini of Milano. The inscription over the gate says Bridge Construction Company. Its offices are to the right. There is an information desk for the official visitors. But you can visit the left part.

The booth reminds me of one of the "One-Minute-Stories" of the 20th century classic István Örkény. In the info cubicle, like that, the hitherto reliable attendant one day doesn't give the usual information about one of the offices, but, looking into the distance, says: "We were all taken from mud, and will one day disappear to the big, filthy nothing". So don't ask anything. Just go and see.

Hungarian Press Building 28E
VI. Andrássy út 101.
The plans for this building are missing from the archives, all we know about this fine example of an art nouveau villa is that it was built sometime between 1900 and 1903 for the "Timber-king of Szolnok" (a country town) and it housed the Turkish Embassy for a short time. No two windows are the same on this building. My favourite ornaments are the bird figures under the windows on the first floor and the stairs to the twin chimney. Above the birds you can see some strange, totally unfunctional iron consoles. They used to support a large sign saying "Huszonötödik Színház" (25th Theatre), which was the 25th professional theatre company in Hungary. In the early 1970s I frequently came here to watch their progressive, modern performances. Later, when the company's fresh and unconventional energies began to fade, they were given an elegant new building. In the end they merged into the National Theatre. One of the three most popular actors remained consistent to his artistic principles and, after fifteen great years in a country theatre, has just established a drama school in the Merlin Theatre; the second comitted suicide; the third has become the celebrated star of a cheap theatre in Pest.

28 **A** Lukács Confectioner's,
B Andrássy út 88—90.,
C Andrássy út 87—89.,
D Andrássy út 98.,
former Pallavicini
palace, **E** Press
House.

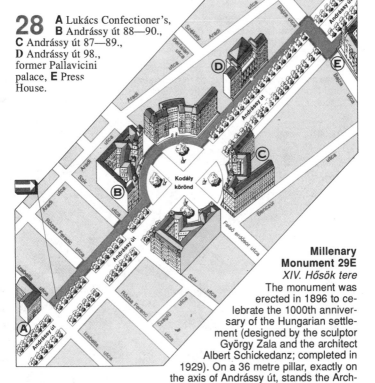

Millenary Monument 29E
XIV. Hősök tere

The monument was erected in 1896 to celebrate the 1000th anniversary of the Hungarian settlement (designed by the sculptor György Zala and the architect Albert Schickedanz; completed in 1929). On a 36 metre pillar, exactly on the axis of Andrássy út, stands the Archangel Gabriel, who, according to the legend, appeared in a dream of King St Stephen I, founder of the Hungarian state, and offered him the crown. Standing opposite the angel, it looks a bit rigid, theatrically solemn. It was awarded the Grand Prix at the 1900 World Exhibition in Paris. Facing the statue, the wings cover the angel's hands, holding the crown. Looking at it from the side, from outside one of the museums you will see how the angel balances on a ball, nearly floating in the air, and how affectionately he hands over the crown, with almost the whole of his body.

At the pedestal are the statues of the legendary "Seven Chieftains" who led their tribes on the conquest of present Hungary. The colonnade has two semicircles and is 85 metres wide, 25 metres in depth. Notice the symbolic figures on top of the corner pillars. The two in the middle are especially remarkable. On the left War whips his horses into an even more frantic gallop, opposite him Peace calmly rides at a slow pace, carrying a palm leaf in his hand. His calmness has apparently communicated itself to the horses.

At the left end of the left colonnade are the figures of Work and Welfare, on the other end those of Knowledge and Glory. Some of the statues of kings on the colonnade have been changed: after World War II those of Hapsburg rulers (Ferdinand I, Charles III, Maria Theresa, Leopold II, and Francis Joseph I) were replaced by Hungarian champions of freedom. Here is also the memorial tablet for our National Heroes. The pavement has recently been relaid and is now as smooth as glass. This turned the square into a meeting place for roller skaters and skateboarders overnight.

Museum of Fine Arts 29B
XIV. Hősök tere

The building to the left at the end of the square was completed in 1906 (designed by Albert Schickedanz and Fülöp Herzog), with the purpose of

housing the city's fine art collection, which by that time was quite remarkable. In the pediment above the main entrance the relief shows the fight
of Centaurs and the Lapiths. The scene is a completed copy of a frag-
ment on the Zeus Temple at Olympia.

Behind the attractive façade, the monumental staircases and spaces paid
no heed to the practical needs of the museum, which had to be rebuilt
several times. Since 1957 the National Gallery has been responsible for

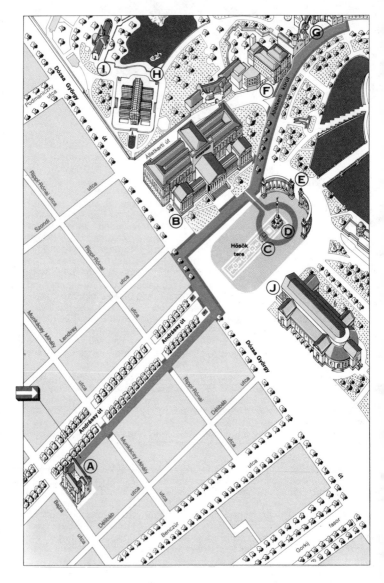

29   **A** Press House, **B** Museum of Fine Arts, **C** Tomb of the Unknown Soldier, **D** Archangel Gabriel and the Seven Chieftains,
E Millenary Monument, **F** Restaurant Gundel, **G** Zoo, **H** Palm House in
the Zoo, **I** Bird house in the Zoo, **J** Exhibition hall.

30 **A** Zoo: the Main Entrance, **B** Artificial Cliff, **C** Elephant House, **D** Municipal Circus, **E** Carousel in the Amusement Park, **F** Amusement Park: main entrance, **G** Széchenyi Baths, **H** Vajdahunyad Castle, **I** Statue of Anonymus, medieval chronicler, **J** Ice Rink, **K** Exhibition Hall, **L** Millenary Monument.

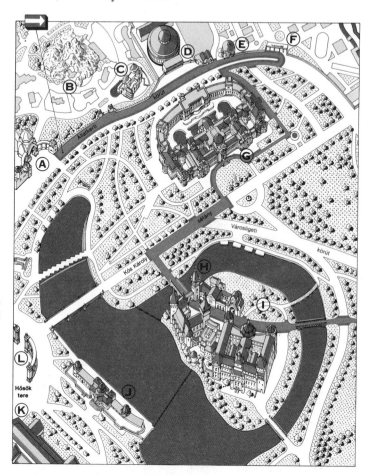

the Hungarian Collection. This museum has the following sections: Egyptian Collection, Antique Collection, Old Paintings (a very rich collection), Old Statues; Old Hungarian Collection, Graphic Art Collection and Modern Paintings and Statues.

At the moment large scale renovation of the building is under way. The "arts robbery of the century" took advantage of this. One night in November 1983, the robbers climbed up the scaffolding and into the museum, rendering the primitive alarm system harmless. Seven priceless paintings, two Raphaels among others, were stolen. It took ten weeks to find the paintings in the garden of a Greek monastery and to arrest the criminals in their homeland, Italy. Since then they have been sentenced to prison, the paintings have came home and the alarm system has been modernized. These paintings were restored then exhibited separately to a public that never before showed such an interest. Perhaps this is the first exhibition in Hungary where the items on display were not chosen by experts.

Városliget, with an area of about 1 square kilometre, is the largest park of the city. It does not take long to walk across it. Our route takes you down *Állatkerti körút*, past the Gundel Restaurant (which has one of the longest traditions in Budapest), past the Zoo (full of small buildings in a Hungarianized version of art nouveau) and past the Circus. Then we come to the

Amusement Park — Vidámpark 30F
XIV. Állatkerti körút 14—16.
This incredibly worn-down, ramshackle fun-fair is a sympathetic, sad place for those of us who cherish happy childhood memories of it. A full view of Városliget can be had from the FERRIS WHEEL. It is very wise to hold on tight when the creaking construction starts moving. If there are only a few visitors, only every second gondola can be used. There is always a very long queue for the ROLLER COASTER, but you should not have to wait more than 20-25 minutes for your turn. Almost one third of the wooden structure is replaced every year.
The SLOT-MACHINE HALL has probably the most worn out American and Soviet machines in the world. If one breaks down, you have to turn to one of the gentlemen wearing a blue coat, chatting in the middle of the hall. They will open the machine but usually just shake their heads and say "Play it on the other one", and point to a similar machine. Near the entrance is the octagonal building of the CAROUSEL. Children, some not so young, go mad with indecision over the ride to choose: the fiery horse, the luxurious triumphal coach or the spinning box. There is a fresco above and the operator peeps out from behind the organ. The other treasure of the fun-fair, the ENCHANTED CASTLE, was set on fire by an employee some ten years ago. His explanation was that he wanted to gain distinction by reporting the fire quickly. Only the exit of the castle, the "Barrel" survived. Its totally modernized successor naturally lacks the old atmosphere.
(From 1st October to 1st April the Amusement Park is only partially open. Most of its attractions, like the Roller Coaster or the Ferris Wheel are closed.)

Széchenyi Baths 30G
XIV. Állatkerti körút 9—11.
This, one of the largest of such buildings in Europe, is visited by 2 million people annually. It has two separate parts, two different worlds of architecture, which attract two different types of regulars. You have to go round the building to see the Medical Baths, which were the first to be built (Győző Czigler, Ede Dvorzsák, 1909—13). It is one of the most relaxed buildings of the turn of the century. The dome of the main entrance, which looks so light from the outside, has such a huge art nouveau mosaic inside, that it keeps visitors busy admiring it for long. The tiles on the floor, the lights, the door-frames, every fitting has been made with exceptional care. You may also walk a bit to the left or to the right, as far as the two side-domes. This is where guests can have a thermal bath in a tub, in a very luxurious environment. The numbers chalked on the doors show what time the guest started his bath.
Of the flood of notices in the entrance hall, those written only in Hungarian tell guests where to find the Complaints Book, or who and on which conditions can use the baths through the National Health Service.
The northern wing of the building was opened in 1927 (designed by Imre Francsek), and its neo-Baroque interior already shows a very modern use of space. The entrance hall has largely preserved its original condition; the newly added parts seem to be glaring mistakes (like the soft-drink machines) and only emphasise the original charm. The atmosphere is quite different here from that of the other wing. This part is always busy. Behind the entrance hall there is a battered but lively restaurant, from where you can see the pools.
In winter the pools are reached through a heated corridor. The water temperature in the large pool is 27, in the warm-water pool 38 Centigrade. A unique local sport is featured here: water-chess, which is played on floating cork chessboards with the normal rules.

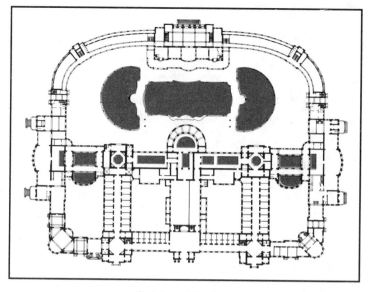

Széchenyi-Baths

The 1,000 years of the Hungarian state was celebrated in 1896 with a huge exhibition, which took up the whole area of Városliget. A popular attraction of the Millenary Exhibition was a group of buildings, set up temporarily with the purpose of showing the various architectural styles of those 1,000 years. Some of these were copies of real buildings. This mixture of buildings, however absurd the idea may now seem, met with such success that the city authorities commissioned a stone-version to be built after the exhibition. Its popular name is:

Vajdahunyad Castle 30H
XIV. Városliget
Part of it was modelled on a Transylvanian castle of that name by the architect, Ignác Alpár (finished by 1904). The building complex consists of four main parts: the Romanesque, Gothic, the Transitional and the Renaissance Baroque.

This bizarre notion was carried out by an architect of exceptional talent and imagination; the impression is rather that of a fairy tale than of kitsch. Naturally, no two turrets are the same, yet the many contrasting forms seem to combine into a unit. In winter the boating lake is turned into an ice rink. The permanent stone-building was planned for the purposes of the Agricultural Museum which still occupies the Castle. Opposite the main entrance is one of the most popular statues in Pest, that of Anonymus, he was the first medieval Hungarian chronicler whose epochal work was modestly signed with the words that appear on the pedestal of the statue: GLORIOSISSIMI BELAE REGIS NOTARIUS. This would be sufficient had not four kings been called Béla in the 12th and 13th century. His identity is still disputed by scholars. The sculptor has given him a hood so that his face cannot be seen (Miklós Ligeti, 1903).

Petőfi Hall 31B
XIV. Zichy Mihály út 14.
This youth centre was opened in 1985 after rebuilding an older exhibition hall. It is now the stronghold of Hungarian rock and pop music. But it also has a fleamarket, theatrical performances for children, a Roller Skate Club and on Saturday evenings the Csillagfény Disco. In summer there is also an open-air cinema but they have organized a new-wave fashion show, an underground theatrical performance, a disco-dancing competition, a "hairshow" too. In brief, it caters for and has caught the imagination of the young who flock to it.

31   **A** Vajdahunyad Castle, **B** Petőfi Csarnok — Metropolitan Youth Centre, **C** Fuit stone, **D** Former Metropolitan Museum (1885), **E** A pavilion from the time of the Budapest International Fair, **F** Statue of George Washington.

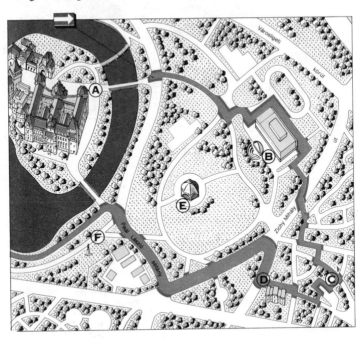

Their 142-4327 telephone number is an important one for you if you want information on what's happening in Budapest and they can usually help you in English or in German. Or you can do what the young do: just turn up and see what's happening.

Statue of George Washington 31F
XIV. Városliget
According to official American statistics, between 1871 and 1913, three and a half million Hungarian immigrants arrived in the United States. Many came frome Bohemia and Slovakia — hence "Bohunk" in American slang. The funds to erect this statue were collected by them (Gyula Beze-rédi, 1906).

Exhibition Hall — Műcsarnok 32B
XIV. Hősök tere
The largest exhibition hall in the country was opened in 1896, at the time of the Millenary celebrations. It was designed by the same architects as the Museum of Fine Arts opposite it. The ground plan shows the influence of the late Renaissance, as does the fine ornamentation of the façade. These were made from "frost-resistant pyrogranite", a contemporary Hungarian invention. Funds ran short when it came to decorating the pediment, the mosaic of "St Stephen, Patron of the Arts" only being put in place in 1941. During World War I it housed a military hospital.

The Exhibition Hall began as a stronghold of conservatism and remained as such until comparatively recently. The youthful lady who is the present director is doing her very best to make it into the home of contemporary arts. Has just been closed for two or three years of renovation.

32 A Ice Rink Building, **B** Exhibition Hall, **C—D** Millenary Monument, **E** Tomb of the Unknown Soldier, **F** Museum of Fine Arts.

*Along the side of Városliget there is a wide concrete pavement which is called **Fel-vonulási tér** (Procession Square). It is here that celebrations involving huge crowds of people, such as those on 4th April or 1st May, were held, and was also the scene of the military parade, which took place only in every fifth year. On such occasions there was a fly-past of fighter planes. In 1990, April 4 ceased to be a holiday — it celebrated the liberation of Hungary by the Red Army — to the sorrow of many a boys, since there would be no more military parades.*
 Opposite Gorkij fasor there stood the huge statue of Stalin, pulled down by the Revolution in 56. It was from the pediment of this statue that the communist leaders waved to the crowds that were passing by in their ten thousands. It was pulled down, just like the statue of Lenin, which was taken away to be repaired, be-cause of "metal fatigue", just when the ancient regime was collapsing. It never re-turned, of course. (It used to stand near the Exhibition Hall.)

This is the end of our walk in Városliget. As I have promised, we shall return to Vörösmarty tér by the Millenary underground. You have to get off at Deák tér.

Danubius Fountain 33B
V. Erzsébet tér
A fountain with three basins, with a male figure (Neptune?) symbolising the Danube on the top. The women sitting on the rim of the lower basin stand for three of the Danube tributaries, the Tisza, Dráva and Száva. The lower basin was carved out of a single piece of rock weighing almost 100 tons. Transporting a rock of this size presented quite a problem at the beginning of the 1880s (Miklós Ybl, Leó Feszler, 1893). This is a copy of the original, destroyed in World War II.

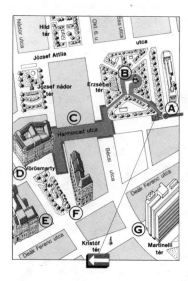

33 A Coach station,
B Danubius Fountain,
C British Embassy, D Gerbeaud,
E Vigadó, F Luxus,
G Office block.

British Council Library 33C
V. Harmincad utca 6.
This Victorian Library can be entered through a side door of the embassy building in which it is housed. The latest British newspapers are available and there is a substantial collection of books. Natural lighting comes through an ingenious crystal ceiling. Leave your bags and coats outside the reading room—the order is a bit soldierly. Library hours: 10 a.m. — 12.45 p.m. and 2.30 p.m. — 5 p.m. only on weekdays.

This walk took me five hours but I did not even look into the Museum of Fine Arts or the Exhibition Hall.
Despite the name, its not a beer hall, but an elegant institution, with more or less reserved tables for some British diplomats. The prices do reflect.

BUDAPEST BESTS :: BUDAPEST BESTS

András Nyerges, language teacher, editor, Budapest freak

My favourite places certainly include the Jazz pub **Billiard fél tízkor** (VIII. Mária utca at Pál). Beacause it's friendly, though trendy. Top Hungarian jazz musicians and Hungarian Dreher beer on draught — and a smile from the barmaid to go with every pint you order.

The most charming small museum is no doubt **Telefónia** (I. Úri utca 49.) Beautiful old telephones, telephone exchanges, and the whole story indeed, from Bell to the present day.

The only fast food place I like at the moment is a small den called **Orient** (V. Párizsi utca at Városház). Reasonable Shish Kebab and Falafel to take away.

Best ice cream for me is in a place called **Marcipán**: about a 100 meters from Orient, at the other end of Párisi utca, near the Váci utca corner. There is Hungarian style ice cream there. It's rewarding to try the other sweets, too — marzipan in all sorts of forms, shapes and colours.

Walk Five

ALONG AND BEHIND THE NAGYKÖRÚT

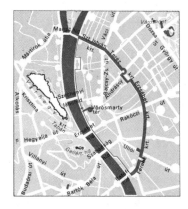

It takes us all the way down the Nagykörút, (or Great Boulevard) from the Danube to the Danube. We shall look into some side-streets and peer behind the plastic cover of the Corvin department store. We shall pay our respects to the site where the National Theatre used to be, visit the Royal Waiting Room, a handsome railway station and see something of Új-Lipótváros and return.

Time: Six hours plus

From Vigadó tér, we board a 2 or 2/A tram coming from the right. This will take us to the south end of the Nagykörút. While waiting you will probably notice how expansive the river panorama is. Budapest is made up of two equally important parts, of totally different character.
Right opposite us is the large building of the Bazaar at the foot of Castle Hill. The intention was that small shops would occupy the ground floor, now this houses sculptors' workshops. On the upper level the legendary rock concerts of the 1960s were held. These concerts affected the foundations of the building which is now awaiting restoration.
We get off at the fourth stop, that is, at the third bridge down from where we boarded the tram. Let's walk to the southern end of the bridge.

Petőfi híd 35A
Linking Boráros tér (Pest) and Goldmann György tér (Buda)
This was the fifth bridge of the city to be built and because of the 1930s recession it has almost no ornamentation (Pál Álgyay Hubert, 1933—37). One third of the construction costs were covered by the state and two thirds by the city through an increased property sales tax. Eight thousand tons of steel were used in the construction. The bridge was in use for less than 8 years before being demolished by the Nazis in January 1944. It was re-opened in 1952 with a lane for cyclists.

On the opposite side of the river is Lágymányos, a part of the XI. district, which was once a marsh.
Over there on the riverbank stands the campus of the Technical University, to the left is the railway bridge (1873—76, designer unknown). The bridge was so far away from the city itself that the designer presumably felt no obligation to any aesthetic principles.

34 **A** Luxus Department Store, **B** Fountain with lions, **C** Gerbeaud, **D** Vigadó, **E** Shipping company headquarters, with sirens.

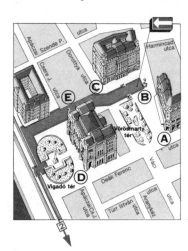

It has just recently been decided that the next of the city's bridges is to be built right beside this one.
Behind the railway bridge you can see the tip of Csepel Island — the proposed site for some ambitions development. Some planners dream of a miniature Manhattan, or Défense there. There is a lot of talk about an express train to Vienna that would only take 53 minutes. Also of incoming Hong Kong businessmen, who are on the way by the thousand to Hun Kong. The centre of the island can be reached in 13 minutes, by way of this commuters' train called HÉV. Its terminus is next to the bridge.
Walking through the subways we come to the beginning of our fifth walk.

Nagykörút — Grand Boulevard

This is the longest thoroughfare of the city, measuring exactly 4,114 metres. At this point the site was once a backwater of the Danube. By the end of the last century, the narrow streets of an unorganised suburb had developed here. Construction began in 1872, at the same time it did on Sugárút, and lasted 35 years. A total of 251 buildings were pulled down and 253, much larger than the original ones, were built. Nagykörút, with a sewerage system running underneath, is 45 metres wide at every point and crosses through 5 districts: hence its sections have different names — Ferenc, József, Erzsébet, Teréz and Szent István körút.

The Nagykörút helped to connect parts of the city, which before its existence, had been separate and socially very distinct. The boulevard was planned to run from the suburb at Boráros tér, through better-off districts, to the ill-famed slums of Margit híd. But by the time construction was completed the situation had changed utterly: the Margit híd area became a fashionable, well-off district as a consequence of the city settling itself around Parliament. So when the boulevard officially opened in 1906, it led from a poorer suburb towards better and better off districts — just as it does today.

Blocks of flats along the Nagykörút are very similar to one another. Their façades are all eclectic, showing elements of all sorts of architectural styles and usually have mortared walls decorated with plaster ornaments. The designs of the buildings imitated those of the townhouses along Andrássy út. On the streetside, light and spacious flats with at least two bedrooms were placed; these usually open into one another but usually have separate entrances from the bathroom, too. Their kitchens are large, with a small room opening from them, which was once the maid's room. The flats at the rear of the buildings, opening from the inner courtyard receive much less light. They have one or two rooms opening from one another, a kitchen and sometimes, a bathroom. The toilets were usually located together, at the end of the courtyard access balcony.
After World War II, when flats were nationalised, the larger front-facing flats were broken up into smaller units, often quite illogically. However, many flats at the rear acquired a bathroom. In the early 1980s the façades all along the Nagykörút were restored and the interiors of some buildings, such as that at Ferenc körút 5., were renovated. Rents are low compared to the cost of modern living. If you go into any building, you will see that they have two separate staircases: the main staircase leads to the front-facing flats and the one at the rear was used by tradesmen and servants. The main staircase is usually much more ornate, though sometimes, as at Ferenc körút 15., it looks just the same as that at the rear. Today everyone uses the main staircase or the lifts which have been since installed; the rear stairs are frequently not even cleaned properly. Inside, in the courtyards, a busy social life used to go on. A reminder of those times is the wooden frame on which carpets were beaten, called the poroló. Maids and later housewives used to take their carpets down to the courtyard and beat them there with a cane carpet beater (the prakker which was also what children were threatened with for misbehaviour). Everyone had to have an agreed upon time for beating their carpets and this gave rise to many arguments. When the ladies made peace, they used to gather in the yard to chat. Sadly, the general use of vacuum-cleaners, which had occurred by the mid- 1960s, brought to an end this busy social life.

Ferenc körút divides Ferencváros, the IXth district. It was named after Emperor Franz I, in 1792 when he came to the throne. This area was agricultural in the last century, but by the end of the 1800s important mills and meat plants had been established here. This soon multiplied the number of inhabitants (1896: 21 thousand, 1910: 88 thousand). It was, and still is, primarily a district where the inhabitants are working class and artisan. The modernization of the district was interrupted by the

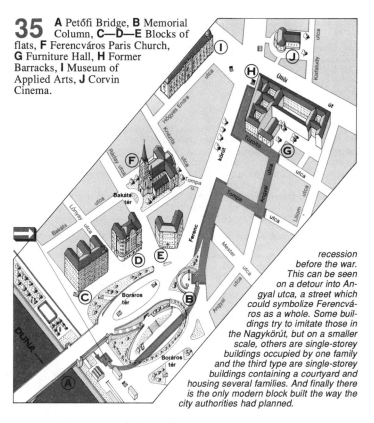

35 A Petőfi Bridge, **B** Memorial Column, **C—D—E** Blocks of flats, **F** Ferencváros Paris Church, **G** Furniture Hall, **H** Former Barracks, **I** Museum of Applied Arts, **J** Corvin Cinema.

recession before the war. This can be seen on a detour into Angyal utca, a street which could symbolize Ferencváros as a whole. Some buildings try to imitate those in the Nagykörút, but on a smaller scale, others are single-storey buildings occupied by one family and the third type are single-storey buildings containing a courtyard and housing several families. And finally there is the only modern block built the way the city authorities had planned.

Second Hand Furniture Store 35G
IX. Tűzoltó utca 14—16.
If you follow Angyal utca, it will lead you straight to this building which, with a slight exaggeration, could be called the museum of forgotten furniture. The ground floor is packed with wardrobes, the upper level with chairs and beds. Usually the furniture comes from older and poorer people without a family to leave it to. Many of the local households are furnished in this way. People who like home carpentry, slumming intellectuals or quite simply the poor come here to buy. If someone comes often enough, they are bound to find something they want among the trash — on the cheap. I once paid 30 Ft here for an armchair — having it re-covered cost me 700 Ft.

Museum of Applied Arts — Iparművészeti Múzeum 35I
IX. Üllői út 33—37.
In contrast to where we have just been, this place contains a collection of objects well worth preserving (Ödön Lechner and Gyula Pártos, 1896). There is an immediate clash between the exterior and the ceiling of the main entrance with the white interior; the aula is covered with a steel-framed glass ceiling. Recently a pendulum was hung from here to show the rotation of the Earth as part of the exhibition on the history of measuring time.

Üllői út separates the IX. district from the VIII. It begins at Kálvin tér and leads out of town as far as the Great Plain, running past the Ferencvárosi Torna Club (FTC) stadium. This is the home of Ferencváros football team, the best supported in the city and in the entire country (see the chapter Entertainment) — with a notorious hooligan following.

Former Army Barracks 35H

IX. Üllői út 49—51.

This large yellow building is the only one that was already here when the Nagykörút was being marked out (József Hild, 1845—46). It presently contains offices, warehouses and temporary housing for people whose home is under reconstruction.

Corvin Cinema 35J

VIII. Kisfaludy köz

The first cinemas in Budapest were usually installed on the ground floor of residential blocks; this is a rare exception (Emil Bauer, 1923). It has a lobby not much smaller than its auditorium, which seats 1,300 people. Along with the buildings surrounding it, it is a good example of architectural design which uses a modern structure but is conservative in style — the façade having neo-Baroque elements.

This was the headquarters of armed resistance in 1956 and close to the fiercest fighting. In 1989 one of the newly formed parties, the Alliance of Free Democrats held its founding Congress here, as a hint to continuity.

József körút the next section of the Nagykörút is thus called because it crosses the VIIIth district, Józsefváros. It was named in 1777 after Emperor Joseph II, who was then heir to the throne. Behind the row of buildings towards Kálvin tér, the area becomes more and more elegant (the aristocrats had their town-houses, **palota** *in Hungarian, built around the National Museum); to the right, however, it is rather less grand with many single-storey houses. A lot of cloak and dagger films have been shot around here and there are whole streets where nothing has changed since the beginning of the century (Futó utca, Nagytemplom utca or another one, blasphemously called Leonardo da Vinci utca). Standing on the corner of Nap utca you can see a stately old hospital building to the left, at the end of the small street on the other side of the Nagykörút, to the right there is a new housing estate. A drastic method of inner-city renewal was adapted here: some ten highrise blocks were built on the site of the old single-storey houses.*

The area along the Nagykörút on the city side and as far as Baross utca was called "Cérnakorzó" (Thread-promenade) before the war. It was only here that needlewomen used to walk after work to become acquainted with the craftsmen in the area. The ladies promenading here now are looking for less long-lasting relationships.

Józsefváros Parish Church

VIII. Horváth Mihály tér 7.

This Baroque church, re-built several times, has a fine location as the gateway of Józsefváros (József Thalherr, 1798). In front of the church there is a statue of Péter Pázmány, the scholarly priest who began the Counter-Reformation in Hungary (Béla Radnai, 1914).

Further down József körút the number of small shops increases: a watchmaker, a pipe shop, a souvenir shop disguised as a tobacconist's and the like. Souvenir shops have been flooded with things like quartz watches from the Far East or key cases which bleep when you whistle to them — it is difficult to find something which is typically Hungarian. Perhaps the plastic donkey which produces a cigarette from its backside when you pull its tail. That I have never seen anywhere else...

Rákóczi tér *is known not only for its market hall and the secondary school that trains dressmakers. It is also the centre of low prostitution. Since 1947 any form of "selling a woman's body for money" has been illegal in Hungary. After years of desperate and vain struggle to end prostitution, the aim now just seems to be to keep it under control. As everywhere in the world, prostitution is interwoven with crime. Women satisfying the needs of fastidious customers can be found only in expensive nightclubs or luxury hotels.*

The buildings here look the same as anywhere else. The value of flats, however, because of the notoriety of the location, is much lower around here. The area beyond the Nagykörút is, if possible, an even more pathetic sight than at other sections. If you peep into the ground floor flats in the dark, narrow streets, although it is not a nice thing to do even here, you can see that the lights have to be on in broad daylight and that some lightbulbs in the chandeliers are gone. A lot of lonely, hopeless, old people live here.

When I lived in this area for some years, I had the impression that alongside the old there lived a lot of young Gipsies settling there from the country — Gipsy musi-

cians with a number of kids or second-hand dealers. The courtyard my flat shared was in a five storey high cauldron and no one could keep any secret from the others. Everyone reached their flat by walking down the long access balcony and in so doing had to walk past the other flats that shared it. In summer, when people left windows open you could hear the baker's alarm clock go off at three in the morning and then, at 15 minute intervals, one after the other. Every district has a couple of pubs or restaurants where you can sense the atmosphere and all the distress of the area. In Józsefváros, it is the **Góbé** restaurant (József körút 28., on the corner of Bérkocsis utca). The regulars here are some of the girls working at Rákóczi tér, family men, often in tracksuits, as they pop in after (or before or even instead of) work and women of unidentifiable ages. The furnishings are quite worn and you have a feeling that should anything new be put in here, it would soon take on the look of the miserable surroundings. I did not try any of the food, though the lamb dishes have a certain reputation. On the other side of the Nagykörút there are computer shops, on this side small shops of various kinds: a ballet-shoe maker, an old fashioned hairdresser or a fountain-pen shop with long traditions. And there is a Totó-Lottó betting office as well. **Lottó** is a form of lottery, you buy a ticket and you tick off 5 numbers of the 90; **totó** is the Hungarian football pools where you have to find the final results of 13 + 1 football matches.

Blaha Lujza tér is one of the central squares in the city. It bisects the Nagykörút, which crosses Rákóczi út at this point. At one end of Rákóczi út there is Erzsébet híd, on the other you can see the great yellow mass of Keleti Railway Station. On the square was the old Nemzeti (National) Theatre and the famous clock standing in front of it, the standard rendezvous spot for ages. "I'll meet you at seven at the Nemzeti, where the number six tram stops", went the old song. The older generation still refer to the spot as the "Nemzeti". It would have been a nice gesture to call this stop of the Metro "Nemzeti" since it was partly due to the construction of the Metro that the old theatre building had to be demolished in 1966. Architects did not consider rebuilding it as at that time the eclectic style that dominates the Nagykörút was held as next to nothing. This was the era of modernization which favoured angular and zig-zag lines.

The editorial offices of the once dreaded communist party paper "Népszabadság" used to be here in the corner block (37A). Now it's by far the most successful and read-

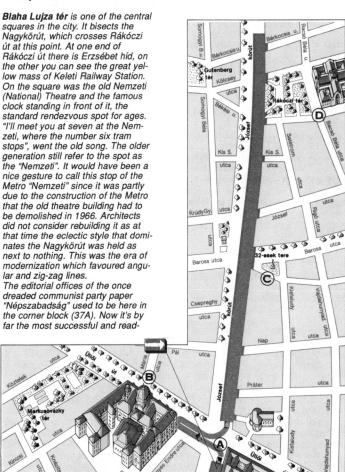

36 **A** Former Barracks, **B** Museum of Applied Arts, **C** War Memorial, **D** Market Hall.

*able daily, independent even of the small, run-of-the-mill left wing Socialist Party.
It now has a very democratic setup and German capital.*
The "new" façade of the Corvin department store
(Ferenc Battka, 1966) is the memorial of this wild rage of modernism.
*If you want to know what the original façade looked like, turn to the left side
of the building, the one which did not get its share of plastic cover.*
*This store can no longer use its not wildly original slogan which went
"The largest store — the largest choice" for there is now a larger department store.
Its customers are mainly people from the country, tourists from our neighbouring
countries or people from the suburbs. I can hardly wait until*
*the plastic façade is taken off and the old wall is painted out of some postmodern
inspiration. It would be a perfect wall for that (37B).*
*In the subway you can buy newspapers day and night and in the early
1960s the first automatic food dispensers were placed here. If you were tall
enough, you inserted the coin — but often nothing happened. You then had to
bang on the machine, whereupon the person who filled it with food from behind,
unwillingly came up and gave you your chosen cake with his own hand or gave
your money back. Now the said person sits behind a window.*
*At New Year's Eve at midnight the carnival-like procession reaches its climax in
streets around here; days before vendors invade the Körút selling the props:
paper trumpets of various sizes, rattles and masks. Police relax all
the parking restrictions on this day and even take flowerboxes away*
*from the corners, whose purpose is partly to stop pedestrians from crossing the
roads. It was at this crossing that the first set of traffic lights
was put up in 1926.*
*The buildings of the Nagykörút are not of much aesthetic value individually but
there is an exception:*

The New York House 37F
VII. Erzsébet körút 9—11.

can be seen from afar as it is situated on the bend in the road. It faces
three streets. Built as the headquarters of the New York Insurance Company (Alajos Hauszmann, 1891—95), it used to house Budapest Fleet
street. The neo-Renaissance building was built of fine long-lasting materials and in a tasteful, unique mixture of styles, which already hinted at
art-nouveau (especially in the formation of the tower). The building is a
little worn inside. Now its up for sale. You can ask in the café if it has already been sold. Mr. Bitai, the scrouge of young waiters, a retired
manager will surely know about it.

Café New York 37F
On the ground floor of the New York House. Budapest had about 500
cafés at the turn of the century but this was the most beautiful, the busiest and the one with the liveliest atmosphere. When it was opened, the
playwright Ferenc Molnár and his friends threw its key into the Danube
so that it should stay open night and day. As the saying goes, at that time
every writer had his own café and every café had its own writer. The New
York had many: virtually all the literary men of the era since those who
were not regulars here often dropped in. Many of them came to work here
from dark, unheated rooms they rented nearby to fill themselves on the
"writers plate" (cold meat, cheese and bread — with a discount for writers) and because the paper and ink was given to them free. The "literary
headwaiters" knew everybody's habits and latest works; better still, they
could eat on credit. A lot of them wrote here but some also sold their
books or looked for a job and everyone read the latest papers. The titles
of the papers the café had were set on a huge noticeboard: "all the dailies
and arts journals of the world". Of course, it was not only writers and
journalists who came here but people of all kinds, depending on the time
of day. Actors, journalists and cinema staff early in the morning, retired
actors later, elegant groups came to dinner, card players, circus artists
and waiters from other places enjoyed the nights. The clock above the
door to the basement restaurant called "Mély víz" (Deep water) must
have worked in those days.
The café had its golden age in the early 1910s, the second in the second

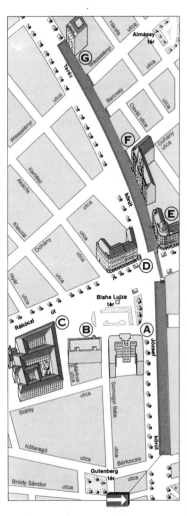

37 **A** The former "Népszabad-ság" House, **B** Corvin Department Store, **C** Rókus Hospital, **D** Block of flats, **E** Block of flats, with a supermarket on the ground floor, **F** New York Palace and the Café, **G** Madách Theatre.

half of the 1920s and in the early 1930s. It was here, up in the gallery that the most influential journals were edited. Caricatures of the old editors are still to be seen on the walls.

After World War II, through the windows of the shelled and burnt out café potatoes, and later, shoes were sold. Still later, as the café was seen as the symbol of the old, useless world, a sports shop was opened within the walls. It reopened as a café again in 1954. Writers came here again for a while but disappeared for good.

The New York is listed in all guide-books and has become the scene of tourist pilgrimage. Nowadays you find just a few newspapers here, but although the Venetian chandeliers were replaced by out-of-style modern ones during a renovation, the interior still retains its splendour. Now it is only open between 9 a.m. and 10 p.m. and the "Mélyvíz" restaurant from 11.30 a.m. to 3 p.m. and 6.30 p.m. to midnight.

Some writers and men of letters have returned. I and my friends are there every Thursday afternoon from 2 to 4, on the gallery. And though the waiters apparently don't read the high-brow literary and social monthly we own and publish, we have a "literary toilet-attendant", a senior lady who does read our paper, and refuses to let us pay if we use her facility. If we are not there on Thursday, the publication of the paper has unfortunately been discontinued.

Horizont Cinema
VII. Erzsébet körút 13.

Most cinemas in Budapest were built in the inter-war period and were quite modern for the time. This cinema opened in 1938 and looks exactly as it used to, only the films have changed. It no longer has a one hour continous programme, which started with a newsreel; it still has, however, the two reliefs depicting the history of mankind on either side of the screen.

*The Horizont is situated on the next section of the Körút, called **Erzsébet körút**. It runs through the VIIth district, Erzsébetváros, named, like the bridge, after Franz Joseph's wife. It is the most densely populated part of the city; 55 thousand people per square kilometre. You can find a number of single-storey buildings in this area, too. Along the Nagykörút itself there are innumerable new, small shops, especially in the entrances of the buildings and some even on the upper levels. Anyone can* *get a licence to run such a shop (providing there are no sanitary or professional objections) and the hope is that competition will lead to an increase in quality and a fall in prices.*

Hunnia Cinema
VII. Erzsébet körút 26.
The name refers to a Hungarian film production company, whose films and other Hungarian movies and art movies are shown here. It has also got something to do with the Hungarian Film Club Association. There is a very pleasant café inside. A trendy place, full of intellectuals.

Madách Theatre 37G
VII. Erzsébet körút 31—33.
This was built on the site of the old Orfeum between 1953 and 1961 (designed by Oszkár Kaufmann). It is very successful in terms of attracting audiences; since in Hungary almost all the theatres belong to the state, box-office success does not mean large profits. It is a repertory theatre, that is, they have several productions on at the same time. After running *Cats* for years, they are now scoring with *Joseph and his Technicolour Dreamcoat*.

Hotel Royal 38B
VII. Erzsébet körút 49.
When it was opened, this hotel was one of the largest in the whole Austro-Hungarian Empire (Rezső Ray, 1896). The four cast iron statues on the façade (the Four Seasons) were brought from Paris. In 1915 its luxurious hall room was converted into a cinema, which is still going strong, the Apollo (for 40 years called the Vörös Csillag, i.e. "Red Star".) Originally the building had a ground plan in the shape of an E but the two courtyards were closed in the early 1960s. The modernized portal has recently been rebuilt in its original form. Bought up by a Canadian hotel chain, it is now undergoing a renovation which is expected to be finished in 1993.

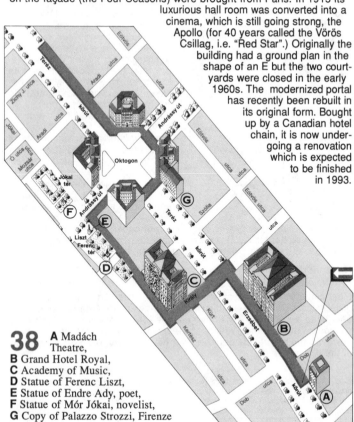

38 **A** Madách Theatre,
B Grand Hotel Royal,
C Academy of Music,
D Statue of Ferenc Liszt,
E Statue of Endre Ady, poet,
F Statue of Mór Jókai, novelist,
G Copy of Palazzo Strozzi, Firenze

The Smallest Shop in Town
VII. Erzsébet körút 48., in the entrance
A record shop in one square metre. The customer can stand just outside the door. Thoughtful service.
(If you find a smaller shop, please let me know by using the postcard at the back of this book.)

Terézváros, the VIth district, starts at Király utca. This street is lined with small shops on both sides. This old trade-district is coming back to life. After a short wide section it narrows and turns to the left. This was the other end of the make-shift ghetto district, where the Jewish population of Budapest was herded together by the German and Hungarian fascists to live in houses marked with a yellow star. Many did not survive. (See Holocaust Memorial, p. 96.)

Academy of Music 38C
VI. Liszt Ferenc tér 8.
The official name of the institution, Liszt Ferenc Zeneművészeti Főiskola, is between the two genii at the top of the building. Music teachers and

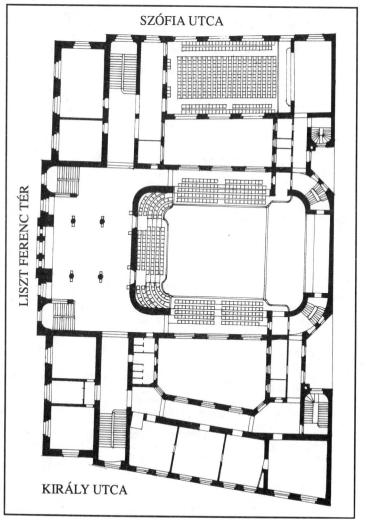

Liszt Academy of Music — the first floor

performing musicians are trained here — about 300 students in all. The building was completed in 1907, after three years to the plans of Flóris Korb and Kálmán Giergl. Above the main entrance the bronze statue of Ferenc Liszt can be seen (by Alajos Stróbl). The main hall (Nagyterem in Hungarian) is 25 by 17 metres and has 1,200 seats, the best of which is obviously the 1st seat in the 8th row — the director of Hungaroton, the Hungarian Record Company, always gets his complimentary ticket for this chair. The "best" just means that you have the best view of the stage from here, the acoustics in the hall are extraordinarily good, you can hear everything even from the back row of the gallery. These seats are usually taken by music students who loudly express their opinions on concerts from there.

On both sides of the recently acquired Walcker organ two inscriptions in Latin ask the audience to behave quietly. There are hundreds of other details to notice on the walls and on the ceiling.

The small concert hall (Kisterem in Hungarian), which you can reach from the first floor, seats 400 people. It too has good acoustics, but sometimes you can hear what is going on in the Nagyterem, as well. This is the venue of examination concerts for music students.

Everywhere in the building you can see the signs of an exceptionally careful and loving shaping of surfaces. This is generally true of most art nouveau buildings, but here the presence can also be felt of a special tranquility. As if this art nouveau building had grown straight out of eclecticism — fire out of water. This reminds me: you should be careful with the marble basin between the ground floor doors — it is always full of water, it is just too clean to be noticed. During term-time you can always walk into the building through the side entrance in Király utca in the lobby. It is worth buying a ticket for a concert that may not be first class just for the sake of the Nagyterem.

Children's Library
VI. Liszt Ferenc tér 6.
This is the library I joined at the age of 10 although it was a long way off from both my school and our home. The library was exactly like that of the adults, only everthing was smaller, including the chairs and the tables. It has a reading room facing the square and many catalogue cases. There used to be a big lady with red hair who helped us to find what we wanted. Above a shelf there used to be the notice: "A selection of adult literature". The red haired lady has now retired.

The New Liszt Statue
VI. Liszt Ferenc tér
The statue was erected to commemorate the 100th anniversary of the composer's death, although there are two full-figure Liszt statues within a distance of a few hundred metres (László Marton, 1986). The statue aroused considerable resistance in musical circles. Critics denounced it as "lukewarm-modern". Passersby ask each other who might the bald man on Liszt's lapel be. (It is the sculptor.)

"Palazzo Strozzi" 38G
VI. Teréz körút 67.
Another work of Alajos Hauszmann, the architect of the New York Palace, this one from 1884.

The original in Florence is larger and better. It houses offices and on the ground floor there is a richly decorated wedding-hall, perhaps the most fashionable in the whole city. Marriage services are conducted at district councils and at such central offices. The bride usually wears a white dress and the bridegroom a dark suit. The young couple are taken to the ceremony in cars decorated with flowers. The state does not recognize marriages in churches, as yet.

In the next section of Teréz körút you will have to forget my promise that we shall walk through better and better-off areas, although the boutiques are of better quality than those in Király utca. The Kőműves Restaurant ("The Bricklayer") is an

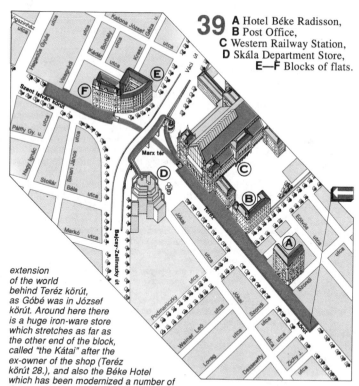

39
A Hotel Béke Radisson,
B Post Office,
C Western Railway Station,
D Skála Department Store,
E—F Blocks of flats.

*extension
of the world
behind Teréz körút,
as Góbé was in József
körút. Around here there
is a huge iron-ware store
which stretches as far as
the other end of the block,
called "the Kátai" after the
ex-owner of the shop (Teréz
körút 28.), and also the Béke Hotel
which has been modernized a number of
times — the last occasion being just recently. The pattiserie of the hotel is very
popular with businessmen for its good coffee, desserts and ice cream. The chubby
gentleman wearing a suit deals with an order as if everything there were his own.
On the façade two sitting lions hold a torch in their paws. Opposite the hotel there
is the Játékszín, a small theatre which does not have its own company (VII. Teréz
körút 48.). Rather unusually for Hungary, here the casts are put together only for
the individual production.*

Western Station — Nyugati pályaudvar 39C
VI. Teréz körút 55.

Trains set out for the North and the East from this finely restored historic
railway station, so the name (Western Railway Station) is misleading. A
long time ago the Vienna train had to make a long detour on its journey
since there was no bridge to cross the Danube. The building was constructed by the Eiffel Company of Paris (August de Serres, 1874—77) in
such a way that the old railway terminal was able to function undisturbed
underneath. Over the next 100 years the 25 thousand square metre hall
deteriorated and plans were made for a new building. Fortunately the
conservationists won and most of the old iron structure has been re-cast;
only the paint has been changed to light blue, the favourite colour of post-
modernism. Towards the end of the hall on the left there is a large closed
door, above the lintel is carved in marble: VIRIBUS UNITIS (With Unity
Strength). This used to be the door to the Royal Waiting Room. Although
pretty from outside it is already not in use. The new wing has been occupied by a row of 26 shops, the Westend Bevásárló Udvar, where you
can have a good idea of what sort of things people put their money into.
The elegant glass screen of the station's main façade lets trains become
part of the city's traffic. Once, about twenty years ago, a train actually
came through, when the brakes failed, and stopped at the tram stop.
The giant restaurant room to the right of the main entrance has been
turned into a McDonald's. The interior is quite a success. Note the ele-

gant, unobtrosive postmodern tower at the corner. Sometimes I come here to smell the odour, it reminds me of my first visits to Western Europe — my youth.

Skála Metro Department Store 39D
VI. Marx tér 1—2.
In the 1970s and the 1980s the Skála Shopping Chain was perhaps the most dramatically developing company in the country. So said TIME magazine in a full page they devoted to this company with the headline "Marks and Spencer of the East". Their store in Buda took over the title of "the largest store" from Corvin. This store in Pest (György Kővári, 1984) is much smaller, occupying only the first and second floors of the building. What they sell is of better quality than what other department stores offer and they are catering for the middle class. With the advent of really free business, the glory of this venture has faded — it turned out to be a success partly due to the good connections of the general manager's — to leading communist party personalities.

The old and the new character of the square is reflected in the two clocks. On the façade of the railway station, just below the copy of the crown, a traditional clock shows the time; in front of the department store, however, there is a digital clock. The time of the two clocks rarely coincide.
*Under **Marx tér** you find an entrance to the Nyugati Pályaudvar Metro station (Third (Blue) Metro Line). It has another entrance from the ticket office of the railway station.*
The last section of Nagykörút, Szent István körút, stretches from Marx tér to the Danube. This part of the road leads through two elegant residential districts, the 19th century Lipótváros and its extension to the north, Új-Lipótváros, built in the 1930s.

Vígszínház 40A
XIII. Szent István körút 14.
When the theatre was built in 1896 this area was so much out of town that the constructor was laughed at: who on earth is going to walk such a long way to see a play? The theatre, however, became very popular through some contemporary naturalist plays and French comedies. This is where Ferenc Molnár started out on his way towards international recognition.

In hardly any other theatre company do actors enjoy a star status such as those of the Vígszínház do. The present management is trying to establish a balance between popular plays and restrained experiments. There have also been produced several musicals.

When the building was constructed by the Viennese Fellner and Helmer company, much simpler and smaller scenery was used for the plays.

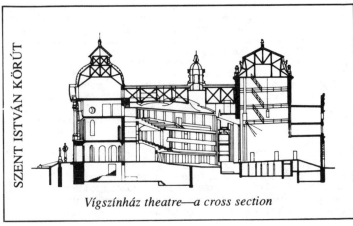

Vígszínház theatre—a cross section

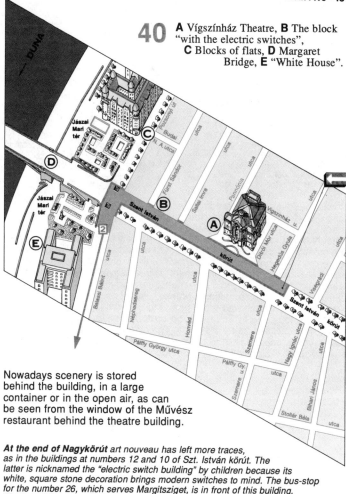

40   **A** Vígszínház Theatre, **B** The block "with the electric switches", **C** Blocks of flats, **D** Margaret Bridge, **E** "White House".

Nowadays scenery is stored behind the building, in a large container or in the open air, as can be seen from the window of the Művész restaurant behind the theatre building.

At the end of Nagykörút *art nouveau has left more traces, as in the buildings at numbers 12 and 10 of Szt. István körút. The latter is nicknamed the "electric switch building" by children because its white, square stone decoration brings modern switches to mind. The bus-stop for the number 26, which serves Margitsziget, is in front of this building. These buildings may look pleasant and interesting, from the inside they are just the typical Nagykörút blocks: narrow and dark. The part of Új-Lipótváros near the river has quite different buildings. On the site of the old factory district dozens of modern blocks of flats were constructed in the 1930s. These blocks, although they seem to be massive, closed structures, enclose large inner courtyards where only the windows of the kitchens and of the maids' rooms opened. The flats had modern practical features built in and were all supplied with central heating. Almost every room has a balcony and the flats receive a lot of light through the large windows.*

The buildings which were strange and unusual at the time were moved into by young, progressive sections of the middle class. The area was described by one of the residents, Antal Szerb, the writer, in his book, A Guidebook to Budapest for Martians (1935): "Nowadays you find the flattest modern palaces here. Inside the palaces young psychoanalysts are laying out each other's souls on the sofas, splendid amazons of bridge games are daydreaming in snow-white bathrooms, extraordinarily intelligent clerks tune their radios to the broadcast from Moscow... Everything is modern, simple, objective and uniformed here. The whole district is made up of two-room flats with a small sitting room and its residents are stubbornly, youthfully and energetically trying to conceal the only reality in their lives: none of them has any money at all." The main street of Új-Lipótváros is Pozsonyi út, which has as its centre the elegant Szent István park. The residents, who once were modern, young people, cling to the area they live in as is clear from the advertisements for changing flats. The value of these flats is almost as high as of those in Buda. Vígszínház draws its audiences from this area. In the auditorium, just as in the shops of the district, there are many elderly people: energetic, talkative, widowed

41 A Thonet House,
B Vigadó, **C** Gerbeaud,
D Luxus Department Store.

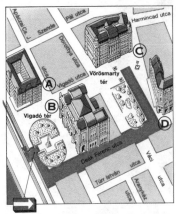

*ladies wearing much jewellery and
neatly dressed gentlemen. Their children often live somewhere around here,
at most, in the housing estate built
further north on the riverbank. There
are a lot of new cars and pretty small
shops around. The whole district apparently enjoys the sparkling life.
If you decide not to finish your walk in
Új-Lipótváros or in Margitsziget, just
board the number 2 tram at the
bridge; the fifth stop is Vigadó tér.*

It was the longest walk, leading a
long way away from the fine
marble tables of the Gerbeaud
café. Not that you cannot discover anything new just by sitting around in
the café. Only after completing this route myself and dropping on a chair
there did I first notice that the surface of the tables fall into two groups:
some are homogeneous some seem to have several layers — like the
Gerbeaud cakes. Surely you have noticed already that the legs of the tables are of three different kinds: bronze, copper and with curved legs...
If you wish to make even more profound observations and have some
more time to spend in Budapest, go on to the chapter For the Second
Time. You can find some distressingly non-touristic tips there — even
less touristic ones than in Walk Five. The those, leaving the city, may I
say "Jó utat" — Bon voyage. I hope you will come back sometime.

For the Second Time

Twelve buildings — Twelve streets and squares — Twelve old shops and workshops — Twelve impressions — Twelve styles

This chapter is for those who are already past the "beginner's stage" in Budapest. It recommends various things to see off the traditional tourist routes.

Twelwe buildings

The Bazaar and Kiosk in the Castle Gardens
I. Groza Péter rakpart
Built in 1872, at the foot of the gardens of the Royal Palace. Two elegant lions guard the gates, the premises, originally planned as shops, are now used by sculptors as workshops. The separate "kiosk" building was built to cover the chimney of the boiler-house, heating the Palace. Both buildings were designed by Miklós Ybl, whose statue is nearby.

The Municipal Library — Központi Szabó Ervin Könyvtár
VIII. Szabó Ervin tér 1.
The neo-Baroque palace of a baron's family from 1889. Except for Wednesdays, it is open daily between 9.00 a.m. and 9 p.m.; on Saturdays and Sundays between 9 a.m. and 1.00 p.m. On the ground floor to the right some lines from a poem hang in the cloakroom: "Oh, what a burdensome life / dressing and undressing every morning and night!" (János Arany).

The Church in Rezső tér
VIII. Rezső tér
This Catholic church, which has a central arrangement with a dome, is situated on the main square of an eighty-odd-year-old housing estate. Only Classicist plans could be submitted for the competition. The church was finished in 1928; the ornamentation recalls the time of the Hungarian settlement (towards the end of the 9th century). The huge bulk of the building can be seen far off from Üllői út, the main road leading south-east, though only few people go near it.

The Clock Villa
XII. Diana utca 25/c.
The villa of a chocolate factory owner, built in the 1840s, is a famous Classicist building. The bronze bell of the clock in the middle of the façade used to strike every quarter of an hour. (It no longer works.)
It was from here that the Hungarian commander watched the reoccupation of Buda in 1849.

The Field-guard Tower in Kőbánya
X. Harmat utca 31.
The tower with an outside spiral staircase used to be the place where the vineyards were watched over from on the hills of eastern Pest (1844). The architect who was commissioned to build the tower totally changed the plans: he favoured the contemporary latest fashion, Romantic style with Gothic elements. Now there is a wine bar in the tower. About 25 minutes from the centre by car.

Gozsdu udvar
Between VII. Dob utca 16. and VII. Király utca 11., near Deák tér

A long row of buildings with a passageway leading through them forming inner courtyards, between Dob utca and Király utca, with small shops and workshops. There is a bend in the middle of the passageway so you cannot see where you started out from if you look back. The area has preserved the atmosphere of the one-time Jewish quarter, which it is in the heart of.

The former House of Representatives
VIII. Bródy Sándor utca 8.

The palace, overlooking the Museum garden, was commissioned by Emperor Franz Joseph on 5th August 1865, the representatives had their first meeting here as little as five months later. During this time the site was assigned, plans drawn and the work done. This kept 800 workers busy day and night. Today it houses the Italian Cultural Institute.

Keleti Railway Station
VIII. Baross tér

This main railway station of the city was at first planned to be built in line with the Nagykörút — like Nyugati Station, which was still Austrian property at that time. In spite of its name (Eastern Railway Station) this is the terminus for the major express trains going westward. It was commissioned by Hungarian Railways (MÁV) and planned by Hungarian architects (Gyula Rochlitz, János Feketeházy, 1884). On each side of the glass main entrance there are the statues of George Stephenson and James Watt.

The Napoleon Courtyard
VI. Hajós utca 25.

This art nouveau block, overlooking three streets, needs to be seen from a large perspective, but it is built in a very narrow street. Notice the fine glass windows and the interesting small details of the building. High above, in the middle of the façade, a Napoleon figure looks down in contempt at the little traffic moving in the street. No one walking there would ever guess that the emperor is watching him.

VIII. Népszínház utca 16.

A typical block in the Józsefváros district, with two inner courtyards, in which I had the pleasure of living for two years. The structure requires wooden timbers for support, enough to make up a forest. The tenants in the rear court are especially dependent on each other. The moving spirit of the building is Mr. Laci, the caretaker, who accepts all sorts of duties, even delivering packages in his old Volkswagen. Naturally he would also bring sodawater bottles up to the tenants and let repairmen into the flats.

The Silk-spinning House
III. Miklós tér 1.

An industrial building, built in 1785 in late-Baroque style, which has an oval ground plan. The inner courtyard has recently been covered over with glass. It houses the Educational Information Centre, an institution which is also supported by UNESCO, which encourages old trades and tries to revive them. Near the restaurant area of Óbuda.

The Water-level Tower
Opposite I. Bem rakpart 3.

An ornamented iron tower of a man's height which keeps a diagram record of the water-level of the Danube. Now it works with electricity. At the Buda end of Lánchíd.

Twelve streets and squares

VII. Barát utca

The short street has only a few houses and looks as if it has been left behind from the 1930s. Uniform buildings with trees in front of them and mostly with their original signboards. It was rumoured that factory owners bought small flats here for their girlfriends, hence the name "Friend Street".

VIII. Baross utca

This is the main street of the Józsefváros district, leading from elegant Kálvin tér through increasingly poorer parts to the suburbs. Many joiners and upholsterers opened workshops here and their typical products are often mocked by the name "Baross utca style". This nickname refers to a richly ornamented, old-fashioned furniture, which has not changed for years and years and is bought almost exclusively by the tradespeople living in the area. From Horváth Mihály tér on the street looks like the main street of a provincial town.

VII. Dob utca

This street leads through the whole Erzsébetváros district from Tanács körút to Rottenbiller utca. The rows of buildings are never in line with each other, there is a wide variety of houses here, from ramshackle one-storey to large, four-storied buildings. The area between Kazinczy utca and Klauzál tér is "block 16", which is where a complex rehabilitation experiment was carried out. Soon after the successful reconstruction, a number of fashionable shops opened here and a postmodern building went up, in perfect harmony with its surroundings. It seems that the deterioration of the area was successfully stopped here.

II. Endrődi Sándor utca

Symbol of the new Rózsadomb. In the early 1980s large villas, breaking with the tradition of being laid out at a right angle, mushroomed on this part of the hill. Large vacant sites bordered by this street, Törökvész út, Fullánk utca and Kapy utca seem to have received building permission at the same time, giving the character of a German suburb to the whole.

See Rómer Flóris utca for an example of the old Rózsadomb.

II. Garas utca

One of the most pleasant streets in Buda, between a park called Városmajor and Fillér utca. This is where the fashionable Rózsadomb area begins. There are some carefully built apartment blocks in the street, which are higher than the villas built at the beginning of the century, and many tall trees. It looks somewhat like the XVIIth arrondisment of Paris.

VI. Gorkij fasor

One of the most attractive streets in Pest, which leads from Lövölde tér to Városliget, that is, it runs parallel to Andrássy út — though it is much quieter. The rows of horse-chestnuts grow unharmed too. There are old and modern villas, embassies, schools and even a factory in the street.

II. Gül Baba utca

A steeply rising, picturesque cobbled street, near the Buda end of Margit híd. This street leads to the tomb of the 16th century Turkish holy man Gül Baba. The "Father of Flowers" died in Buda in 1541. His memorial is the northernmost Islamic holy place kept up with subsidies from the Turkish government. Next to the tomb there is a small look-out tower.

XV. Hevesi Gyula út

The main street of a housing estate called Újpalota, all ten-story blocks. Now they already have a good confectioner's and even a second-hand bookshop. Unfortunately the trees are growing slowly and perhaps will never be as high as the tenth floor.

VIII. Mátyás tér

A square with a unique atmosphere in the heart of the Józsefváros district. It is surrounded by single-story and six-story buildings, workshops and pubs. The atmosphere perhaps comes from the fact that the traditional Jewish middleclass lives here together with gypsies who have come up to Budapest from the country. Near the edge of the square, at the corner of Koszorú utca and Tavaszmező utca, there is a touching statue of a tin-plate Christ.

VIII. Mikszáth Kálmán tér

A hidden gem in the inner Józsefváros area. It takes its name from one of the great Hungarian novelists (1847—1910), who spent the last years of his life here. His corpulent figure can be seen in the middle of the square. (Theodore Roosevelt's favourite novel was his "St Peter's Umbrella".)
Another building overlooking the square is the traditionally strict and high-standard grammar school of the Piarist Order.

II. Napraforgó utca

Called the "experimental housing estate" and of real interest to those who like architecture. It was built in 1931, with the support of the city, by a building entrepreneur. The twenty-two small buildings are on a small site but in a very clever arrangement. On one side, the back of the buildings overlook a small stream called Ördögárok. The names of the architects can be seen on a memorial column in the middle of the plot.

Twelwe old shops and workshops

A butcher's in the Lehel market
XIII. Lehel tér

This shop, entirely of wood, is at the southern edge of the market, near Váci út. The walls are blue and from the ceiling hangs a huge metal fan which I have never seen in operation. The butchers, just like their predecessors must have done a hundred years ago, produce their pencil stubs from behind their ears to write the price of the meat on the wrapping paper. The diploma hanging above the door certifies that it is an "Excellent shop". The better-looking a lady-customer is, the better the meat she gets — as everywhere, butchers are great admirers of the gentle sex.

A car electrics workshop
VI. Podmaniczky utca 75.

The tall, bespectacled, good-humoured man, Master Csizmadia, is always surrounded by 4-5 busy assistants. He is the guardian angel of taxi drivers and gives his help immediately if he can. He also gives an immediate and accurate diagnosis, free of charge. The workshop is partly equipped with 50-60 year old instruments and, at the back, he also has a classic American roll-top desk, always full of piles of documents.

The Fleischer shirt-making workshop
The corner of VI. Paulay Ede utca and VI. Nagymező utca

There are very few people who still buy their shirts bespoke. This shop has remained here, almost unchanged, from the 1920s. Between the shopwindow and the shop itself the partition is made from the traditional, vertically striped engraved glass.

Mrs. Klein, suitcase maker
V. Bihari János utca 20.

A couple of steps lead down into the basement. The customer is received by a lively, old lady who puts a chalkmark on the part of the suitcase needing to be repaired. In the back room behind her there are antediluvian sewing machines. At one of them, an elderly man is working, taking his time. They have so much work that they do not do any job with a deadline shorter than a month. On the shelf at the entrance there are suitcases, bags, handbags whose owners have not come to collect them — some have been there for years and years. They are for sale now. "Will you please give me a ring just in case? Perhaps we'll be ready before that", is her farewell greeting.

László Klem, furrier
XIII. Sallai Imre utca 18.

The small shop was modernized in the early 1960s and it still has the curved plastic letters. The notice "Latest models" must have been there since that time. At the entrance to the right a puppet dressed in a tailcoat offers notepaper and the card of the shop.

Lajos Libál, optician
V. Veres Pálné utca 7.

Some of the furniture might well be a hundred years old — the small drawers for example. Contact lenses are now increasingly common. Several state opticians have computers to examine their customers eyes. They also have lengthy queues.

Sándor Puskás, sign-painter
VI. Podmaniczky utca 18.

A traditional sign-painter's workshop very near Nyugati Railway Station. Everything is done by hand here, the brushes are put against a stick to measure the spacing. Behind the shopwindow, to the left of the entrance, one or two ageing assistants work. In the shopwindow a display of samples can be seen, not much influenced by changes in fashion.

A soda water workshop
The corner of VIII. Kisfaludy utca and VIII. Nap utca

A huge metal container, the size of a man, can be seen in this corner shop. Once the soda-water man used to do his round every day and wherever he stopped, rang his bell. Then the women came out and changed their empty bottles for full ones. Today there are only 5-6 soda-water men left in the whole of Budapest.

A tobacconist
XII. Márvány utca 24/b.

The usual, run-down tobacconist with everything under the sun in the shop from shoelaces through fresh wafers to magnifying glasses fastened on pens. But there are hardly any souvenirs, which makes it different from the tobacconists in the City area, which have been flooded with various bits of kitsch, electronic games and expensive perfumes.

Dénes Vándorffy, button shop
V. Váci utca 75.

This shop is in the southern end of Váci utca, the section not a pedestrian precinct, close to Szabadság híd. The bespectacled gentleman in a white coat, belying his age, briskly moves about in his small shop. There are some quite extraordinary buttons in his drawers. If he needs some special material, he goes and gets it even if he has to seek it out at the ends of the world for it. He specializes exclusively in women's buttons.

The Velvárt bicycle workshop
VII. Wesselényi utca 56.

Nándor Velvárt was a champion cyclist in the 1920s, winning several big international races. There are old photos, drawings and newspapers in the shopwindow. Everybody thinks that it is the ex-cyclist himself who runs the workshop. In fact, the manager is a friend of his, also a famous one-time cyclist. Every year the word goes around that he is retiring but then he changes his mind. He simply cannot stop working. His workshop is a fine example of poetic disorder.

Lajos Zsurek, cabinet maker
V. Irányi utca 9.

You can peep into the workshop through the door and the window. "Contemporary" furniture is made here. There are torsos, unfinished pieces on the gallery. The light is always on until late at night.

Twelve impressions

The "Ecseri" second-hand market
XIX. Nagykőrösi út 156.

The market, which has been driven out further and further of town step by step, is more interesting and varied than flea-markets in many western cities. It is rather like an antique shop crossed with a junk store, having all sorts of tit-bits some western treasure hunters are looking for. There are silver pocket watches, Thonet chairs, re-cast copper lamps; there are also trendy Italian jeans, the latest pop records and plastic carrier bags just for the price of 3-5 litres of milk. There are folk costumes, art nouveau blankets, "Everything-for-20-Forints" piles of clothes and all sorts of goods which may not be available in state shops. Although foreigners are usually over-charged, they can usually find something which is in fashion again at home but is still rubbish here. Bauhaus furniture is now becoming fashionable here but that from the 1950s still counts as trash. As it is quite difficult to get good quality modern furniture, some of the young furnish their homes from here. They fight over a piece with property men from theatres or with dealers over from Austria. The market is a museum of man-created forms, where there is a mixture of old and new, poor and rich; fine and chaotic. Nobody likes being photographed here but you can get old pictures and postcards.

The Ecseri Market can be found at the opening of the E5 motorway, coming from the city, next to the first footbridge over the road. Accessible by bus 54.

The Walled-in Lady, awaiting her husband
XIV. Thököly út 61.

On the side-wall of a yellow apartment block a strange, life-size statue is watching the street. According to the legend, this woman, her hair in a bun, spent many a day on this balcony, waiting for her husband's return from the Great War. She died of the Spanish influenza, two days before he arrived home. The husband had the statue erected in honour of his wife's fidelity.

The Fuit-stone
XIV. Városliget, between Olof Palme sétány and Hermina út

A simple tomb stone with the one Latin word carved into it: FUIT (was). A lawyer in Pest, who wished to remain unknown, left a large amount of money to the city and asked in return to be buried here and in this manner. On All Souls Day, November 1st, many people light candles at this stone, remembering their own loved ones. Near the Museum of Transport, in the direction of Dózsa György út.

The Botanical Garden — Hortus botanicus
VIII. Illés utca 25. T.: 133-4333

A pathetically neglected garden, full of the scents of the six thousand types of exotic plants, attracting almost as many birds. The buildings, among them the octagonal, glass-covered palm-house in the middle (József Drescher, 1867), are in an awful state, some of them used as dwelling places for families. Buying tickets is not taken seriously, nor is closing time. The huge, old, white dog hardly moves. Plants can be seen in taxonomical arrangement, from 9 a.m. to 4 p.m. on weekdays and from 9 a.m. to 1 p.m. at the weekend. The city has not protected this treasure. A large high-rise block now stands right next to it.

The second-hand shop in Hernád utca
VII. Hernád utca 7.

The shop offers things like bronze chandeliers, used prams and cheap chinaware. They have probably the widest range of the products of the East-European souvenir industry: glass fish, tapestry, plates to hang on the wall. There is no danger of being accused of smuggling art treasure on leaving the country if you buy anything here.

The Lukács Garden and the thanksgiving tablets
II. Frankel Leó út 25—29.

There has been a spa on the site of this 100-year-old building since the 16th century. It is also since then that those cured have placed tablets here to express their gratitude. The tablets on the wall praise the medicinal power of the spa in all languages, there are even Eastern scripts. Social life is very busy in the spa itself. It is frequented by many senior journalists close to the Establishment, and other leading lights. They complain the institution of private dressing-boxes has been abolished.

A cinema-tour

The most attractive cinemas in Budapest are the following: Apollo (VII. Erzsébet körút 45.), Atrium (II., Mártírok útja 55.), Bartók (XI. Bartók Béla út 64.), Horizont (VII. Erzsébet körút 13.), Puskin (V. Kossuth Lajos utca 18.), Uránia (VIII. Rákóczi út 21.), Zuglói (XIV. Angol utca 26.).

The main hall of the Polyclinic in Péterfy Sándor utca
VII. Péterfy Sándor utca 8.

The hospital was built for the Private Insurance Company for Civil Servants in 1934. Seeing the gaunt outside of the building, you would not guess how elegant the two-floor high hall is inside, with its glass roof that could be opened. In the hospital wing there used to be sitting rooms and small kitchenettes on every floor. Even a roof garden was built for sunbathing and the wards had only 3-5 patients in them. Not any more, when the author of this book was born here.

A self-service restaurant in Móricz Zsigmond körtér
XI. Móricz Zsigmond körtér 3/b.

A breakfast place and a restaurant, which smells of stale food. When you finally get your food after a considerable time spent in queuing, it is very unwise to leave it unattended even for a second, as a gentleman may come (the "marksman") who gets the impression that you have already finished your meal. (And goes for it.) Not recommended for its gastronomy. Also known as the "House of Lords".

XIV. Örs vezér tér — the eastern gate of the city

The Örs vezér tér terminal of the Second (Red) Metro Line decants people by the thousand into the subway. Some are hurrying towards the housing estate, some are travelling on to neighbouring villages by suburban train. 300,000 people use this subway every morning. This is where one of the funniest newsagents in the city can be found. His most famous shout is: "Ma még van még" (Some more left, just today). Here they shout out real or made-up headlines. The popular, bearded newsagent collects about 60-70 kilograms of coins every single day. One of his famous "headlines" is: "The wandering knife-grinder drank himself to death".

The Sunday car market
X. Albertirsai út
In the carpark next to the Budapest International Fair area every Sunday. If you just want to look around, it is better to go by the 100 bus than by car (the bus starts from the terminus of the Second (Red) Metro Line).

XIX. Kós Károly tér
Construction work on this working-class housing estate started in 1909, and was named after the Prime Minister who initiated the work, hence the name: Wekerle-telep. 650 single-storey and 270 one-storey houses were built here in very varied formations. Its centre, Kós Károly tér, can be approached through four ornamented gates, which were built in a style common in Transylvania. The whole gives the impression of a large village which has been swalloved up by the city. This square can be visited on the way to Ecseri Market.

Twelwe styles

The most typical buildings of the city are listed here, some of them have already been mentioned in our Walks. No styles are mentioned from the times before the 18th century, only those which have created the present face of the city.

Baroque
especially its Austrian version
St Anna Church (I. Batthyány tér), Egyetemi templom (The University Church — V. Eötvös Loránd utca 5.), Orthodox Serbian Church (V. Szerb utca 4.), Franciscan Monastery and Church in Buda (II. Mártírok útja 23.), the Town Hall in Buda (I. Szentháromság utca 2.), Erdődy palace (I. Táncsics Mihály utca 3.), the Semmelweis-house (I. Apród utca 1—3.), the Central City Hall, previously a hospital for disabled soldiers, "Invalidusház" (V. Városház utca 9—11.), the Castle in Nagytétény (XXII. Csókási Pál utca 9—11.).

Classicism
The National Museum (VIII. Múzeum körút 14—16.), the former Valero Silk Factory (V. Honvéd utca 26—30.), the Synagogue in Óbuda (III. Lajos utca 163.), the County Hall (V. Városház utca 7.), the former Ludovika Academy of Military Sciences (VIII. Kun Béla tér), the Trattner-house (V. Petőfi Sándor utca 2.), Károlyi Palace (V. Károlyi Mihály utca 16.), the former István Főherceg szálló (Archduke Stephen Hotel — V. Akadémia utca 16.).

Romantic
The Vigadó in Pest (V. Vigadó tér), the Synagogue (VII. Dohány utca 2—8.), the Unger-house (V. Múzeum körút 7.), the Pekáry-house (VII. Király utca 47.), the Kauser-house (VIII. Gyulai Pál utca 5.), Toldy Grammar School (I. Toldy Ferenc utca 9.), Nyugati Railway Station (VI. Marx tér), the former House of Representatives (VIII. Bródy Sándor utca 8.).

Eclectic
(We have seen so many examples of this style during the Walks that here only some less known but fine buildings are mentioned:) The new Town Hall

(V. Váci utca 62—64.), the Palace of Alajos Károlyi (VIII. Pollack Mihály tér), the Parish Church in Ferencváros (IX. Bakáts tér), the Parish Church in Erzsébetváros (VII. Rózsák tere), the Ádám-house (VIII. Bródy Sándor utca 4.).

Art Nouveau

The Museum of Applied Arts (IX. Üllői út 33—37.), the Parish Church in Kőbánya (X. Szent László tér), a block of flats (V. Honvéd utca 3.), Gresham Palace (V. Roosevelt tér 5.), the Geological Institute (XIV. Stefánia út 14.), the Academy of Music (VI. Liszt Ferenc tér 8.), the Post Office Savings Bank (V. Hold utca 4.), the Gellért Hotel and the Baths (XI. Szent Gellért tér).

Folkloristic-Modern ("National Romanticism")

Elementary School (XII. Városmajor utca 59.), a residential block (VIII. Népszínház utca 19.), the Nerve Surgery Institute (XIV. Amerikai út 57.), a residential block (XIII. Váci út 36.), the Calvinist Church in Gorkij fasor (VI. Gorkij fasor 4.), the Palatinus-houses (XIII. Pozsonyi út 2.).

Neo-Neo-Baroque ("Corvin-cinema style")

The Corvin cinema (VIII. Kisfaludy köz), Kaffka Margit Grammar School (XI. Villányi út 5—7.), the former Cistercian Grammar School (XI. Villányi út 27.), the block of flats of a mining company (V. Kossuth Lajos tér 13—15.), the former Cyclop Garage (VII. Kertész utca 24.), the new part of Széchenyi Baths (XIV. Állatkerti körút), the original façade of Corvin Department Store (VIII. Blaha Lujza tér).

Bauhaus

The row of apartment blocks lining XIII. Szent István park, the Atrium-houses and the cinema (II. Mártírok útja 55.), an apartment block (V. Régiposta utca 13.), the airport in Budaörs, the bell tower of the Catholic church in Városmajor (XII. Csaba utca 7.), an apartment block (VII. Rákóczi út 4.), the Post Office headquarters (VII. Hársfa utca 47.), Calvinist church and office buildings (V. Szabadság tér 2.), the housing estate in Napraforgó utca (IInd district).

The Style of the 1950s

The Council House of the IInd District (II. Mechwart tér), the Dubbing Film Studio (II. Vöröshadsereg útja 68.), the College of Applied Arts (II. Zugligeti út 9—25.), a building complex (XIV. Pákozdi tér area), the Party Headquarters in Óbuda (III. Flórián tér), a student hostel (XI. Bercsényi utca 28—30.), the MOM Cultural centre (XII. Csörsz utca 18.).

The Style of the 1960s

An office building (V. Bécsi utca 3.), a transmission station (IX. Csarnok tér 3.), Trade Union Centre (XIII. Váci út 73.), Kőbánya Cinema (X. Szent László tér), an apartment block (VIII. Luther utca 2.), an apartment block (V. József nádor tér 8.), the Budapest Hotel (II. Szilágyi Erzsébet fasor 47.), the headquarters of the Hungarian Automobile Association (II. Rómer Flóris utca 4.), the staircase block (I. Gellérthegy utca 35.), the temporary National Theatre (VII. Hevesi Sándor tér 4.), the false façade of Corvin Department Store (VIII. Blaha Lujza tér), The Aluminium Industry Trust Building (XIII. Pozsonyi út 56.).

The Style of the 1970s

Skála Budapest department store and the market (XI. Schönherz Zoltán utca 6—10.), office building and car-park (V. Martinelli tér), Duna Intercontinental Hotel, University of Horticulture, the lecture-hall wing (XI. Villányi út 35.), Party Educational Centre (XI. Villányi út 35.), the central buildings of the Medical University (IX. Nagyvárad tér 1.), Athenaeum Printing House (X. Kozma utca 2.), Domus furniture store (XIII. Róbert Károly körút 67.), Hilton Hotel (I. Hess András tér).

The End of Modernism
The Novotel, Penta, Forum and the Hyatt Hotels, the Institute of Haematology (XI. Daróczi út 24.), the Recreation Centre in Almássy tér (VII. Almássy tér 6.), the Krisztina Telephone Exchange (XII. Városmajor utca 35—37.), Skála Metro Department Store and office building (VI. Marx tér 1—2.), the new section of the Museum of Transport (XIV. Városligeti körút 11.), Waste Re-cycling Works (XV. Ifjú Gárda út 119—121.).

Postmodern
The Taverna Hotel and Trade Centre (V. Váci utca 20. and 19.), a block of flats (VII. Klauzál tér 12.), the Villa District in Endrődi Sándor utca (IInd district), the Bartók memorial building (II. Csalán utca 29.), the Ady Endre Cultural Centre (IV. Tavasz utca 4.), an apartment block (V. the corner of Semmelweis utca and Vitkovics Mihály utca), International Trade Centre (V. Bajcsy-Zsilinszky út 12.), Hotel Liget (VI. Dózsa György út 106.), Office block (I. Hegyalja út 21.).

BUDAPEST BESTS :: BUDAPEST BESTS

István Rév, historian, maverick political scientist and a true son of Buda

By taking a 91 bus from the Vígszínház and, after it winds its way up **Rózsadomb,** by getting off in the quietness of Áfonya utca to a stroll up to the József-hegy look-out point on the very top of Rózsa- domb, a truly charming view is to be had. In clear weather, looking north, not only all the Danube bridges and the hills lying beyond the city but the contours of the Carpathians themselves can be seen. A clear view all around is blocked only to the south-east by two boorish houses that obscure the hill known as Svábhegy. In the house that ruins one of the city's finest views, on Józsefhegy, lives A- J-, who at the time he moved in was responsible for the city's development and planning.

At the beginning of the century, Rózsadomb was essentially a place of parks, vineyards, gardens and kitchen gardens; it was between the too wars that building started here. Out of the noisy city there mainly came Christian middle-class citizens to build their detached houses and their rented-off villas of various sizes. After the WWII, Rózsadomb became the quarter for the déclassé: wives of arms manufacturers who painted scarves, of business magnates who became daily helps, widows of distillery proprietors who survived by giving German lessons, barons reduced to smuggling codices, chairmen of foundations, retrained as carpenters. Here they all lived in their seized and expropriated houses.

During the fifties communist functionaries began moving into the vacant expropriated villas. On the streets of the hill could be seen the Chevrolets from before the war and the Soviet makes brought immediately after the war, the Zims, the Zils, the Pobyedas. After 1956 János Kádár, the dictator himself came to live at number 19-23 Cserje utca at the foot of the Józsefhegy lookout tower. For 33 years he stood at the helm of the country and the Party... It is because of him it is still difficult to reach the vantage point by car, the streets being one-way and filled with no halting signs.

From the mid-sixties, as constraints on the real estate market if not on the country began to be relaxed, the *nouveaux riches* who had made their fortunes in the second economy began to appear on the hill. Their dull apartment houses gradually gave way to suburban villas copied from West German magazines, and to Disneyland dreamhouses.

To a Central European Beverly Hills.

Who was who

Periods of Hungarian History

895—896	THE SETTLEMENT (Hungarian tribes reach the Carpathian Basin)
TO 955	Raids and incursions into Western Europe
1000	CONVERSION TO CHRISTIANITY
1000—1541	INDEPENDENT HUNGARIAN KINGDOM
	1241—42 Mongolian Invasion
	1458—1490 King Mátyás (Matthias)
	1526 Utter defeat of the Hungarian army by the Turks
1541—1686	TURKISH OCCUPATION
1686—1867	AUSTRIAN RULE
	1703—1711 War of Independence led by Ferenc Rákóczi II
	1848—49 Revolution and War of Independence
	1867 The Austro—Hungarian Compromise
1867—1918	AUSTRO—HUNGARIAN MONARCHY
1918—19	HUNGARIAN REPUBLIC
	1918 The "Aster Revolution"
	1919 Hungarian Soviet Republic
1919—1946	KINGDOM WITHOUT A KING
	Miklós Horthy as Regent
	The Trianon Treaty of 1920 assigned 3/5 of Hungary's territory to the successor states
	1941 Entry into the war as ally of Germany
	1944 Attempts to negotiate armistice
1944	GERMAN INVASION
1946—48	HUNGARIAN REPUBLIC
	(Coalition government)
1948	"Year of the Turnover": Communist coup d'état.
1956 23 Oct	REVOLUTION
1956 4 Nov	János Kádár returns with Russian tanks.
1956—58	The Revenge. Over 400 executions, including Imre Nagy and his circle
1963	Amnesty to most political prisoners
1968	New Economic Management
1972—73	Reforms refrozen
1979	Stagnation starts
1984—86	Debts doubled — but boosting policies fail
1988 May	Ailing, outmanoevred Kádár deposed after 32 years in power.
1988—89	The disintegration of the "party-state"
1990 25 March	RETURN TO PARLAMENTARY DEMOCRACY

The Kings of Hungary

1. THE ÁRPÁD DYNASTY

1000—1038 St Stephen I	1141—1162 Géza II
1038—1041 (Orseolo) Péter	1162—1172 István III
1041—1044 Aba Sámuel	1162—1163 László II
1044—1046 (Orseolo) Péter recrowned	1163—1165 István IV
1046—1060 András I	1172—1196 Béla III
1060—1063 Béla I	1196—1204 Imre
1063—1074 Salamon	1204—1205 László III
1074—1077 Géza I	1205—1235 András II
1077—1095 St László I	1235—1270 Béla IV
1095—1116 Kálmán (of the Books)	1270—1272 István V
1116—1131 István II	1272—1290 László IV (the Kun)
1131—1141 Béla (the Blind)	1290—1301 András III

2. KINGS OF VARIOUS HOUSES

1301—1305 Vencel (of Premysl)	1444—1446 Interregnum
1305—1307 Ottó (of Wittelsbach)	1446—1453 János Hunyadi Regent
1307—1342 Károly Róbert (of Anjou)	1453—1457 László V (of Habsburg)
1342—1382 Lajos the Great (of Anjou)	1458—1490 Mátyás I (Hunyadi)
1382—1385 Mária (of Anjou)	1490—1516 Ulászló (of Jagello)
1385—1386 Károly II (of Anjou)	1516—1526 Lajos II (of Jagello)
1387—1437 Zsigmond (of Luxemburg)	1526—1540 János I (Szapolyai)
1437—1439 Albert (of Hapsburg)	1540—1553 János Zsigmond
1440—1444 Ulászló I (of Jagello)	

3. KINGS OF THE HOUSE OF HABSBURG

1526—1564 Ferdinánd I	1705—1711 Ferenc Rákóczi II
1564—1576 Miksa I	— Regent
1576—1608 Rudolf I	1711—1740 Károly III
1605—1606 István Bocskai — Regent	1740—1780 Mária Terézia
1608—1619 Mátyás II	1780—1790 József II
1619—1637 Ferdinánd II	1790—1792 Lipót II
1637—1657 Ferdinánd III	1792—1835 Ferenc I
1647—1654 Ferdinánd IV	1835—1848 Ferdinánd V
1657—1705 Lipót I	1849 —Lajos Kossuth — Regent
1705—1711 József I	1848—1916 Franz Joseph I
	1916—1918 Károly IV

People on Streetsigns

This is a selective list of people whose names we have met in street names. Law does not permit the naming of a street after people deceased less than 5 years before.

Ady, Endre (1877—1919) Poet, journalist, founder of modern Hungarian lyric poetry; central figure of intellectual life at the beginning of the century.

Anonymus (late 11th century—early 12th century?) Chronicler, author of the earliest Hungarian historical work, Gesta Hungarorum. See Walk Four, Vajdahunyad Castle, about him and his statue.

Apáczai Csere, János (1625—1659) Hungarian theologian in Transylvania, writer, teacher. Author of the Hungarian Encyclopedia.

Arany, János (1817—1882) The greatest Hungarian epic poet. His statue is in front of the National Museum.

Árpád, Prince (?—907?) Leader of the alliance of tribes which conquered the territory of present-day Hungary, chieftain of the "Magyar" tribe. Ancestor of Hungarian kings.

Aulich, Lajos (1792—1849) General, Minister of War during the 1848 War of Independence. One of the 13 generals executed after the defeat.

Babits, Mihály (1883—1941) Poet, literary translator and novelist. Major influence on literary life.

Bajcsy-Zsilinszky, Endre (1886—1944) Political writer and politician, a leader of the resistance during World War II. Executed at Christmas 1944.

Balassi, Bálint (1554—1594) Great poet and womanizer of the Hungarian Renaissance. One of the first to write poetry in Hungarian, not Latin. His statue is in Kodály körönd.

Baross, Gábor (1848—1892) Politician, the Iron Minister. Initiator of the nationalization of the railway system and the organisation of cheap transport. His statue is in the square named after him.

Bartók, Béla (1881—1945) Composer, pianist, musicologist and teacher. A major figure in 20th European century music. Died in New York. He declared in his will that no street can bear his name until there is a Hitler Square and a Mussolini Square in Budapest.

Báthori, István (1533—1586) Prince of Transylvania, from 1576 King of Poland.

Batthyány, Lajos (1806—1849) Landowner, politician. The first Prime Minister in 1848. Executed after the defeat.

Bem, József (1794—1850) Polish army officer, Hungarian general, leading figure in the 1848—49 War of Independence.

Blaha, Lujza (1850—1926) Leading actress and prima donna, the "Nightingale of the Nation".

Boráros, János (1755—1834) Chief Justice, later Mayor of Pest. He opened Városliget to the public.

Bródy, Sándor (1863—1924) Writer, dramatist and muckraker journalist. Helped naturalism to be accepted in Hungary.

Clark, Ádám (1811—1866) English architect, directed the construction of Lánchíd, designed the Tunnel. Settled in Hungary.

Csokonai, Vitéz Mihály (1773—1805) Poet, dramatist, teacher. The major figure in the Hungarian Enlightenment.

Deák, Ferenc (1803—1876) Politician, lawyer, the "Sage of the Nation". Had a decisive role in the Compromise with the Hapsburgs (1867). His statue is in Roosevelt tér.

Dürer, Albrecht "Ajtósi" (1471—1528) German painter and graphic artist. His father immigrated to Nürnberg from a Hungarian village called Ajtós. The "Dürer" name is a literal translation of the name of the Hungarian village.

Eötvös, József (1813—1871) Writer, poet and politician. Introduced Public Education Law. His statue is outside the Forum Hotel.

Eötvös, Loránd (1848—1919) University professor of physics, minister, son of József Eötvös, inventor of the pendulum named after him.

Erkel, Ferenc (1810—1893) Composer, conductor and pianist. Founded the national opera and composed the music for the national anthem.

Erzsébet (Elizabeth), Queen (1837—1898) Wife of Franz Joseph Austrian Emperor and King of Hungary. She learned the Hungarian language and spent a great deal of time in Hungary.

Gárdonyi, Géza (1863—1922) Writer, poet and teacher. Still one of the most widely read writers.

Hunyadi, János (1407?—1456) Regent and army leader. His victories over the Turkish army temporarily held up the Turkish onslought. Father of King Mátyás. His statue is on Halászbástya.

Innocent XI, (1611—1689) Benedetto Odeschalchi as Pope called for the liberation of Hungary from Turkish rule. His statue is in the Castle district in Hess András tér.

Jászai, Mari (1850—1926) Great Hungarian tragic actress. Played many leading Shakespearian roles in the National Theatre.

Jókai, Mór (1825—1904) Novelist, the greatest figure of Hungarian romantic prose. Hero of the 1848 Revolution, keeping the spirit of the revolution alive later. Still later, he was Member of Parliament for a while.

József, Attila (1905—1937) Poet, the greatest figure in 20th century Hungarian poetry. His statue is near Parliament, at the bank of the Danube.

József, Palatine of Hungary (1776—1847) Austrian regent, who helped the development of Pest. His statue is in József nádor tér, the square named after him.

Julianus the Monk (?—1289?) Hungarian monk and traveller who, on his journey in Asia, found the original home of the Hungarians and warned of the Mongolian invasion. His statue is behind the Hilton Hotel.

Kapisztrán, (St) János (1386—1456) Monk, inquisitor and army leader. Had a major role in the victory over the Turks in 1456.

Karinthy, Frigyes (1887—1938) Writer, poet, classic Hungarian humourist, legendary jester.

Károlyi, Mihály (1875—1955) Landowner, politician, the first President of the Hungarian Republic (1918). His ashes were ceremoniously brought back to Hungary in 1962. His statue is to the right of the Parliament.

Kodály, Zoltán (1882—1967) Composer, musicologist, teacher of music. Colleague and friend of Bartók's.

Kossuth, Lajos (1802—1894) Lawyer, journalist, politician. Outstanding figure in the Reform Age just before the 1848 War of Independence, then Hungarian leader during the War as Regent. Died in exile in Torino.

Kosztolányi, Dezső (1885—1936) Poet, novelist, literary translator, journalist. One of the first to use urban life in large cities as a subject of novels. See Reading.

Lechner, Ödön (1845—1914) Architect, philosopher of architecture, master of the Hungarian art nouveau.

Liszt, Ferenc (1811—1886) romantic composer, pianist, founder of the Academy of Music.

Madách, Imre (1823—1864) Dramatist who lived in isolation in the country. Writer of "The Tragedy of Man", the classic Hungarian drama. His statue is on Margitsziget.

Mikszáth, Kálmán (1847—1910) Novelist, journalist. Member of Parliament. The central classic writer in the last third of the last century. Widely read even today.

Móricz, Zsigmond (1879—1942) Novelist, polemicist on social issues. The prolific literary figure who revived popular prose.

Munkácsy, Mihály (1844—1900) Realist painter, well known in Europe. His paintings are in the National Gallery.

Pázmány, Péter (1570—1637) Archbishop of Esztergom, cardinal, writer. Leading figure of the Counter-Reformation in Hungary.

Petermann, Judge (late 13th century—early 14th century) Justice in Buda of Hungarian nationality between 1302—9, when the citizens of Buda excommunicated the Pope.

Petőfi, Sándor (1823—1849) Prolific romantic poet, revolutionary politician. His statue is on the bank of the Danube.

Rákóczi, Ferenc II (1676—1735) Hungarian prince who became the Regent who led the War of Independence between 1703 and 1711. Died in exile in Turkey.

Savoy, Eugene of (1663—1736) Austrian politican, army general. His statue is in front of the Royal Palace.

Semmelweis, Ignác (1818—1865) Professor of Medicine, the "Saviour of Mothers". The surgeon to first realise the importance of antisepsis.

Széchenyi, István (1791—1860) Hungarian count, politician and writer, called 'the Greatest of Hungarians'. The prime mover behind innumerable Hungarian public institutions and enterprises. His statue is in Roosevelt tér.

Szent István, St. Stephen (?977—1038) King, founder of the Hungarian state, converted to Christianity in 1000. His statue is on Halászbástya.

Szondi, György (?—1552) Soldier, commander of a castle which he defended with a garrison of 150 Hungarians against 10,000 Turks. He fell there with all his soldiers. His statue is in Kodály körönd.

Táncsics, Mihály (1799—1884) Politician, journalist. Imprisoned for his ideas several times in the street which now bears his name. His portrait is on the wall of his former prison.

Vak Bottyán, János (?1643—1709) Commander of the army made up of peasants at the time of the Rákóczi War of Independence, a talented strategist. In a battle he lost one eye, hence his nickname of 'vak' (blind). His statue is in Kodály körönd.

Vörösmarty, Mihály (1800—1855) Romantic poet, author of one of the most influential patriotic poems in the last century. His statue is in the square named after him in the City.

Wesselényi, Miklós (1796—1850) Political writer, reformer, the Hero of the Flood of 1838. One of the leaders of the anti-Austrian opposition before the Revolution.

Ybl, Miklós (1814—1891) Leading Hungarian architect, designer of the Opera House, the Basilica and many other public buildings, master of the neo-Renaissance style. His statue is on the bank of the Danube, at the foot of Castle Hill.

Zichy, Mihály (1827—1906) Painter, graphic artist, welcomed in several European royal courts. He died in St Petersburg.

Zrínyi, Miklós (?1508—1566) Hungarian nobleman, who was killed at the siege of Szigetvár, defending the castle. His statue is in Kodály körönd.

Zrínyi, Miklós (1620—1664) Army commander, poet, the Hero of the Sword and the Lute. Wrote a famous epic on the heroic deeds of his aforementioned great grandfather. His statue is in front of the Vígszínház.

Richard Baltimore III, Deputy Chief of Mission, US Embassy, Budapest

Budapest, if you want to get to know this town well, plan on hoofing it. While downtown, look up, you may discover a seldom noticed recessed statue, elegant turret or an original turn of the century roof design. Meandering into apartment courtyards may reveal anything from an elaborate iron gate to an antique elevator. Hungarians are a very friendly people, dogs or small children often help break the ice quickly. Although I have travelled in 78 countries, this is the only city in which a kind smiling restaurant hatcheck *néni* returned my overcoat and and commented nonchalantly that she decided to sew its loose button while I was eating. On an entirely subjective basis, here are a few of my personal choices.

— **Best soup in town:** venison with tarragon at Kispipa restaurant, in Akácfa utca.

— **Finest turkey dishes:** Szindbád restaurant, in Markó utca.

— **Most unusual brew:** "fig coffee", at Museum restaurant, at the National Museum.

— **Choice local throat drop:** "*Negro*, a torok kéményseprője: the chimney sweeper of the throat."

— **Waiters with the best memory:** Hotel Forum Grill where following a forty month absence my favourite dish was served as casually as if I had been away for a weekend.

— **A hidden first class restaurant in Óbuda:** Garvics at Ürömi köz 2.

— **Architectural eclecticism at its best:** the upper portion of the former stock exchange, now Hungarian TV headquarters, on Szabad-ság tér which has been described as "Angkor Vat meets the Greek Temple".

— **One of the few (two) American statues to an American in Budapest:** General Henry H. Bandholtz who saved singlehandedly the treasures of the National Museum from being looted by foreign troops at the end of WWI. After an absence of decades, Bandholtz was returned to Szabadság tér in 1989.

— **Most misleadingly labeled statue:** Raoul Wallenberg in Buda, commissioned by then US ambassador Nicholas Salgo. Plaque gives credit to local city council.

— **Best place to browse for books and records at bargain prices:** Könyvesház in Váci út (not the pedestrian, downtown Váci utca).

— **Kindest museum curator and guide:** Mrs Ilona Benoschofsky at the Jewish Museum next to the great synagogue.

— **Most Impressive Museum Interior:** The Etnographic, on Kossuth tér.

— **One of the most enjoyable tram rides:** number 4 between Buda's Moszkva tér and Skála department store at Fehérvári út via Pest's Grand Boulevard (avoid rush hour); **least enjoyable:** the so-called "Pioneer Railway" in the Buda hills.

— **Most Likely and Annoying Petty Theft:** any Western car insignia.

— **Last but not least, best all-night piano bar:** Piaf's in Nagymező utca.

A CITY TO ENJOY

Day by Day

Food shops — Markets — Baths, strands, swimming pools — Jogging —
Cycling — Some laundries and dry cleaners

Food Shops

Here in Hungary smaller shops do not necessarily offer better goods or service. There are several shops, though, which can compare with the supermarkets of larger Western towns. Here are some of them.

Skála Metró
VI. Marx tér 1—2. Open 7 a.m. to 8 p.m., Saturday closing 3 p.m., Sundays 8 a.m. to 3 p.m.

Skála Budapest
XI. Schönherz Zoltán utca 6—10. Open 7 a.m. to 7 p.m., Saturday closing 3 p.m., Sunday closed.

Skála Csarnok
VII. Klauzál tér 11. Lovingly restored old market-hall in the centre of Erzsébetváros. Open 7 a.m. to 8 p.m., Saturday closing 5 p.m., Sundays closed.

Sugár Shopping Centre — Ground Floor
XIV. Örs vezér tér Open 6 a.m. to 8 p.m., Saturday closing 5 p.m., Sundays open 6 a.m. to 3 p.m.

Batthyány ABC — First Floor
I. Batthyány tér Open 6 a.m. to 8 p.m., Saturday closing 5 p.m., Sundays open 7 a.m. to 1 p.m.

Csemege-Meinl Supermarket
I. Erzsébet körút 1. Open 6 a.m. to 9 p.m., 7 a.m. to 5 p.m. on Saturdays.

Real brown bread can be bought in all these shops: it is slowly becoming popular, though rather more expensive than the traditional Hungarian white bread. (Bread is very cheap compared to meat and fruit.) All these shops are self-service: you just pile everything into a basket or cart. They usually have about 10 cashiers in operation, those nearer the entrance normally having shorter queues.

The title "ABC" for some shops derives from the fact that supposedly all kinds of goods can be bought there. They are always self-service and cover between 100 to 300 square metres; they do in fact stock a wide range but their layout often confounds all rationality. At certain times of the day the queues can be large. Most housing estates contain one, at least, of these shops. The one on the corner of Szent István körút and Fürst Sándor utca, used to have a celebrated and famous old lady who sits on a podium beside the baskets keeping an eye out for would-be shoplifters.

The word **"közért"** which appears on many corner shops used to mean that the shop was part of a larger retail chain, now it has come to mean "grocer's". These too are self-service, of 50 to 100 square metres, with a limited selection; basic foodstuffs are always in stock. **Bejárat** means entrance and **kijárat**, exit. However it is usual to go in by the exit door as it is often only there that the baskets are to be found.

A development of the 1980s has been the opening of smaller, privately run shops both in the inner city and in the suburb. They almost always have a speciality, whether it be home-made bread, sausages or a dessert speciality. But very soon all small shops will be in private hands — and the "special" features will disappear.

There is a growing number of health-food shops, but still a far cry from the numbers in the rest of Europe.

Health Food

Koleszterin Stop V. Garibaldi utca 5.
Bio-bolt. VI. Nagymező utca 23.
Kenyérbolt. XIII. Pannónia utca 7.
Bio bolt. XIII. Katona József utca 22.

Markets

Food is worth buying in one of the markets. In these prices of fruit, vegetables and bread fluctuate freely between wide limits. People can often be seen queuing to buy piping-hot white bread. However it goes stale within a day. In our Third Walk we mentioned the five markets that were opened on the same day at the end of the last century. They are as follows:

V. Hold utca 13.
VI. Hunyadi tér 4.
VII. Klauzál tér 11.
(See SKÁLA CSARNOK above under FOOD SHOPS)
VIII. Rákóczi tér 7—9.
IX. Vámház körút 1—3. (Now closed for repairs.)

Other markets of interest are:

II. Fény utca
The most expensive in Budapest, serving a better off area with wide choice. Beside Moszkva tér.

VII. Garay tér
Interesting building that went up in the thirties in an area that has come down in the world. A very influential muck-raking novel of the sixties was set here. Many small shops around here. Near Keleti Railway Terminal.

Lehel Market
XIII. Lehel tér
Behind a large church, the cheapest of the markets with a large choice and many small shops nearby. Open Sundays as well. Take Third (Blue) Metro to Lehel tér.

Swimming Pools and Baths

Of all the world's large cities, Budapest is the one richest in medicinal springs. Their waters, between 22 and 76°C, were enjoyed by the Romans; there is so much that some people living near the Széchenyi Baths have hot mineral water piped direct to their bathrooms. From 1937 the International Association of Spas have had their headquarters here.

There is a total of 30 medicinal baths, swimming pools and strands open to the public; of these we will mention those which are of interest because of their waters, atmosphere or sports facilities.

MEDICINAL BATHS

Gellért Fürdő
XI. Kelenhegyi út 4.

Remarkable art nouveau building at the Buda end of the Szabadság híd, beside hotel of same name. See Third Walk. Opening hours: Thermal bath 6.30 a.m. to 7 p.m.; bubble bath in winter 6 a.m. to 4 p.m. on Sundays. Closed for maintenance on the fourth Wednesday of every month.

Lukács Fürdő
II. Frankel Leó út 25—29.

Long established, many times rebuilt, centuries old plane trees, fine old drinking well. See For the Second Time / Twelve Impressions. Open: Thermal baths 6 a.m. to 7 p.m., Sundays to 1 p.m.; swimming pool 6 a.m. to 7 p.m., Sundays to 5 p.m. in summer, to 1 p.m. in winter. Thermal baths reserved for men on Tuesdays, Thursdays, Saturdays and Sundays — other days for women. Closed on the third Tuesday of every month except for the pool.

Király Fürdő
II. Fő utca 84.

See Second Walk. Dating from Turkish times though in a Classical building. Open: 6.30 a.m. to 7 p.m., on Saturdays 12 p.m. Closed on Sundays. The steam bath reserved for women on Tuesdays, Thursdays, Saturdays and Sundays — rest of the week for men. Closed on the first Thursday of every month.

Margitsziget "Thermal" Hotel
XIII. Margitsziget

Modern hotel and baths built on the thermal springs of an old spa and possessing the most modern facilities. Can be reached by car from Árpád híd, which is close by. (Cars may not come onto the island from Margit híd.)

Széchenyi Fürdő
XIV. Állatkerti körút 11.

See Fourth Walk. Exceptional range of facilities in this original building from the beginning of the century. Open: Thermal baths 6.30 a.m. to 8 p.m., Saturdays and Sundays to 1 p.m.; Strand 6 a.m. to 7 p.m., Sundays to 7 p.m. in summer and 4 p.m. in winter.

STRANDS

Csillaghegyi Strand
III. Pusztakúti út 3.

Hot and cold water on a 12 hectare site. A large part is on a southern slope and here nude sunbathing is allowed. Modest hotel, bungalows, sauna and one of the pools is covered in winter. Take Szentendre HÉV to Csillaghegy stop, about 15 minutes by car from centre. Open: 7 a.m. to 7 p.m. (in winter to 6 p.m. and on Sundays from 6.30 a.m. to 1 p.m.)

Palatinus Strand
XIII. Margitsziget

Enormous, holding up to 10,000 at a time and open from early May to the end of September. Seven pools, of which the biggest is 118 x 43 metres. Artificial waves, water chute, playing area and fenced area for ball games. The 26 bus starting from Marx tér gets you there; it is 15 minutes walk from Margit híd.

Római Strand
III. Rozgonyi Piroska utca 2.

Originally used by the Romans — hence the name — this 7 hectare site has many reminders of their presence. Childrens' pool, water chute and swimming pool is addition to strand itself. Chilly water. Take Szentendre HÉV to Római Fürdő stop or 10 minutes by car from centre. Open: May to September, 8 a.m. to 7 p.m., Sundays from 7 a.m.

Dagály Strandfürdő
XIII. Népfürdő utca 36.

Dagály, the name means high tide; up to 12,000 people at a time can use it. On the Danube, to the north of Árpád híd. Many warm and cold water pools. The 25 meter pool is covered and usable in winter too. Food stalls under every tree and a sauna and keep-fit room. Access: Bus 133; Third (Blue) Metro to Árpád híd; by boat on the Boráros tér—Pünkösdfürdő line. Open 7 a.m. to 7 p.m., in winter and on Sundays 7 a.m. to 4 p.m.

SPORTS POOLS

There are very few and only two can be recommended and even then non-competitive swimmers may have trouble in gaining entry.

Komjádi Béla Sports Pool
III. Árpád fejedelem útja 8.
Near Margit híd at Buda end. Easily seen because of its size and large curved aluminium roof. There is an Olympic-standard pool and an older pool beside it. Non-competitive swimmers may use the facilities between 11 a.m. and 2 p.m. weekdays and from 6 a.m. weekends, if and only there is no competition that day. Children's pool. Comfortable place to sunbathe. You deposit 100 Ft or your watch to use cloakroom facilities on entry.
This is the venue for the big water polo matches. Sadly Hungarian water polo teams are no longer the force they used to be.

Hajós Alfréd Sports Pool
XIII. Margitsziget
One of the architects gave his name to the complex: he was the winner of the first (and second) Hungarian Olympic gold medal, in Athens in 1896 (100 and 1200 metres freestyle). Five minutes walk from Margit híd or take the 26 bus to door. Three pools, one (33,3 x 18 m) is covered, the largest (50 x 20 m) is open and there is a diving pool too, the only standard one in Hungary. Very pleasant place but it tends to be dominated by competitors past and present. Open: 6 a.m. to 4 p.m., weekends to 6 p.m.; limited during competitions.

Jogging

No longer considered as an absurd way of spending free time here — not surprisingly in view of the cardiac figures. The most pleasant run is what joggers and runners call "the island circuit": this is around Margitsziget and is about 5 kilometres. (Some turn back at the Rose garden in the middle of the island.) If coming onto the island by car, park it by the hotels.
The two large parks, Városliget and Népliget, along with the embankments, are also pleasant — though the latter is not recommended during rush hours.

Cycling

Cyclists are barred only from Lánchíd and the subsequent Tunnel, the access roads to motorways and to the airport. Despite this the visitor will probably notice very few cyclists in Budapest. The reason is quite simply the combination of dense traffic and high level of air-pollution. You may, however enjoy cycling at night, or at the weekend. Some essential addresses:

Hungarian Cycling Association — Magyar Kerékpáros Szövetség
XIV. Szabó József utca 3. T.: 252-0879

The Repair Shop of the Hungarian Cycling Association
XIV. Erzsébet királyné útja 14/a.
Spare parts, immediate small repairs.

Kerékpár Centrum
V. Kálmán Imre u. 23.

László Bicycle Workshop
I. Hunyadi János út 4. T.: 201-0713

Repairs and bikes on sale. Fluent English and German. Tips on where you can rent a bike in Budapest.

See also the Velvárt Bicycle Workshop, in the chapter *For the Second Time / Twelve Old Shops and Workshops.* (VII. Wesselényi utca 56.)

Some Laundries and Dry Cleaners

These are either automats or will do laundry within a day — within 6 hours if you are in luck.

I. Fő utca 10.

V. József Nádor tér 9.

V. Városház utca 3—5.

VI. Liszt Ferenc tér 9.

VII. Rákóczi út 8/b.

VIII. József körút 44.

BUDAPEST BESTS :: BUDAPEST BESTS

András Kepes, television talkshow host

Just like in other major cities, there are sights **worth** visiting, besides things that are a **pleasure** to see. The latter gives away the exclusive secrets of the insiders.

I usually take my friends on a kind of social safari, way off the tourist path. Coming from downtown, we get off at Klinikák metro station and turn right to see a rather impoverished, run-down area, which is definitely not for the faint-hearted.

The area of Király utca and Dob utca in the deep VIIth district is also usually on the agenda. In a couple of years' time quite a number of blocks were renovated, without the neighbourhood being gentrified. This was the ghetto area in 1944. The most evocative scene is an arcade of seven yards between the two streets mentioned above, called Gozsdu Udvar. (Entrance through 13 Király utca — See also Budapest for the Second Time / Twelve Buildings, p. 134)

Upper middle-class **Rózsadomb** can also be part of our social safari. Margaret bridge — Vérhalom utca — Vérhalom tér is a route to see an old fashioned villa neighbourhood. Endrődi Sándor utca and vicinity boasts with recent luxury apartments.

But my real favourite in Buda is obviously **Gül baba utca**, above Margaret bridge. It's lovely to climb up to the top and then back to Török utca, to sniff the air of the centuries of Turkish domination. If you liked it you can resort to a Turkish bath in Water town, the Király for instance.

When in Buda Castle, (especially in Tárnok utca or Táncsics Mihály utca) don't forget to peep into the **courtyards.** It's really a treat to walk into the Dominican Church courtyard of Hotel Hilton. There is a fantastic panorama of Pest there, with the Houses of Parliament in the centre.

My top **art nouveau** landmarks are Gresham palace in Roosevelt Square and the Museum of Applied Arts in Üllői út. The foyer of the latter is really not to be missed. If you have been converted to art nouveau, you should go to Városliget and see the original part of **Széchenyi Baths** there. It's especially overwhelming in winter afternoons, through the yellowish mist, up to the chin in one of the pools.

Eating

Those with long memories speak nostalgically of the Budapest restaurants of the inter-war years. In what was "the most peaceful, easygoing and least expensive city in Europe", an enormous number of restaurants competed for the discerning customer. Then came the war and the lean years that followed. In a dictionary of mine, published in the fifties, the entry at "banana" is an illustration with minimal attempt at explanation of a phenomenon so outside ordinary experience. Like many other children of the sixties I felt that things were getting better, improving all the time. The exception, however, was eating out. My childhood memories are of rows with waiters and of food left barely touched on the table. I later came to understand that all restaurants had the dead and rigid hand of large catering companies on them. The new hotels that went up in the seventies brought new standards with them and they attracted the talented and ambitious to them. Eventually in the early eighties a system of contract leasing whereby restaurants were let out on three to five year leases to the highest (sealed) bid, came into being. This has led to a proliferation of privately run restaurants — often in impossible locations, for example in a street famous only for its courts of justice and rows of ambulances parked on standby alert. Over the past five years establishments ranging from those serving hamburgers to those using silverware have sprung up. Even in suburban housing estates adventurous housewives have joined together to provide good home cooking for their delighted neighbours.

It was a bad system: the contractors had a sense of insecurity — some of them wanted to get rich overnight. It was better than the state-only-system, though.

Within two years, all state restaurants will be privatized. Thank God.

Hungarian Cooking

The predominant influence on Hungarian cooking has long been Austrian and thus, indirectly, French. Interestingly enough it was French chefs, mainly employed at the great houses, who "liberated" Hungarian cooking from the Austrian. Just as French cuisine turned to peasant and traditional dishes for inspiration, so too did these chefs look to Hungarian peasant cooking and brought it into the mainstream of European tastes.

The basis of Hungarian peasant cooking is a heavy **rántás**, a roux of rich flour and pork lard. This naturally requires rich spicing and gets it from red paprika. Yet the use of paprika, now thought of as a defining feature of Hungarian cooking, only dates from the latter half of the eighteenth century. Ground paprika, however, is a Hungarian innovation. Slowly the eating of the fiery pepper became a Hungarian virtus and as the saying goes, "a real Magyar can handle his strong paprika well". Another feature of Hungarian cooking is the use of sour cream. Soups and pasta also figure strongly — the latter because of the excellence of our flour. Our traditional cooking was only "Europeanized" about a hundred years ago: this conjoining is Hungarian cooking.

The heyday of hospitality and eating out was that commonly evoked European golden age — the two decades before the outbreak of the First World War. In Hungary it has its own chronicler: the novelist and short story writer, Gyula Krúdy (1878—1933, his statue is in III. Szentlélek tér). His work, still as popular as ever, abounds in the sensuous evocation and celebration of food and its eating. His name has been bequeathed to more than 100 dishes, all of which are worth trying.

It would be only a slight exaggeration to say that Hungarian cooking of today is his mediation of the peasant cooking already referred to. For many of us Krúdy's name evokes a marrowbone. Let me explain. Zoltán Huszárik's film **Szindbád** (1971) was based on Krúdy's stories of the same name. (The film deservedly features high on a recent critics' poll of the twelve best Hungarian films ever, see *Entertainment*.) It contains a scene in which the eponymous hero — and the camera — gaze lovingly on a golden-coloured bowl of soup. Szindbád expertly cracks the marrowbone and the camera closes in onto the marrow as it shimmers on the surface of a crispy slice of toast. Audiences inevitably and involuntarily gasped with pleasure. The scene has passed into the subjective consciousness of the nation and may well have contributed to the revival and rejuvenation of traditional dishes.

This process has gone far even though Budapest can still not bear comparison with a French or an Italian city for the range and quality of its cooking. (Hungarian cooking has not encompassed a wide usage of herbs or vegetables and the recent revolution in French taste is still in the offing.) Nevertheless I doubt that anyone will be seriously disappointed in any of the establishments I list below. They have all been checked personally and in consultation with two restaurateurs. This selection from the more than 5,000 eating establishments should provide sustenance and more to the visitor. For good cookery books see *Reading*.

Elegant Restaurants

Listed below are those which do not cater for block-booked tourist groups — hence the omission of one or two wellknown names. This is not to say their food is bad, but I feel that the individual customer tends to have difficulty in getting reasonable attention from a staff busy with and harrassed by these groups. Nor are restaurants of the major hotels included since what they serve is, in general, standard international hotel fare. I am told that the restaurants of the Gellért, the Intercontinental and the Forum enjoy a high reputation within the profession.

Fehér Bölény — The White Bison
V. Bank utca 5. T.: 112-2825.
Open: 6 p.m. to 2 a.m. Closed on Sundays.

The menu doesn't contain much more then a dozen kinds of steaks — but they are apparently the best available East of Munich (maybe of Grenoble). The décor is as kitsch as it can be — it reminds one of a wild west bar that imitates a wild west bar in the suburb of a Bavarian city.

A downtown address, a block away from the National Bank, two blocks from the American embassy. The Stars and Stripes plus President Bush on the counter.

Not cheap even for New Yorkers.

Gundel
XIV. Állatkerti körút 2.
T.: 121-3550
Open: Noon to 4 p.m., 7 p.m. to 12 p.m. daily.

Situated in Városliget, close to the Zoo, whose lions can be frequently heard from within this restaurant of longstanding repute and tradition. Margaret Thatcher was dined here on her 1984 visit. Among its specialities are various pork dishes and, of course, the rich pancake to which it has given its name. The new proprietor, George Lang, a Hungarian-born New York restaurateur will surely restore it to its former ranking as the first real restaurant east of Vienna. Once he attends to minor details — like serving the food hot, to name one.

Kacsa — The Duck

II. Fő utca 75. (Corner of Kacsa utca). T.: 135-3357.
Open: 6 p.m. to 4 a.m. every day.
A rising star on the elegant scene. Immaculate service, outstanding pianist, well-versed both in classical and light music. A not very extensive menu of international and Hungarian dishes. English-speaking waiters.
50 meters from the river, on the Buda side, between Lánchíd and Margit-híd.

Kéhli Vendéglő — Mrs Kéhli's Place

III. Mókus utca 22. T.: 188-6938.
Perhaps the only more or less genuine place left of the many that used to be patronized by the immortal gourmet writer, Gyula Krúdy. You can still see a plaque commemorating his table. His spirit is everywhere — in the menu, in the décor, in the witty inscriptions on the wall. The recent facelift fortunately didn't spoil the atmosphere (it used to be much smaller, dirtier and much cheaper). To include the cobblestoned gate area was a good idea, to flaunt the Gösser beer signs was not. The menu is a delight in itself (in several languages). If you want to try the famous scene in the film "Sindbad", you should order Forró fazék velőscsonttal (Hot pot with marrow-bone), which is served in the cosy red pot that is used by impoverished old ladies. Other favourites (there is a full explanation in the menu): Szindbád margitszigeti étke ("What Sindbad liked to eat on Margaret Island"), and Fidó Apó magyarkúti medvetalpa ("The Magyarkút Bear Sole").
Live accordion music. Miscellaneous music from a very cheap stereo rack — less than a perfect sight here.

Kisbuda — Little Buda

II. Frankel Leó út 34. T.: 115-2244
Open: Noon to midnight, Sundays noon to 3 p.m.
At the Buda end of Margit híd. Seats 60 inside and, in summer, a further 100 in the pleasant courtyard at the rear. (Beside it runs the cobble-stoned lane, Gül Baba utca, which is mentioned in For the Second Time.) Service is outstanding. Booking advisable.

Kisbudagyöngye — The Small Pearl of Buda

III. Kenyeres utca 34., T.: 168-6402.
Open: 4 p.m. to midnight every day. Essential to book..
A brand new place reborn out of a well known, shabby but charming place. Miraculously, the new owner did listen to the designers, who wanted to blend the postmodern with the *fin-de-siécle*. They ransacked all the low quality antique shops and the Ecseri flea market. All the walls are panelled with sides and doors of cupboards, pieces of drawers; with hard wood of all kinds, tints and patterns. It all amounts to a very elegant and intimate atmosphere. Hungarian and international dishes. A beautiful, three-language menu, with very few misprints. A pianist and a violinist — two virtuosos. The latter looks like a 19th century anarchist just back from Siberia.
The place seems to be thirty years old — a real compliment in Budapest.

Légrádi testvérek — Légrádi brothers

V. Magyar utca 23. T.: 118-6804
Open: 5 p.m. to midnight, closed Saturdays and Sundays.
In a cellar in a winding street in the centre, just opposite one-time "Maison Frida", a red-lamp house, later turned old actresses' home, this establishment, opened in the mid 80s has entirely by word of mouth become the trendiest place in town, gaining inclusion in a number of European gourmet guides. Air-conditioned, oil-paintings on its white walls and antique furniture provide the décor. Herend china, silver cutlery, tailcoated waiters and the white-tied Légrádi brothers who have given their name to the establishment watch over quiet unhurried service. Seems an age-old established place. Essential to book. Quiet guitar music. Ladies get menues without prices.

Marco Polo

V. Vigadó tér 3. T.: 138-3354.
Open: 11.30 a.m. to 2.30 p.m. and 7.30 to 11 p.m. Closed on Sundays.
Built three years ago, in the place of a seriously underused science library, by an Italian businessman, who imports a lot of beef. His vans bring fresh spices from Italy apparently every day. A very elegant décor from the late eighties, with slight hints to the fifties. The restaurant proper is on the L-shaped second floor, which can be lethal in the summer when — for some curious reason they leave the main door open, thus killing the air conditioning.
A really top class restaurant, "one of the best Italian restaurants in Europe". This comment, exclusive, to this book, by the great restaurateur, Paul Kovi, of the Four Seasons, New York.
The atmosphere is casually elegant. Try to be served by the Uruguay-born wizard, Sergio. He even speaks Hungarian.
Half a month's pay — for a Hungarian couple.

Robinson
*XIV. Városliget, Állatkerti körút,
on a small island on the lake,
overlooking the right side of the
Museum of Fine Arts and Restaurant Gundel. T.: 142-3776.
Open: 6 a.m. to 3 p.m. and 6
p.m. to midnight.*

A very elegant place in a singular environment. Views to a fountain on a lake. Several rooms, all kinds of tables. Very smooth service, even on the somewhat less elegant open-air terrace. International menu.

You shouldn't miss Robinson palacsinta, a sort of crêpe stuffed with vanilla cream and fresh fruit salad.

Szindbád
*V. Markó utca 33. T.: 132-2966.
Open: Noon to midnight, Saturday and Sunday 6 p.m. to
midnight.*

Takes its name from Krúdy's hero (see introduction to this section) and not

from the Arabian Nights, which gives a hint to its culinary ambitions. A sensibly restricted menu á la carte, fully detailed, is a true delight. Excellent desserts and a good wine and spirit list. The atmospherical arches of the ceiling permit clear listening-in to every conversation in the room.

A speciality: Báránycomb mentamártással. (A fine lamb dish with mint).

Vörös Sárkány — The Red Dragon
*VI. Andrássy út 80.
T.: 131-8757.
Open: 12 p.m. to 1 a.m. Closed
on Sunday.*

Mr. Kassai, the famous icehockey player, journalist and socialite has been running the place for 10 years, and made it a Budapest institution. The favourite meeting place of journalists, actors, other comedians. One of the best Chinese restaurants in East Central Europe.

"Shirtsleeve" Gourmet Restaurants

To my mind it is these restaurants which are rejuvenating Hungarian cooking. Their menus generally list many dishes cooked in the manner of the last century and they make an effort to make use of ingredients which are fresh to hand and in season. 'Shirtsleeve' indicates that they have no desire to overwhelm their guests by their ambiance. Service is straightforward and friendly. Cordon Bleu is not (usually) mis-spelled on their menus — a mark of their culinary ambitions.

Bécsi Liesinger söröző — Vienna Beerhall
*V. Eötvös Loránd utca 8.
T.: 117-4504
Open 11 a.m. to 10 p.m. Saturday
closed, Sundays 11 a.m. to 4 p.m.*

Named after the Viennese beer (Liesinger) it served once, this small cheerful beerhouse is very centrally located near the University Church. Portions are enormous and the cooking is truely Viennese — both reasons for its success. Menu in German and Hungarian, beer on draught.

Csülök vendéglő — The Knuckle
*IV. Reviczky utca 36.
T.: 169-0202
Open: Noon to 9.45 p.m. daily.
Closed late July and early August.*

Located in rather drab northern end of town, a district of factories and box-like high rise housing developments. It may be relatively unknown but not I suspect for long. Apples and scones on the table and a menu which is extensive. On entering turn to the left for a better atmosphere. They take orders in six languages.

Ezüst ponty — The Silver Carp
*XII. Németvölgyi út 96.
T.: 181-0139
Open: Noon to midnight daily.*

The proprietress, a retired famous athlete, has made fish dishes the speciality of the house — 20 are listed in a tri-lingual menu. The décor tries for a folk effect and the service gives no indication that the establishment has become popular. Good selection of drinks too. In the summer you can eat outside in the garden. Reservation is essential.

Kiskakukk — The Little Cuckoo
*XIII. Pozsonyi út 12. T.: 132-1732
Open: Noon to 11 p.m. noon to 4
p.m. on Sunday. Closed on Sunday in summer.*

On the Pest side of Margit híd, near the bridge. (See Fifth Walk.) Has held its name for a good ten years. Menu specializes in game (with an Italian bias). Service can be fitful. And they have done something about their carpet and chairs — not enough yet. The red-haired proprietress, from a village near Pest, is said to be complaining that it is hardly worth going on with the lease, prices being what they are. That would be a great pity.

Kispipa — The Small Pipe

VII. Akácfa utca 38. T.: 142-2587
Open: Noon to midnight, daily.

Hidden away in a street running parallel with the Nagykörút. Fish swimming in their tank, forty year old posters on the wall, the charm didn't disappear, despite several facelifts that added more and more brass to the once shabby décor. The restaurant has its devoted regulars. Mr. Aubel, its proud proprietor, supervises his waiters and personally serves regulars, copes with accidents. He will cook anything to order which is not on the extensive menu. Advisable to book for lunch, essential for an evening meal. There are four-course "full dinners", which are worth a try.

Náncsi néni

II. Ördögárok út 80. T.: 176-5809
Open: Noon to 9 p.m.

In Hungarian you don't tell it to the marines, you tell it to Auntie Náncsi. The lady in question was a simple credulous countrywoman. The restaurant is in a charming district, quite far from the centre, called Hűvösvölgy — around 20 minutes by car. It has a pleasant garden and a formidable menu. The most expensive items are just over the 200 Ft mark and it has a regular clientele who swear by it. Busy at all times so be prepared for a wait. Live music, menu in English and German.

Tabáni kakas — The Tabán Rooster

I. Attila út 27. T.: 175-7165
Open: Noon to midnight, Saturdays and Sundays 1 p.m. to midnight.

The Tabán is the name for the area lying on the southern slope of the Gellért-hegy. (See the First Walk.) The proprietress of this fashionable restaurant is known for her handling of the cloakroom — no matter how busy, she can put a face to every article deposited with her. One corner of the rather featureless room has a bar with an upright piano beside it, played with unusual discretion. They specialise in game — especially fowl — which comes in various Hungarian and other European styles. (Everything is cooked in goose dripping.) Service particularly attentive.

Small Restaurants

"Kisvendéglő" in Hungarian means a small dining area with room for up to 60 people, whose food is relatively cheap and which most often has a villagy feel to it (checkered table-cloths, candles, wine jugs). Although they may not pay too much attention to their furnishings and fittings, they most usually have a family atmosphere about them. You are expected to share your table if the place is full.

With the advent of total privatization this is an endangered species. Everyone will be tempted to turn his/her just acquired place into a luxury establisment — but sure to upgrade it.

Apród csárda — The Page

VI. Szondi utca 17.
Open: 9 a.m. to 9 p.m., Saturdays and Sundays closing 4.30 p.m.

Three minutes from the Nagykörút, hot food is served as soon as it opens. The fittings have a folk flavour with peasant boots on the wall, wooden seats and a gallery; wine served in carafe, many brands of beer. Hungarian country cooking and service.

Bohémtanya — Bohemian Den

VI. Paulay Ede utca 6.
T.: 122-1453
Open: Noon to 10 p.m. daily.

The sign above the door simply says "Söröző" — beerhouse. At the bar at the back there are always half a dozen customers having a beer while they wait. Only seats 52. Has large, well-cooked dishes and real beer-hall atmosphere. Deserves the loyalty it has from its regulars.

Boszorkánytanya — Witch's den
III. Pacsirtamező utca 36.
T.: 168-9413
Open: Noon to midnight, daily.
Near the Buda end of Árpád híd, one of the friendliest small restaurants, run by the Bátkis. Air-conditioned, semielegant, with a TV-set and a huge white device for heating with a notice: "Forbidden to touch it". German—Hungarian, printed menu. The staff is very casual, swift and attentive. With a small drinkbar, with witches on top of the poles.
Specialities: Treasure of Belzebub and the like.

Csarnok étterem — The Market-Hall
V. Hold utca 11. T.: 112-2016
Open: 9 a.m. to 10 p.m., Saturdays and Sundays closed.
Close to the market (csarnok), this contains a few snugs in which you can eat and where you drink "real" (cheap and less fine) draught Kőbányai beer. Market stall-holders come here as well as a famous staff member of the Department of Philosophy with her students. There is a rather uncomfortable terrace open in the summer. Specialities are lamb, mutton and marrowbone dishes.

Csendes — The Quiet
V. Múzeum körút 13., entrance from side-street. T.: 117-3704
Open: 12 p.m. to 10 p.m., closed Sundays.
Quartier Latin atmosphere for this is a favoured meeting place of university students and alumni. Rather uncomfortable seats contribute to the "rustic" feel. Transylvanian and Slovak dishes usually on the menu — try them.

Görög taverna — Greek Tavern
VII. Csengery utca 24.
T.: 141-0772
Open: Noon to 11 p.m., daily.
Five minutes from the Nagykörút, neat, white, air-conditioned cellar. Two rooms, seven tables, for a maximum of forty people. Oil paintings (Greek ruins) and black and white photos (Greek peasants). Huge, Greek flag, out of silk. Soft Greek musaka — live music on Wednesday and Saturday. Bilingual menu.

Harold kisvendéglő
VIII. Baross utca 122. T.: 114-0192
Open: Noon to 4 a.m. daily.
On the fringe of the inner city, this cross between a small restaurant and a cocktail bar can seat 45. Décor is dark-brown, including the espresso machine. Like in all new privately-run places, the service is warm and fast.

Három pintér — The Three Coopers
V. Váci utca 69. (in the middle of Pintér utca). T.: 118-0452.
Open: 11 a.m. to 11 p.m., every day.
In an ultra-narrow alley way, between the not fashionable part of Váci utca and Molnár utca, in a block that seems to be 200 years old. Simple homespun Hungarian food. Self-service. Choose your dish from the large wall menu, then go to the counter. Some nice furniture and old fittings. Nightmarish "modern paintings" on the wall — for sale. Avoid the place between 12.15 a.m. and 2.30. p.m. Customers spill out. Cheap drinks to go with your meal. A recent change: it becomes a Thai place in the evenings and at the weekend.

Horgásztanya — The Angler's Hut
I. Fő utca 27. T.: 201-0683
Open: Noon to midnight daily.
On the corner of a street parallel to the Buda bank, not far from Clark Ádám tér. The awkward combination of the fittings create the ambiance: a whisky advertisement, a fishing net hanging from the ceiling and a boat at the rear. The food has a country taste to it, the service can be a bit fitful and the foliage is rich.

Kisbojtár — The Small Shepherd Boy
XIII. Dagály utca 17.
T.: 129-5657.
Open: 12 a.m. to 11 p.m. Closed on Sunday.
A museum piece of a restaurant that preserves the genuine coziness of the late fifties, early sixties. The small shepherd boy can be seen on an incredibly kitschy oil painting and the iron railings on the windows. Several rooms each with unforgettable design subtleties. A camp experience proper, to use the term established by Susan Sontag.
Food is delicious — all dishes represent Hungarian home cooking tradition. The head waitress is exceptionally warm and unobtrusive, who speaks with a slight ac-

cent in Hungarian. She is of Slovakian origin. She also speaks German.

Kis Itália — Small Italy
V. Szemere utca 22. T.: 111-46-46.
Open 11 a.m. to 9 p.m. Closed on Sundays.

A very simple, reliable place just off the Grand Boulevard, with about 8 tables. Quick and attentive service. Very few mistakes in the Italian menu. A small drinks counter. Their slogan: If you've been satisfied, come again, and recommend us to friends, if not, send your enemies. Moderate prices.

Makkhetes — Seven of Clubs
XII. Németvölgyi út 56.
T.: 155-7330.
Open: 11 a.m. to 8 p.m. daily.

Named after a playing card — we call them "magyar" but they are of Swiss origin. Of this type of place, it tends to be one of the neglected ones. Nice intimate family atmosphere and it is packed by local families for Sunday lunch. Service is cheerful and very fast — even when crowded. Good country cooking.

Megálló — The Bus Stop
VII. Tanács körút 23. T.: 122-3015
Open: 11 a.m. to 11 p.m., closed Sundays.

With a rather frightening grim look to it, they are busy at lunchtime. They have some 120 items on their menu, including frog legs as part of their Hungarian fare. Service is exceptionally fast and the ambience is relaxed. The recent renovation has created a drinkbar at the rear end, but has left the toilet-curtains intact. The text on the wall is mentioned at the end of the Second Walk. They claim to speak English, but they fail to write it — see front door.

Specialities: Tequila Beefsteak, Game dishes.

Sport
XVI. (Rákosszentmihály),
Csömöri út 198. T.: 183-3364
Open: 10 a.m. to 10 p.m. Closed on Monday and Tuesday.

Anyone willing to make the pilgrimage out to this end of town is in for a pleasant surprise. One of Pest's best restaurants is located in what appears to be a shambly, tumble-down barn. Inside however it is an entirely different story for the food has no connection with the place's exterior: Well worth the 25 minute drive from the centre of town. Uncommonly rich selection of beer and wine.

Specialities: Frogleg stew with gnocchi, Roast Duck with crepes filled with marrow, Beefsteak Nivernaise.

Tüköry söröző — Tüköry Beerbar
V. Hold utca 15. T.: 131-1931
Open: 10 a.m. to midnight, closed Saturdays and Sundays and on all public holidays except August 20th.

In the centre of Lipótváros and our Second Walk. It can get almost unbearably hot in summer, even in the closed-in terrace. Inside are snugs and a long central table. Serves Dreher (Hungarian) draught beer. At noon it is full of clerks from the banks nearby. It can be full in the afternoon as well. One has the feeling that the customers always talk about business here. The décor is unbelievably shabby. On the walls youll will find paper reproductions of a modern Hungarian painter just glued to the wall. The pony-tailed waitress has the nicest smile all over twon. The food is plain Hungarian village cooking at its best.

The Kifőzde: A Genre of its Own

Called "kifőzde" in Hungarian, this is the sort of place where there are rarely more than 10 dishes available and where you would expect to find a stew of heart or of tripe or even of tongue — all cooked in the peasant style. Where there are tables, they are shared automatically. The kitchen is thinly partitioned off, but every comment can be heard. They get less busy around two o'clock. Most of them close around four o'clock (unless stated otherwise). They tend to have a two-three week holiday in August.

Ádám étkezde
XIII. Sallai Imre utca 5.

Bakáts étkezde
IX. Bakáts tér 9.
Near the Danube, in the more elegant part of Ferencváros. The owner doesn't accept tips from the apprentices working around.

Étkezde
I. Várfok utca 8.
Closed on Saturday, on Sunday: noon to 5 p.m.

Étkezde
VII. Damjanich utca 26/A.

Étkezde
III. Vörösvári út 31.

Kádár étkezde
VII. Klauzál tér 9.
Open: 11.30 a.m. to 15.30 p.m., on weekdays.
A charming, legendary establishment of the heavily Jewish neighbourhood. With two soda water bottles on each table and celebrity photos on the wall (Mastroianni included). Jewish dishes on Friday.

Kék Ibolya
VII. Wesselényi utca 45.
On the corner of Nagykörút. Ibolya (or Violet in English) is not the energetic lady in the white smock, but her daughter. She does however speak excellent German.

Kistitok falatozó
VI. Nagymező utca 41.
Open: 8 a.m. to 8 p.m, on weekdays.

Kívánság étkezde
VII. Alsóerdősor utca 36.
Open: 11 a.m. to 5 p.m. On Saturday: 9 a.m. to 1 p.m. Closed on Sunday.

Oliva Ételbár
VII. Murányi utca 61.
Open: 9 a.m. to 10 p.m. Egyptian specialities.

Toldi falatozó
I. Batthyány utca 14.
Open: 10 a.m. to 5 p.m., on weekdays.

Zamat étkezde
VII. Izabella utca 34.

An Appendix: expensive places with gipsy music for tourists

The following places are not among my favourite ones. However, they should be mentioned in a book for tourists.

Gipsy music is a highly problematic genre. My generation that has been taught genuine folk music from an early age somewhat unanimously sneers at this music that is confused with Hungarian folk music all over Europe (Ferenc Liszt was no exception here). The pieces the bands play are called "magyar nóta" (Hungarian song) — a sugary, quasi-folkloristic song, originally written for the hundreds of thousands who migrated to Budapest. Later it was adopted by the upper classes as well. Nowadays it is rapidly losing its audience, even in the country. Twenty years ago there were about twenty thousand professional gipsy musicians in Hungary, as opposed to two thousand today — living largely off the tourists. The classic gipsy band originally consisted of no less than eight musicians: the "primás" (violin), the "kontrás" (second violin), the bass, the cymbalo-player, the clarinettist, the second kontrás, the cellist and the second primás. They are rarely seen in bands of more than four or five any more.

Interestingly enough, a number of outstanding figures of Hungarian jazz come from gipsy musician families (from the Lakatos dynasty, among others).

If you, Gentle Reader, are interested in genuine gipsy music, you might buy two brilliant recordings of a band called "Kalyi Jag" (Black Flame). Also on CD.

Alabárdos
I. Országház utca 2. T.: 156-0851
Open: 6 to 12 p.m. (from 1 May to 15 September: 10 a.m. to midnight.) Closed on Sunday.

Apostolok
V. Kígyó utca 4—6. T.: 118-3704.
Open: 10 a.m. to midnight, daily.

Aranyhordó
I. Tárnok utca 16. T.: 156-6765.
Open: Noon to midnight, daily.

Margitkert
II. Margit utca 15. T.: 135-4791.
Open: Noon to midnight, daily.

Márványmenyasszony
I. Márvány utca 6. T.: 175-3165
Open: 11 a.m. to midnight.

Mátyás Pince
V. Március 15 tér 7. T.: 118-1693
Open: 11 a.m. to 1 a.m.

Ménes csárda
V. Apáczai Csere János utca 15.
T.: 117-0803
Open: Noon to midnight, daily.

New York
VII. Erzsébet körút 9—11.
T.: 122-3849
Open: 11.30 a.m. to 3 p.m. and 6.30. p.m. to midnight.

Pest-Buda
I. Fortuna utca 3. T.: 156-9849.
Open 5 p.m. to 1 a.m., on Sunday: noon to midnight.

Postakocsi
III. Fő tér 2. T.: 168-7801
Open: 11 a.m. to midnight, daily.

Régi Országház
I. Országház utca 17.
T.: 175-0650.
Open: 11 a.m. to midnight, daily.

Vasmacska
III. Laktanya utca 3—5.
T.: 188-7123
Open: Noon to midnight. Closed on Sunday.

Drinking

Hungarian wines — Some shops — Wine drinking — Wine bars — Beer and beer drinking — Spirits — Cafés and cocktail bars

The old pub joke goes that Hungarians only like drinks beginning with the letter "a"—"a bor" (wine), "a sör" (beer) and "a pálinka" (spirits). The joke is that the letter "a" in Hungarian is the article. Anyway we are going to treat them in that order.

Hungarian Wines

When a Tokaji was given pride of place among the white wines at the Paris International Exhibition of 1900, a new wine was registered by wine-lovers everywhere. (The wine in question was a Tokaji Aszú.) This is still the best known Hungarian wine abroad. However there are quite a few wines worth tasting. Hungary has many hours of sunshine and, usually, a long and warm autumn. Most of our wine-producing areas have sandy soil. Here too as elsewhere the best location for vines is where there is a combination of a southern slope (for sunshine) and a good water-table to nourish the roots. This combination occurs in the Balaton and Tokaj areas, the latter's water-table being replenished by the Tisza, the second largest of the rivers flowing through the country. Both areas have volcanic soil. Only twenty-eight villages may use the name Tokaji to describe the wine they produce.

Hungarian wines are classified as cheap by international standard but this is a result of poor marketing as much as anything else. Apart from the wines of Tokaj, those from Badacsony, Eger, Szekszárd, Pécs, Villány, Somló, Mór and Sopron are worthy of mention. If the neck of any bottle labelled as coming from the above areas has a red, white and green collar with a number stamped on it, then it's definitely worth buying. The winning Tokaji in Paris was an **aszú**, a wine produced from grapes left to rot on the vine and thus affected by the pourriture noble. The quality is indicated by the **puttony** number: the higher the number the higher the quality. The year of vintage is also of crucial importance. Other well-known wines from Tokaj are the **Szamorodni**, the **Hárslevelű** and the **Furmint** — all whites.

Wine labels always indicate whether the wine is **édes**—sweet, **félszáraz**—half-dry or **száraz**—dry.

Since much of our good wine goes abroad, the quality of what turns up in the shops can fluctuate wildly. However the **Pinot Noir** from **Pécs** and the **Egri Bikavér** reds — the latter only in the squat bottle — are usually reliable. Of whites, so too are the **Badacsonyi kéknyelű**, **Egerszóláti olaszrizling** and the **Móri ezerjó**.

SOME SHOPS

Csemege
VI. Oktogon 1.
Hungarian and imported drinks. Giftwrapped if desired.

Curioso
VII. Király utca 69.
Especially imported drinks.

Delikátesz
II. Retek utca 6.
Wines from Tokaj.

Mozaik
V. Múzeum körút 27.
Imported and Hungarian drinks. Open round the clock, except for 6 a.m. Sunday to 6 a.m. Tuesday.

Csemege-Meinl
VII. Rákóczi út and Erzsébet körút corner.
Very busy at rush hour.

Mézes mackó
V. Kígyó utca 4—6.
Good selection of wines and spirits.

**Palackozott italok boltja
(Shop of Bottled Drinks)**
V. Régiposta utca 11., off Váci utca, opposite McDonald's.

Wine Drinking

Real wine-lovers here do not rely on shops to indulge their passion but buy from the producer by going direct to the vineyard. To keep their spirits up they also drop into the occasional wine-bar **borozó**, many of the best of which are supplied by wine growers' co-operatives. (There is another type of place called a **talponálló**, a wine counter, which is generally filthy and full of drunks.) However the wine-bar here, unlike its counterpart in London or New York, is neither overpriced nor pretentious. Many a borozó has stand-up tables where customers take their wine at leisure, occasionally helping it down with slices of **zsíros kenyér** which they buy at the counter. (Try it: it's bread and pork dripping sprinkled with paprika, often topped with fresh onion slices.) In Hungary it is common to add soda to your wine. Our word for this is **fröccs** and there are five varieties of this spritzer.

	wine	soda	meaning
kisfröccs	10cl	10cl	small spritzer
nagyfröccs	20cl	10cl	large spritzer
hosszúlépés	10cl	20cl	long step
házmester	30cl	20cl	janitor
viceházmester	20cl	30cl	under-janitor

The selection below took into account general ambiance as well as the quality of the wine served. They usually open at 9 a.m., but bear in mind that most of them close between 8 p.m. and 10 p.m.

Wine Bars

Szarvas pince
I. Szarvas tér 2.
Expensive, beside the restaurant of the same name.

Hattyú
I. Hattyú utca 1.
Stands back off the bottom of Castle Hill. Cheap and cheerful.

Állami gazdaságok borozója
II. Török utca 1.
Very large with benches, hot food.

Kertészeti Egyetem Tangazdaság
II. Keleti Károly utca 4.
Outlet for the vineyards of the Horticultural Uuniversity.

Postakocsi borozó
III. Fő tér 2.
Expensive and favoured by tourists. Bar in form of coach, meals served.

Gresham borozó
V. Roosevelt tér 5.
See Second Walk for information on the building. Entry into bar is from Mérleg utca. Marble tables but not pricey.

Grinzingi
V. Veres Pálné utca 10.
Table and counter service. Hard-boiled eggs, sandwiches and salads, wine from the barrel. Middle price range and off the tourist track.

Rondella borozó
V. Régiposta utca 4.
Touristy and the prices are San Francisco.

Tokaj-Hegyaljai Szövetkezet
V. Vigyázó Ferenc utca 4.
A pleasant little cellar on the Pest side of the Lánchíd. Zsíros kenyér.

Villány-Siklósi borozó
V. Gerlóczy utca 13.
Close to Deák tér. A wine-counter but serves wine from two interesting areas.

Tokaji borozó
VI. Andrássy út 20.
All the Tokaji wines, right beside the Opera House.

Kiskőrösi borozó
VI. Zichy Jenő utca 4.

Móri borozó
XIII. Pozsonyi út 39.

Tortilla borbár
XIII. Budai Nagy Antal utca 3.
Hungarian drinks and Spanish tortilla. Tiny figurine of Bacchus on the wall.

Beer and Beer Drinking

It is only in the last dozen years or so that Hungary has become a beer drinking country. Now the figure has come up to about 100 litres per head per year, around four times the figure for wine. We have a preference for **világos**, that is lager or light beers although **barna** (dark) beer is also brewed. (This latter tends to be sweetish to the English palate.) The beer most popular in the shops is **Kőbányai Világos**, the cheapest type, brewed in the Kőbánya district of Pest. This brewery is an old established one. The Kőbányai Brewery runs two beer halls of its own, serving what a native of Budapest considers as the only real beer on draught: the **Sörcsárda** on the brewery premises themselves and the **Aranyászok** in the inner city.
Three Kőbányai beers are sold in the shops: the **Világos** (pale), the **Korona** and the **Jubileum**. Look out also for the excellent Czech bottled beers such as **Pilsner Urquell** and **Budweiser** (Budavár) and their German counterparts such as **Wernesgrüner** and **Radeberger**. **Tuborg** and **Holsten** are brewed here under licence. Beer sold in small 33cl bottles or cans is rather more expensive than that in the half litre bottles. All these bottled beers taste the better for being chilled.
Over the last few years, several foreign companies — mainly Austrian and German—have sponsored beer-houses selling their products.
The list that follows has no claims to be complete.

Ászok söröző
I. Győző utca 5.
Open: 9 a.m. to 2 a.m. daily.
Not for the faint-hearted! Video, serving the Ászok and Alpesi beers from Sopron.

Fortuna söröző
I. Fortuna utca tér 4.
Castle district beer-house that is popular with tourists.

Csalogány snack bar
I. Csalogány utca 26.
Younger, up-market regulars. Lively, serving **Egger** and **Kaiser** beers.

Négy szürke
II. Mártírok útja 60.

Open: 9 a.m. to 4 a.m. daily.
At the sign of the grey horse, on one of Buda's main streets. Draught **Pilsner**, snacks.

Radeberger söröző
III. Hídfő utca 16.
Wernesgrüner on draught and **Radeberger** in bottles.

Aranyászok söröző
V. József nádor tér 12.
Open: 11 a.m. to 10 p.m., closed Sundays.
Owned by the Kőbányai brewery. **Jubileum** (light) and **Bak** (dark) beer on draught.

Gilde sörbár
V. Ferenciek tere 7.
Open: 11 a.m. to 11 p.m.
Gilde beer in bottles and on draught.

Borsodi söröző
V. Honvéd utca 18.
Open: 8 a.m. to 10.30 p.m., Saturday closing 8 p.m., Sundays open noon to 4 p.m.
In the heart of the city, behind the Ethnographic Museum. Select from around ten beers.

Dóm sörbár
V. Szent István tér 2.
Open: 9 a.m. to 5 a.m. daily.
Looks onto the Basilica. **Wernesgrüner** on draught and a very wide choice of bottled beers.

Dönci's Rendezvous
V. Kecskeméti utca 15.
Gösser beer in bottles and on draught. Remarkably nice sandwiches and hot snacks. Some say this is the best beer available in town.

Fregatt söröző
V. Molnár utca 26.
First attempt in Eastern Europe to create an English pub — and pretty successful at that — both in appearance and atmosphere.
(Food infinitely superior to English pub food.) Young crowd, in which resident foreign students figure largely. Often live jazz music. **Holsten** beer.

Gösser sörpatika
V. Régiposta utca 4.
Open: 10 a.m. to 10 p.m. from Monday to Saturday. Sunday 5 p.m. to 10 p.m.
First of the Gösser houses in Budapest. Name means "beer pharmacy". Excellent sandwiches and lively atmosphere. In a side-street off Váci utca.

Pilseni sörbár
V. Irányi utca 25.
Open: 8 a.m. to 4 a.m. daily.
Very busy and small. Despite the name and the ad in the window, it does *not* serve Pilsner (Czech), but plain Hungarian "Aranyászok" beer. Cheapest draught in town. Can get a bit heavy at night.

Trojka söröző
VI. Andrássy út 28.

Open: 10 a.m. to 6 a.m. daily.
Known to all taxi-drivers, catering for an amazing assortment of night-birds. Films on video upstairs, general weirdness downstairs. **Egger, Ratskeller** and other beers.

Hági söröző
VII. Huszár utca 7.
Open: 9 a.m. to 5 a.m. daily.
On a side-street off Rákóczi út. Traditional, frequented by local residents. Rings the changes on a number of Austrian beers.

Prágai Svejk vendéglő
VII. Király utca 59/b.
Named after the good soldier of Hasek's novel, this is an imitation of his favourite Prague beer-hall, right down to the faded portrait of Franz Joseph. Excellent beer, reasonable Czech food.

Kaltenberg bajor királyi söröző
IX. Kinizsi utca 30—36.
A well-conceived, but somewhat posh house. Beer brewed on premises. Essential to reserve for the evening. T.: 118-9792

Sörcsárda
X. Jászberényi út 7.
Open: 9 a.m. to 8 p.m., closing at 3 p.m. on Saturdays and Sundays.
House owned by the Kőbányai brewery and not for the faint-hearted.

Italcsarnok
XI. Budafoki út 35.
Open: 9 a.m. to 9 p.m., Sundays 7 a.m. to 9 p.m.
German style beer-hall a few steps from the Technical University. **Kőbányai** on draught and a selection of bottled beers.

Mészöly söröző
XI. Bartók Béla út 21.
Open: 9 a.m. to 3 a.m., closing 11 p.m. Saturdays and Sundays.
Hungarian beers only.

Bécsi city söröző
XIII. Sallai Imre utca 18.
Open: 9 a.m. to 11 p.m. daily.
Kaiser beer.

Vidor sörbár
XIII. Katona József utca 22.
Open: 10 a.m. to 10 p.m.,
Saturdays 3 p.m. to 10 p.m.,
closed Sundays.
Holsten beer.

Piccolo sörbár
XIII. Pozsonyi út 3.
Pilsner Urquell on draught.

Spirits

The best known of Hungarian spirits is **barackpálinka**, apricot brandy, which is perversely drunk as an aperitif, thus numbing the taste-buds well and truely. A variation is **óbarack**, old apricot. The other fruit brandies are **cseresznye**, cherry, **szilva**, plum and **körte**, pear: the brand of the latter called **Vilmos Körte** should be noted. The best cognac-type drink distilled here is **Tokaji Borpárlat**. Another drink worth noting is **Unicum**, a dark brown liqueur containing 23 herbs and which has a passing resemblance to Unterberg and Fernet Branca. (The old pre-war placards for Unicum are much sought after to decorate walls.) After decades of shortage, you can get it in practically every shop selling spirits. (Opt for the ones with red-white and green top if there is a choice. The emigré former owner, Mr Zwack came back to re-buy his own factory. He is the Hungarian ambassador in Washington at the moment...)

Tourists may often be offered a lethal concoction that was invented for their benefit a few decades back: **puszta-koktél**, which is 3 parts apricot brandy to 2 parts Mecseki liqueur and to 3 parts Tokaji Szamorodni wine and all parts lethal.

All cafés and coffee-houses serve spirits in a measure of 5 cl called **féldeci** or **feles** (a half decilitre) and waiters tend to turn up their nose if asked for a **kis** (small) measure of spirits, this being "only" 3 cl. It is advisable to ask for a **kis szóda** or **kísérő**, which will get you a glass of soda water. Mixers and ice are generally unknown. If you ask for a vodka and tonic you will get a glass of vodka and a glass of tonic.

Cocktails have made some penetration in the larger hotels and a few of the places calling themselves **drinkbár**, cocktail bars, are recognizably such.

Cafés and Cocktail Bars

Angelika
I. Batthyány tér 7.
Open: 10 a.m. to 8 p.m. daily.
Entrance a few steps below street level in an old house. Furnishings neo-baroque. An old — fashioned, though not old place, ideal for discussing the meaning of life.

Café Pierrot
I. Fortuna utca 14.
Open: 5 p.m. to 1 a.m.; Sundays 10 a.m. to 11 p.m.
On the site of a six hundred year old baker's. Great lengths gone to in finding the Far Eastern fixtures. The pianist is eager to play your favourites. Music from 8 p.m. when the piano is uncovered.

Ruszwurm
I. Szentháromság utca 3.
Open: 10 a.m. to 8 p.m. Closed on Wednesdays.
A baroque coffee-house dating from 1824, still with its ambiance intact. Its confectionary was so famous that couriers from Vienna were sent. Marvellous ice-creams too. It is swamped by tourists, although you may be able to get a table in its tiny salon between 2 and 3 on a winter afternoon. Its famous speciality is its Linzer, given the name by an owner who shared a prison-cell with a man of that name in the aftermath of the 1848—1849 Revolutionary War.

Foundue bár
II. Keleti Károly utca 25.
Open: 3.30 p.m. to midnight.
Saturday 6.30 to midnight,
closed Sunday.
Opened in a half-completed block and immediately acquired a following. Can just about hold three small groups. If someone manages to drop bread into the food, he has to drink 10cl of white wine.

Miniatűr presszó
II. Rózsahegy utca 1.
Open: 7 p.m. to 3 a.m., closed Sundays.
A genuine Pest place, though in Buda, with red silk décor, intact from the sixties. Not anybody is let into the inner room. Full of aged burghers, bohemians, and couples wildly in love. Service is old-fashioned and very attentive. Music from 9 onwards, by a real classy Budapest pianist.

New Wave drinkbár
II. Mártírok útja 67.
When first opened it had a wave-sweep in its window—the Waterworks are supposed to have banned that.

Acapulco drink
V. Kecskeméti utca 7.
Open: 1 p.m. to 4 a.m.Saturdays and Sundays 4 p.m. to 4 a.m.
Air conditioned.

Alibi kávébár
V. Szemere utca 19.
A very small, tidy bar. Good coffee and cocktails.

Csendes drink
V. Múzeum körút 13.
Open: 12 p.m. to 8 p.m., closed Sunday.
Entry from side street.

Dani drink
V. Szent István körút 21.
Open: 10 a.m. to 10 p.m.,
Saturday 9 a.m. to 2 p.m.,
closed Sunday.
Take stairs up from small shop — to another bar with own bottles. Any cocktail made to order.

Galéria drink bár
V. Vitkovics Mihály utca 6.
Open: 11 a.m. to midnight daily.
Pleasant fin de siécle bar. Pottery and pictures on display are for sale. Remarkably nice and friendly barmaids, not for sale but innovative mixers.

Gerbeaud cukrászda
V. Vörösmarty tér 7.
Open: Main hall—9 a.m. to 9 p.m. daily. Side-room 7 a.m. to 9 p.m.
Discussed in the introduction to the walks, the great monument to the old coffeehouse life. Due to huge number of foreign visitors, service can be fitful. If an elderly lady in a blue smock comes to the table and reaches for your coat, do not be alarmed — she is the cloakroom attendant. The side-room, which has a separate entrance is less busy and less elegant.

John Bull
V. Apáczai Csere János utca 17.
An English pub — as real and expensire as its location suggests. In the middle of the tourist reservation, opposite the back of Forum Hotel.

Otard drink bár
V. Kristóf tér 8.
A beautiful tapestry shows the whereabouts of Otard county (adjacent to Cognac). Drinks of the same brand. Possibly the most expensive place in town.

Pertu drink
V. Váci utca 39.
American cocktails — has made the Manhattan stylish.

Balettcipő
VI. Hajós utca 14.
Open: 10 a.m. to 10 p.m. At the weekend 3 p.m. to 10 p.m.
At the rear of the Opera and much favoured by actors for a drink after work. The American Heating stove, a favourite of the customers, was stolen during a recent reconstruction.

Ballantines Club
VI. Andrássy út 19.
Open: 10 a.m. to 3 a.m. Saturdays and Sundays from 6 p.m.
Members only from 9 p.m. to 3 a.m. Lavishly furnished and very expensive. Piano music, billiards, and the richest selection of whiskies in the city.

Broadway drink
VI. Nagymező utca 49.
Open: 9 a.m. to 1 a.m., Saturdays and Sundays opening at 4 p.m.
Two young proprietors created here the first modern cocktail bar. Cocktails fine, introduction of television set recently not. Try the **Zöld Özvegy**, the Green Widow.

Éva
VI. Andrássy út 41.
Open: Noon to 3 a.m. daily.
A cross between a restaurant and cock-tail bar.

Lukács cukrászda
VI. Andrássy út 70.
Open: 9 a.m. to 8 p.m.
(summer to 9.30) daily.
Our Fourth Walk brought us to this patisserie. Worth a visit just to see the fixtures.

Művész cukrászda
VI. Andrássy út 29.
Open: 8 a.m. to 8 p.m., Saturday 10 a.m. to 8 p.m., closed Sunday.
Mirrors, statues, paintings surround the rather elderly regulars who sit over their papers. The terrace is pleasant though a little noisy. The chairs are chained up at evening — in order not to be stolen. For more, see *Walk Four*.

Pardon Eszpresszó
VI. Szondi utca 11.

A very pleasant, never crowded place just opposite the side of Hotel Béke Radisson. A good selection of drinks and coctails.

Rigoletto
XIII. Visegrádi utca 9.

Called that way because of the huge stained glass windows illustrating the well-known plot. Two floors, billiard room. A shabby, dark, but (apparently) not dangerous place. Younger crowd. Moderately expensive drinks.

Entertainment

Sources of Information — Theatres — Theatres in Summer — Concerts and Recitals — Jazz — Folk music and dance houses — The pop scene — Discos — Museums — Exhibition halls — Galleries — Films and cinemas — Twelve Hungarian films — Radio and television — Sports events — Horse racing

Most, expensive hotels provide an extra TV channel with up to date information, compiled by the Hungarian news agency in English. (You can also have access to CNN News, and a couple of other channels.)

Sources of Information

Apart from **Budapest Week:** a bilingual monthly called PROGRAMME IN UNGARN/IN HUNGARY, which supplies much basic information. The concert information is reliable but its restaurant listings are not: there might be a third class place listed among the good ones while the best might be missing. For a visitor it does not make much sense to offer literary evenings in Hungarian or the museum about the history of a Hungarian magazine.

PESTI MŰSOR, the programme weekly, comes out on Thursdays and has 96 pages, including all kinds of mainstream events. Most short previews in the magazine are too easy-going but the information it gives covers more and more areas. It has even got a humour column. ("An envelope, please", the customer says in a stationer's. "A lined one?" "No, it's not that cold yet..." 1987/1.)

I have never seen this magazine in the hands of a tourist, even though it could be a superb source for making up your own plans. Pesti Műsor is often sold out by the weekend but you might try the box-offices of cinemas.

The columns in Pesti Műsor: **színház** (theatre), **zene** (music), **képzőművészet** (fine arts), **pop, film.**

MERLIN THEATRE is now a year old: in the summer months it houses the first English language Theatre in East/Central Europe. It is within the Budapest City Hall, the entrance is from V. Gerlóczy utca 4., near Astoria and Deák tér underground stations. It also houses a good restaurant with live jazz every evening at 10 p.m. and 12 p.m.

In the Summer of 1992, the Merlin will probably re-stage it's 1991 hit, a comedy by Ferenc Molnár, THE PLAY'S THE THING (translated by P. G. eodehouse), again with some leading London actors. The new production will be the English version of a Hungarian play *Gloomy Sunday,* about the life of a café-pianist between the two world wars.

From autumn to spring the theatre hosts other Hungarian-speaking productions, including those by students of the Merlin Drama School, which is run by a couple legendary in the Hungarian theatre of the seventies and eighties: Tamás Jordán and Kati Lázár. It is also a venue for chamber concerts, so it's always worth keeping an eye on its programme, either in *Budapest Week* or in *Pesti Műsor.*

Other Theatres

Visitors are usually recommended to see some musical piece and it is most often a performance at the magnificent OPERA HOUSE (See *Fourth Walk*) that first comes to mind. The word "bérlet" (season ticket) in Pesti Műsor refers to a performance for which most tickets have been sold on subscription. A family may buy a season ticket, usually for six performances perhaps without knowing the casts. There are families that have been keeping their usual seats for many years.

On the occasion of its 100th anniversary, the building was restored inside and outside, a task which took four years to accomplish. Even the stage machinery was modernized, but, as the director of the Opera House confessed at a press conference, they are sorry to have opted for the cheaper East German equipment, since it does not work perfectly.

More popular operas, attracting larger audiences, are performed in the ERKEL THEATRE by the company. With 2400 seats, this is the largest theatre in the country. The building, which shows almost nothing of its original art nouveau character, due to a major modernization, is situated in VIII. Köztársaság tér, close to Rákóczi út between the Nagykörút and Keleti Railway station. There are other musical pieces performed in the OPERETTA THEATRE (VI. Nagymező utca 17.), some classic Hungarian operettas, some modern musicals. Besides these places, three of the ordinary theatres have also staged musicals recently. The biggest hit for years has been Cats, produced by the MADÁCH THEATRE company (VII. Erzsébet körút 29—33.), soon after its London première, with some dancers of the Opera House. It is still difficult to get tickets. The hotels have a limited number of tickets available for US dollars.

The recent period has been called the "seven lean years of Hungarian theatre" by a well-known critic. There are two exceptions: the Csiky Gergely Theatre in the town of Kaposvár (189 kilometres south-west of Budapest) and the KATONA JÓZSEF THEATRE in Budapest. Let us focus on the latter in more detail; not that the performances of other theatres have no value (for example, the Nemzeti lays stress upon clear Hungarian speech), but from a visitor's point of view most other theatres in Budapest are out of the question.

The KATONA JÓZSEF COMPANY was established in the spring of 1982, by separating from the Nemzeti. The new company was formed within a few days, its members chosing others. The thirty-odd actors and actresses of the company work as a genuine company without the rigid hierarchy which is characteristic of Hungarian companies. Someone who plays the lead in one production, holds a spear in another. The company's primary strength is in theatrical spectacle and the best designers have been commissioned to create sets that are often very expensive. The theatre itself is situated in the block next to Párisi udvar, occupying a totally rebuilt ground floor of an early twentieth century building at V. Petőfi Sándor utca 6.

The directors of the company believe in fanatic work at rehearsals, and this comes over in every single production; the company has managed to establish a very intense and authentic style of acting, unique in the country. Even the back-stage situations are given in the smallest details, the emotions directed in and by the characters are true and tense: a complex, organic reality is present in the Katona József Theatre. Critics have called the success of the company "a landslide victory of aesthetics and ethics" and have been very laudatory.

They have become one of the most successful companies in Europe — receiving ovations in the Odéon of Paris and the Old Vic in London. Their production of Chekhov's Platonov had its première abroad! The box office opens at 2.00 p.m. At about 6 o'clock people begin to line up for tickets marked "for any unoccupied seat", which are sold at 7, just before the performance. (The seat you get depends on who does not turn up.) Some productions on their repertory: Gogol: The Government Inspector, Jarry: Ubu Roi, Shakespeare: Twelfth Night, Chekhov: Three Sisters.

The evening performances generally start at 7.00. Tickets to all theatres in Budapest are available at the **Central Box Office (Színházak Központi Jegyirodája) at VI. Andrássy út 18.** (near the Opera House), **T.: 112-0000**, or at their other office in Buda, at **II. Moszkva tér 3. (T.: 135-9136**). Every morning between 9 and 11 o'clock, information on theatre listings can be had by calling 111-7220 in Hungarian.

The Tourinform staff are helpful with theatre matters (T.: 117-9800): they usually look up Pesti Műsor but are happy to pass on their personal experiences as well.

Theatres in Summer

Summer is not the season for serious plays, not even the ones with music. The better known premises: the Budai Parkszínpad, the Hild Yard, the Dominican Churchyard of Hotel Hilton, the Margitsziget Open Air Theatre, the Városmajor Stage, the Zichy Castle. Tickets available from June 1st at:

PR OFFICE OF OPEN AIR THEATRES (VI. Jókai utca 24. T.: 132-4721).

ADVANCE BOOKINGS OFFICE (VI. Teréz körút 48. T.: 112-0430).

CENTRAL BOX OFFICE (VI. Andrássy út 18. T.: 112-0000).

Concerts and Recitals

Concerts and recitals can be found in Pesti Műsor in the column called ZENE, where the events are listed by venue. Most evening performances start at 7.30.

The main venue is the ZENEAKADÉMIA (Academy of Music). Hardly a single day passes without a major event here. Along with these are often others, given by the students of the Academy, which are open to the public. Their concerts are advertised on a noticeboard in the building of the Academy next to the side entrance in Király utca. (For the building see the *Fifth Walk* — VI. Liszt Ferenc tér 8.) As the main concert hall has no air conditioning, there are usually no concerts here in summer. Another location is the Main Hall of the VIGADÓ. (See the *Third Walk* — V. Vigadó tér 2. T.: 118-9903.) The acoustics here are not nearly as good as those of the Academy of Music. Only concerts likely to attract a large audience are given in the BUDAPEST CONVENTION CENTRE, which has a large, air-conditioned hall (XII. Jagelló út 1—3. T.: 161-2869). It is situated in very pleasant surroundings, in the "Chestnut-garden", next to the Novotel Hotel. There are musical events organized in the BARTÓK MEMORIAL BUILDING (Bartók Emlékház, II. Csalán út 29., T.: 116-4123), in the Liszt Museum, in Mátyás Church and at many other occasional venues. Hungarian concert life is based on three symphony orchestras, more or less equal in quality. The Hungarian State Symphony Orchestra is run by the largest concert organizing agency; the Hungarian Radio and Television Symphony Orchestra, or the Radio Orchestra in short, was originally established to function within the radio. (For their records and concerts abroad they use the name "Budapest Symphony Orchestra".) The third orchestra, that of the Philharmonic Society, is made up of members of the Opera House. There are some more orchestras, such as that attached to the Trade Union of Post Office Workers or to the Hungarian Railways, or even that of I. István Secondary School; they give regular concerts but quality is lower. The announcement in 1983 by two young musicians, Iván Fischer, a conductor and Zoltán Kocsis, the acknowledged pianist, both in their early thirties, that they would found a new orchestra, the Budapest Festival Orchestra, caused a great stir. The orchestra was to come together for occasional concerts. In musical circles the orchestra was mocked as the "Supergroup", whose musicians were drawn from the other three orchestras, from young musicians just beginning their careers (or even undergraduates of the Academy) and music teachers. Their Boxing Day concerts and summer concert series have become a tradition, and they have taken part in the Budapest Spring Festival. The Festival Orchestra set themselves the task of gaining European recognition; the Liszt Ferenc Chamber Orchestra has already earned a world reputation. It was founded twenty-five years ago by young musicians just completing their studies at the Academy of Music.

One of the founders of the Festival Symphony Orchestra, Zoltán Kocsis, is one of the exceptionally talented generation who were given special infant prodigy training at the Academy. These whiz kids were tutored from around the age of eight and were kept off the concert platform for a while. Dezső Ránki and András Schiff, who has settled in Britain went through the same training. They more or less still regard as their master the legendary musician, Ferenc Rados, who follows a contrary policy to the late Glenn Gould, who was willing to make recordings but not to have concerts. Rados, however, occasionally gives concerts in Hungary, politely rejecting a whole series of requests to record.

The annual musical competitions are important events. Some, such as the conductor competitions have a very high rating on TV. The winner of the first such competition, Kobayashi Ken-Ichiro of Japan is still a great favourite here and has recently become the leading conductor of the State Symphony Orchestra. He allegedly appeared in front of the orchestra with tears in his eyes, saying in broken Hungarian: "I cry... — such a good orchestra... such a bad conductor..."

Since the death of Zoltán Kodály (1967) no one has held a status as important and popular in Hungarian musical life. The greatest audience interest is shown at the premieres of György Kurtág's pieces; he is possibly the only one who attracts a large number of people outside the musical circles. Zsolt Durkó, Sándor Szokolay, Sándor Balassa and András Szöllősy have produced successful compositions for international competitions. Lately "Group 180", who play their own music and compositions by foreign composers, as well as the "Amadinda" percussion group have attracted much interest.

Tickets to concerts are available at the **Central Ticket Office** on the ground floor at **Vörösmarty tér 1. (117-6222)**, and before each concert at the venue. Since you do not have to produce your ticket again to return to your seat after the interval often you can just walk in to listen to the second half of a concert. At the Academy of Music, if the concert hall is not too packed, you can usually sit in the dress circle seats without having a ticket right from the beginning.

Jazz

Jazz is popular in Hungary and has overcome the recession in the 1950s. Yet despite a number of brilliant musicians, there are still many problems. Jazz musicians do not have enough opportunities or venues for playing together, they often make their living playing blandly in restaurants or night-clubs or, at best, they teach music. Groups break up too often. Jazz-fans are dissatisfied, too, most of them belonging to some fraction or another. There are not enough jazz events to make up a separate column in Pesti Műsor, where they are listed together with discos and pop under **Koncertmenü**, in the Pop column.

The only lasting success in Hungarian Jazz life is the Benkó Dixieland Band, who have been together for more than twenty years. They play traditional dixieland with long, joyful solos.)

At the time of going to press there are only two places devoted to jazz every night — one elegant and the other a genuine, smoke-filled den. **Merlin Jazz Club** is in the theatre of the same name Performances: 10 p.m. and 12 p.m., reservations advisable (T.: 117-9338; bear in mind, it's also a restaurant).

Billiárd fél tízkor (VIII., Mária utca 48., near Ferenc körút underground) is a different kind of lively, always crowded club. The name ("Billiards at nine thirty" comes from Heinrich Böll's novel.

Some more or less permanent premises of the ever changing scene:

BELVÁROSI MŰVELŐDÉSI HÁZ (V. Molnár utca 9. T.: 117-5928).

EÖTVÖS-KLUB (V. Károlyi Mihály utca 9. T.: 117-0602).

The one time splendid café — at present the student club of Eötvös University.

KASSÁK KLUB (XIV. Uzsoki utca 57. T.: 183-3974).

KOSZTOLÁNYI MŰVELŐDÉSI HÁZ (IX. Török Pál utca 3. T.: 118-0193).

The club of Benkó Dixieland. Every Wednesday, when the band is not abroad.

KÖZGÁZ JAZZ KLUB (IX. Kinizsi utca 2—4. T.: 117-3033).

Club of the University of Economic Sciences. Progressive tendencies, young formations, foreign guests.

FIRST DISTRICT COMMUNITY CENTER (I. Bem rakpart 6. T.: 115-2430).

Facing the Danube. The Dresch Quartet every Friday. A legendary venue in the story of Hungarian rock music.

The most important patron of Hungarian jazz is the Radio, which on its Bartók Rádió channel brings news of jazz events from all over the world and broadcasts the latest records. The Radio also subsidises jazz-weekends in two provincial cities, Debrecen (226 kilometres east of Budapest) and Nagykanizsa (209 kilometres southwest). Tourinform (117-9800) provides information about concert times, programmes and transport facilities.

Folk Music and Dance Houses

The end of the last century saw a large number of people moving up to the capital; here they cherished their folk songs for a while but rarely passed them on the next generation. The middle class favoured (as they still do) a type of folk-music-like romantic songs, called "Hungarian songs". (They are analogous to "Loch Lomond" in its connection to real Scottish folk-music.) Then around 1970, quite out of the blue, two young musicians, Ferenc Sebő and Béla Halmos, brought the real thing into fashion overnight. This music is still alive around the province of Szék in Transylvania, a part of Romania which used to belong to Hungary. It was not only folk-music that became trendy at that time, traditional dancing also captured the imagination of the young. Many gathered in "dance houses" week after week to dance to live Transylvanian music, to learn new dances and to enjoy the melodies. Anyone could join at any time and newcomers were taught the already mastered dances. Soon dance-houses for children also appeared. A national dance-house festival has been organized annually for a few years now in Budapest, where folk musicians and dancers come together from all over the country and thousands of people dance together. These occasions are usually accompanied by a busy market of folk crafts. Dance houses have a unique atmosphere — the devotees regard each other as members of a large family. This rising interest in folk-music is reflected in a number of records.

Information on dance house events can be obtained from the information service of Petőfi Csarnok (T.: 142-4327).

The Pop Scene

The mid-1960s saw the arrival of rock (or 'beat' in Hungarian) groups which started to write their own music and lyrics in Hungarian; they had to fight a desperate battle for recognition. Of the "holy trinity" of the 1960s (Illés, Metro and Omega), only the latter still exists today. They tour the whole country, roadies, truckloads of equipment and all; their concerts are replete with special effects and they make a record almost every year, introducing a new generation of teeny-boppers to consumption.

Illés successfully assimilated certain motifs of Hungarian folk-music. After they broke up, some members continued in another group, Fonográf, which has also broken up. Levente Szörényi and János Bródy, who wrote most of the music and the lyrics for both these groups, came out with the first Hungarian rock opera, István a király.

They established a luxurious community centre up on Szabadság hill, which quickly became the club of Hungarian pop musicians and entrepreneurs.

The pop singer, Zsuzsa Koncz, who frequently appeared with both groups in concert has also retained her popularity: she still sells out when she puts on a concert.

Some members of the, Omega group, founded a new group called Locomotiv GT. They rarely give concerts but are involved in most of the musical productions at the Vígszínház. Gábor Presser ("Pici"), their leading figure, is a very talented song-writer and a great discoverer of new talent.

In the second half of the 1970s heavy metal arrived, in 1980 punk. As elsewhere, the young divided themselves by clothes and music. The number of amateur groups mushroomed. Now the most interesting thing happening here is a form of "post-punk", which is heavily based on lyrics. Some of the longer-established marginal groups have made some records as well (Európa Kiadó, which means Europe Publishing House, also Europe To Let). A popular new wave band is called "Vágtázó Halottkémek" (Galloping Coroners).

The PETŐFI CSARNOK, or Metropolitan Youth Centre is an important venue for such events, while the younger groups have made a workshop out of the ALMÁSSY TÉR COMMUNITY CENTRE (VII. Almássy tér 6., T.: 142-4144) and VÖRÖSMARTY COMMUNITY CENTRE (VIII. Golgota utca 3. T.: 113-9488). Concerts which are not listed in Pesti Műsor are advertised in the downtown area through simple, photocopied posters, especially along the arcades of Rákóczi út and in most subways.

There is a huge following for the Hobo Blues Band (HBB), which has a self-given mission to introduce the rhythm-and-blues of the 1950s, since Hungary missed out on this music at the time. Hobo (László Földes) wrote a book on the Rolling Stones, and has shared a concert stage with Allen Ginsberg, who can also be heard on one of the band's records.

THE BUDAPEST SPORTCSARNOK (Budapest Sports Hall) is both a blessing and a curse on Hungarian rock life. It accomodates ten thousand people, consequently Budapest suddenly became a fixture on world tours. Everyone was happy about this fact except for the Hungarian "mainstream" groups. The trade union of Hungarian pop musicians even tried to get the authorities to limit the number of foreign big names, because, as they said, these groups would detract from the demand for Hungarian concerts. Visitors to date have included Johnny Cash, Queen, James Brown, Santana and Genesis. Posters for these big concerts compete with the conspicuous posters of the Laser Theatre, where the words "Pink Floyd" do not refer to the rock group but to a laser light show produced to accompany their music.

Pesti Műsor lists the week's pop, jazz and folk events under **Koncertmenü** in the **Pop** column. The abbreviations refer to the various types of community centres. First they give the location, then, after the date list the groups giving concerts. The most noted venues are "KEK", that is, the club of the Horticultural University (XI. Villányi út 35., T.: 185-0666), the "R-CLUB", which is located on the campus of the Technical University in Building R on the first floor (XI. Műegyetem rakpart 9., T.: 166-4011 or, between 6.30 p.m. and 9.00 a.m., 185-0313). Another important place is I. KERÜLETI MŰVE-LŐDÉSI HÁZ (I. Bem rakpart 6.), which often features what is new in music.

The most important venue, however, is PETŐFI CSARNOK (seen on the Fourth Walk). It is usually open between 10.00 a.m. and 10.00 p.m. The office stays open until this time anyway (if some event lasts longer than that, the office stays open longer, as well) and they provide information on all the most important events taking place. They do this in English as well all the time (also is German, French, Italian and in Russian occasionally). The address is XIV. Zichy Mihály út 14. (on the route of trolley buses 70, 72 and 74), T.: 142-4327.

The most important regular event in the Petőfi Csarnok is the Holdfény-Csillagfény ("Moonlight-Starlight") Disco on Saturday nights, hosted in turn by one of the three most fashionable disc jockeys in town.

Discos

The most popular disco in Budapest is that in the Petőfi Csarnok on Saturday nights. It attracts 3500-4000 at a time. (Tickets cost some 50 per cent more for boys.) It has the lot: flashing and spinning lights, a round stage like a rocket ready to take off, which is the DJ's platform. From here he runs the show and the audience. The top 10 for the following week is voted on every Saturday.

Some other discos:

Rock Café
VII. Dohány utca 20. Open: 6 p.m. to 2 a.m.
Above the entrance a red motorcycle coming out of the façade. It does not resemble its spacious New York and Amsterdam namesakes. It is a rather cramped cellar, with giraffe-skin patterned walls. Live set every night at 9.30 p.m. and 11.30 p.m. In between a high quality disco by a British disc jockey. Full most of the time. As we are duly warned at the entrance, humidity is very high.

Levi's 501
VI. Nagymező utca 41.
T.: 132-3857.
Open: 4 p.m. to 4 a.m.
An elegant, air-conditioned disco-bar. All the seats are upholstered with Levi's jeans. Recently I haven't seen the black London cab that used to be parked in front of it.

Blue Box
IX. Kinizsi utca 28. T.: 117-9574.
Open: 8 p.m. to 2 a.m.
(changeable).
In the same building as an art kino called M.I.T. that stands for Motion Picture Innovation Partnership. The rooms where the actual disco is held, upstairs, are painted blue.

Razzia Rock Lokál
V. Bajcsy-Zsilinszky út 36. Open: 4 p.m. to 4 a.m.
Inside and under the Toldi Cinema, an avantgarde establishment. There is a bar in the foyer with good beer (after 10 p.m. you have to pay a cover charge to get in). The crowded disco is downstairs. Note the huge projectors from the sixties. In the bar there are all kinds of textiles hung from the ceiling, in the usual deconstructivist manner. Their number seems to grow with time.

Black Hole
VIII. Golgota utca 3.
Open: 8 p.m. to 4 a.m.
In a huge community center of a huge state train manufacturer. The place for alternative music. Live concert almost every day. The shabbiest of shabby Budapest places.

Tölgyfa Kávéház
II. district, corner of Tölgyfa utca and Henger utca, in the building of the Tölgyfa gallery. Both of them parts of the Academy of Arts and Crafts, a design school. Nicest, best dressed girls in the Budapest night, with an intellectual bias, though. At the Buda end of Margit-híd.

Tilos az Á
VIII. Mikszáth Kálmán tér 2.
T.:118-0684.
The name is taken from Milne's Winnie-the-Pooh, cult teenager reading in Budapest. That's what left of the sign at Piglet's House: "Tresspassers will be prosecuted". (And Piglet says it's his Grandfather's name.)A smoke filled, lively place, with a very young crowd . A stronghold of the Fidesz Party (The Young Democrats). There is a cover only when there is live music. It's not really a disco, rather a place to get together.

Mediterran Club Disco
In the Bowling Beer Hall of Hotel Novotel, XII. Alkotás utca 63—67. T.: 166-8007. Reservation advisable. Expensive. Thursdays, 9 p.m. to 2 a.m.

Expo 25 Disco
On the site of Budapest International Fair, in Pavilion 25, hence the name. Entrance through Gate Two in Dobi István út.
Open: 9 p.m. to 3 a.m.
"The" disco right now. Big crowds, large floor, live music, go-go show. High prices.

Star Club
(In Hotel Atrium Hyatt, near Lánchíd.)
Very much up-market, very expensive. Every Friday, from 9 p.m.

Vén Diák
V. Egyetem tér 5. T.:117-4603
Open: 10 p.m. to 5 a.m.
A very trendy and very crowded place just opposite the Law School of Eötvös University. The name literally means "aged student", i.e. "former student". The abbreviation, seen all over the place, is of course "VD".

Museums

Museums are usually open between 10.00 a.m. and 6.00 p.m. and are closed on Mondays (unless stated otherwise). On Tuesdays every museum in Hungary can be visited free. The following includes only those which would be of interest to a visitor.

Aquincum Museum
III. Szentendrei út 139. Open from April to October. Access: Szentendre HÉV to Aquincum; Buses 42, 134. T.: 180-4650)
A major Roman site with the ruins of the civilian town.

"Arany Sas" Pharmacy Museum
I. Tárnok utca 18., on Castle Hill. T.: 175-9772.
Pharmacology in Renaissance and Baroque times, in the surroundings of an old chemist's shop.

Béla Bartók Memorial Building
II. Csalán út 29. T.: 116-4123
Bartók exhibits and concerts in the authentically restored home of Bartók.

Bélyegmúzeum — Stamp-Museum
VII. Hársfa utca 47. T.: 142-0960.
The huge building was constructed on the line of a planned boulevard. The boulevard was never completed — it was left unfinished at Madách tér.

Budapesti Történeti Múzeum — Budapest History Museum
Building E of the Royal Palace. T.: 175-7533.
Archaeological excavations in Budapest. The two thousand years of Budapest. The Royal Palace of medieval Buda and surviving Gothic sculptures.

Evangélikus Országos Múzeum — National Lutheran Museum
V. Deák tér 4. T.: 117-4173.
See the *Fourth Walk.*

Hadtörténeti Múzeum — Military History Museum
I. Tóth Árpád sétány 40. T.: 156-9522.
Open: 9 a.m. to 5 p.m., Sundays 10 a.m. to 6 p.m. Closed on Monday.
The War of Independence in 1848—49. The Austro-Hungarian Monarchy and World War I. The history of small arms. Guns and military vehicles in the courtyard. Great for children. See the *First Walk.*

Ferenc Hopp Museum of Eastern Asian Arts
VI. Andrássy út 103. T.: 122-8476.
The art of India and South-East India.

Iparművészeti Múzeum — Museum of Applied Arts
IX. Üllői út 33—37. T.: 117-5222.
Marvellous displays which use large models to illustrate applied techniques such as weaving and crochet. Exhibits and presentation both of great interest. For the building, see the *Fifth Walk.*

Kereskedelmi és Vendéglátó-ipari Múzeum — Museum Of Commerce and Catering Trade
I. Fortuna utca 4. On Castle Hill. T.: 175-6249.

Presentation on Hungarian trade of the first half of this century. History of Confectionary. See **First Walk**.

Közlekedési Múzeum — Transport Museum
XIV. Városligeti körút 11. Opposite the Petőfi Csarnok.
T.: 142-0565.
Displays on rail, shipping and road transport. Large-scaled working models. New extension recently opened with relics from city transport. The air exhibition is on first floor of Petőfi Csarnok, which is a short walk away. (The latter from Wednesday to Sunday and only from spring to autumn.) Great for children.

Ferenc Liszt Museum
VI. Vörösmarty utca 35. On corner of Andrássy út. T.: 122-9804.
See our *Fourth Walk*. Complicated hours: open Mondays to Fridays 10 a.m. to 6 p.m., Saturdays 9 a.m. to 5 p.m. and closed Sundays. Original furniture and instruments. Records and books related to Liszt on sale.

Mátyás Church
I. Szentháromság tér.
Open: 9 a.m. to 7 p.m. daily. A collection of religious art objects. Enter through church and go up to choir gallery. See First Walk.

Mezőgazdasági Múzeum — Agricultural Museum
Széchenyi sziget in Városliget. Rear of the Vajdahunyad Castle group in a Baroque wing. T.: 142-0573.
Open daily except Monday, 10 a.m. to 5 p.m., Sunday to 6 p.m.
See our Fourth Walk. Mainly on animal husbandry, horse and pig breeding.

Molnár C. Pál gyűjtemény — Pál C. Molnár Collection
XI. Ménesi út 65.
Open Tuesday, Wednesday and Thursday between 3 p.m. and 6 p.m., Sundays 10 a.m. to 1 p.m.
A collection devoted to the twentieth century master who was much influenced by Art Déco. Located in a charming old-fashioned street.

Legújabbkori Történeti Múzeum — Modern History Museum
In Wing A of Buda Castle.
Formerly called Museum of Working

Class Movement. Even at that time it could equally well be called a museum of sociography. Particularly striking collection of photographs.

Nagytétényi Múzeum — Nagytétény Castle Museum
XXII. Csókási Pál utca 9—11. The district is some 10 kilometres from town. T.: 173-8547.
Calm, non-assertive collection. Stately home, Hungarian style. European furniture of 15th and 16th centuries, Hungarian of the 18th.

György Ráth Museum
VI. Gorkij fasor 12. T.: 142-3916.
Exhibits from China downstairs, Japanese collection upstairs, in a beautifully preserved Art Nouveau villa, that used to belong to the famous collector — hence the name.

Nemzeti Galéria — National Gallery
Wings B, C and D of the Royal Palace. T.: 175-7533.
See our *First Walk*. Late Gothic winged altars. Gothic wood sculptures and paintings. Late Renaissance and Baroque works. Two important Hungarian painters of the 19th century, Paál and Munkácsy — the latter well-known in France. Hungarian painting and sculpture of our century.

Nemzeti Múzeum — National Museum
V. Múzeum körút 14—16.
Open: 10 a.m. to 17.45 p.m.
See Third Walk. On the history of Hungary from pre-historical times to 1849. Houses the Hungarian coronation regalia.

Néprajzi Múzeum — Ethnology Museum
V. Kossuth Lajos tér 12.
T.: 132-6349.
See Second Walk. Entrancing museum which usually has four or so special exhibitions to see in addition to its permanent display.

Semmelweis Orvostörténeti Múzeum — Semmelweis Museum of Medicine
I. Apród utca 1—3. T.: 175-3533.
Ignác Semmelweis was the Hungarian doctor who made the connection between puerperal fever and infection to become the pioneer of obstetrical antisepsis. The museum is housed in the house in which the "saviour of

mothers" was born. Fascinates doctors. Permanent display of medical treatment of the past. Open daily 10.30 a.m. to 5.30 p.m. except Mondays.

Szépművészeti Múzeum — Museum of Fine Arts
XIV. Hősök tere. T.: 142-9759.

See Fourth Walk. This enormous building houses the works of non-Hungarian art which are owned by the state, several private collections having been donated to it during its existence. So great is the collection that the 23 rooms on the first floor can only display one third of the classical paintings at a time. The other sections are the Egyptian Room, Greek-Roman Exhibition, Graphics Collection, Twentieth Century Foreign Paintings, Old Paintings, Modern Foreign Painting (namely 19th century), Old Foreign Sculpture. This is a major European museum and surprises every visitor to it. Paintings and statues may be handed in for identification and evaluation on Tuesdays between 10 a.m. and 1 p.m. — entry through Dózsa György út — and are normally returned by the following week.

Varga Imre gyűjteménye — Imre Varga Collection
III. Laktanya utca 7.

From the sixties on Varga has been one of the most important Hungarian sculptors. Venice Biennale 1984. The modern for the widest public. The tall, short silver-haired artist is often seen on the spot, guiding around foreign friends fluently in several languages.

Vasarely Múzeum
III. Szentlélek tér 1.

From the oeuvre of the celebrated Hungarian-born French artist. Quite a large collection in a converted part of an 18th century castle. Easily accessible from the Buda end of Árpád-híd.

Zenetörténeti Múzeum — Music History Museum
I. Táncsics Mihály utca 7.
T.: 175-9782.

History of music and musical life in Hungary. Open daily except Tuesdays 10 a.m. to 6 p.m., Mondays 4 p.m. to 9 p.m.

"Exhibition Halls"

There is a clear distinction in Hungary between galleries which simply mount exhibitions and those in which the exhibits are for sale. All of the former are state owned and subsidized. The list that immediately follows is of this type of gallery. ("Kiállítóterem" in Hungarian.)

Several state companies handle them and the most adventurous is the MŰCSARNOK, which also possesses the largest exhibition hall in the country. (*See Fourth Walk.*) Here are mounted the more important exhibitions which aspire to survey the artist or the movement. The rear of the building has many small offices whose function is to arrange the paperwork. They have for their own use three distinct rooms for mounting exhibitions. (For these consult a monthly published brochure which is distributed free.)

Dorottya Utcai Kiállítóterem
V. Dorottya utca 8. T.: 118-3899.

Photography, graphics and applied arts follow each other into this small but important gallery — this is one of the windows that is automatically looked through when passing by and one of the doors that, as a result, is often passed through. Closed on Sundays.

Ernst Múzeum
VI. Nagymező utca 8.
T.: 141-4355.

This progressive gallery dates back to 1912. The painter of Art Nouveau, József Rippl-Rónai designed the window in the staircase. It is once again bearing the progressive banner.

Árkád Galéria
VII. Rákóczi út 30. T.: 122-5818.

In a rather unfortunate location on a busy shopping street and on the first floor of a residential block — no casual dropping in here! Has a reputation for displaying peripheral works, which is not really justified. A modern art market is only now in the process of formation and rankings are still in a very fluid state.

Stúdió Galéria
V. Bajcsy-Zsilinszky Endre út 52.

A tiny one for artists just leaving the Academy.

Vigadó Galéria
V. Vigadó tér 2. T.: 117-6222.

See Third Walk for details on the building. Essentially for the "establishment" of middle-aged and older artists and keeps at a distance from the new. Its exhibitions, which change monthly, get a full television programme devoted to them before-hand.

Further galleries of this type are to be found in Pesti Műsor. Although objects may not be bought from these galleries, they do sell catalogues which normally contain the artist's address and telephone number — you can always deal directly with the artist. Art objects may only be taken out of the country with a permit from the Nemzeti Galéria; for information ring 175-7533.

Howewer galleries which act as dealers normally handle the export permit formalities for their foreign customers and you should ask for this help.

Galleries

Dovin Gallery
I. Tigris utca 46. T.:156-9155.

A small, professional organization in a nice Bauhaus villa — but no gallery on the spot. So call ahead. They organize shows of their artists in other galleries.

Galéria
V. Petőfi Sándor utca 18.

Those who run it include painters and sculptors, some of high reputation.

Gulácsy Galéria
V. Tanács körút 6.

A big one selling traditional modern art

Kilátó Galéria — Lookout Gallery
XIII. Margitsziget

In the top part of the watertower. Miscellaneous shows.

Knoll Gallery
VI. Liszt Ferenc tér 10.

The branch of a Vienna gallery of the same name — the only one in Budapest that deserves the name of a modern art gallery at the moment. Extensive information about Budapest and Eastern European art market on the spot.

Műgyűjtők Galériája
V. Kossuth Lajos u. 12.

Mainly traditional Hungarian artists — not alive any more. For those who look at investment possibilities first.

Na-Ne Gallery
IX. Lónyay utca 41.

Hungarian avantguard designers, a closed group. Worth visiting. One of them, László Rajk Jr. sits in Parliament all day, so it's unlikely to meet him there.

Qualitas Galéria
V. Bécsi utca 2.

Inner room for old Hungarian masters, outer devoted to works from the P'anno 2000 group.

Vár Galéria
I. Táncsics Mihály utca 17.

Conservative though high quality; good graphics and paintings of old school, plastic works too.

Képcsarnok

Chain of commercial galleries. Paintings, graphics and various objects. Occasional good piece among all the dross and kitsch. Branches at:

Csók István Galéria
(V. Váci utca 25.)

Csontváry Terem
(V. Vörösmarty tér 1.)

Derkovits Terem
(VII. Teréz körút 9.)

Dürer Terem
(V. Váci utca 16/b.)

Mednyánszky Terem
(V. Tanács körút 26.)

Paál László Terem
(VIII. Rákóczi út 57/b.)

Poór Bertalan Terem
(VIII. József körút 70.)

Films and Cinemas

There have been two important events recently. First, to counterbalance the avalanche of American action films, the Art Kino network was formed. The other: Cinema names with political connotations (!) were changed. There is no more Red Star, May 1, Victory, Spark cinemas, and the like...

Pesti Műsor probably best serves the film buff. The section is in two parts: listing by cinemas and by films. There is a review of films premiering that week in the capital.

The listing by cinemas is headed **A budapesti mozik műsora**. (There is no connection between the word mozi and movie!)

The asterisks indicate the gradings. *means Not Recommended for Under-14s; **means For Over 16s Only and ***means For Over 18s Only. The *Szín.* means "in colour" and *Mb.* means "dubbed". (The absence of Mb. means that the film has been subtitled.) *NH* simply means that hearing-aids are supplied for the deaf. *IM* refers to a type of subscription ticket which is valid for the show in question. (These can only be obtained by Hungarian citizens.) The pictogram shows wheelchair access.

E refers to the times of shows. Here you have to bear in mind that **n8** means 7.15, **f8** means 7.30 and **h8** means 7.45. (These are abbreviations for the Hungarian words meaning "a quarter of", a "half of" and "three-quarters of" respectively. Thus **1/4 8** means 7.15, **1/2 8** means 7.30 and **3/4 8** means. 7.45. (You have been warned!)

The larger cinemas have six shows a day, the smaller three. No cinema in Budapest has continuous performances. **De** means "mornings" and **Du** means "afternoons and evenings", **este** refers to an evening, **éjjel** refers to a (late) night show. The nationality of the film is also given. Here you should be aware that **Magyar** is "Hungarian", **Lengyel** is "Polish", **Német** is "German" and **Olasz** is "Italian". The entry that indicates that a film has been held over is **Prol.**, thus **3 hétre Prol.** means "now in its third week". The second part of the Cinema section in Pesti Műsor is headed **A hét filmjei** and under this films are listed in alphabetical order. Here the films' origins, director and leading players are given. Then comes a short outline of the film and the names of the cinemas playing it. For times of shows, dates and even if the film is dubbed or not, you have to return to the first section. (It is not always easy to work out the original title — you have to use the director's and players' names and guess!)

There then comes a section called GYERMEKEKNEK AJÁNLOTT FIL-MEK: films recommended for children. More importantly for the foreign visitor is the list NYELVGYAKORLÓK FIGYELMÉBE (literally "for those who want to practise foreign languages"). These films are grouped by languages. After the title of each film comes the name of the cinema it is playing in. Beware: "angolul" means *in English*. All films featuring in this list are in the original, undubbed version, with subtitles. Budapest Week carries a listing of films in English.

Normally tickets can be ordered over the phone but must be collected fifteen minutes before the show. You have to show your ticket to one of the old ladies who guards the door into the auditorium. Heaven help you if your ticket is marked **bal** (left) and you present it at the door marked **jobb** (right). You are sent on your way with withering scorn. They remain at the door until the film begins. If there are plenty of empty seats, the custom is to remove yourself to a better one. The real trouble begins when a late-comer is brought in by one of the usherettes: she usually manages to give a performance worthy of something from a folk-tale. (We do not tip usherettes but although the cloakroom charge is marked clearly it is customary to add one or two forints.)

Over the last year a tidal wave of American action films forced out everything else from the Budapest movies. There are a couple of oases, though:

THE ART KINO NETWORK

Európa
VII. Rákóczi út 82. T.:122-5419.

Hunnia
VII. Erzsébet körút 26.
T.: 122-3471.
See *Walk Five* about details.

Blue Box Moziklub
IX. Kinizsi utca 28.
T.: 117-9574.

Művész
VI. Teréz körút 30. T.: 132-6726.

Tabán
I. Krisztina körút 87-89.
T.: 156-8162.

Tivoli
VI. Nagymező utca 8.
T.: 142-0549.

Toldi
V. Bajcsy-Zsilinszky út 36-38.
T.: 131-8129.

Vörösmarty
VIII. Üllői út 4. T.: 133-8125.

OTHER SPECIALIZED CINEMAS

Broadway (Filmmúzeum)
VII. Tanács körút 3.
T.: 122-0230.
Run by the Film Institute, showing both box-office films and archive films. Usually has seven or eight films in repertory at one time, among which will be pre-war films. A large board above the box-office window displays what is showing and when. If a lamp is on beside one of the performance times, that means that it isn't sold out yet. The auditorium is below ground level and used to be known as the Barlang Mozi — The Cave.

Örökmozgó
VII. Erzsébet körút 39.
T.: 142-2167.
The name means "perpetuum mobile". It has a conplicated programme. To see most of the performances you have to be a member of the film club here. Also a café and a bookshop — a very pleasant, trendy place, run buy enthusiastic film buffs, who tend to speak English. On Saturday and Sunday afternoons there are Kids' programmes.

Szindbád
XIII. Szt. István körút 16. T.: 131-8573.
All-Hungarian programme in two rooms, which bear the name of two immortals of Hungarian cinema. Recently redecorated in a somewhat posh manner.

When I was a student I won a bet by seeing seven films in the same day. (Video wasn't heard of then.) I saw the last at ten o'clock in the Bástya, which is still one of the to cinemas to have a late-night show every evening. The regulars consist of those who give encouragement to and a running commentary on the actors, those who snore loudly and those who protest against the activities of the first two groups. The manager tries to book in the more exciting type of film — and occasionally succeeds.

LATE-NIGHT SHOWS:

Bástya
VII. Erzsébet körút 8.
T.: 122-2426.
10 p.m. daily.

Metro
VI. Teréz körút 62.
T.: 153-4266.
Friday and Saturday at 10 p.m.

Duna
XIII. Fürst Sándor utca 7. Two minutes from the Pest end of the Margit híd. T.: 112-7446.
10 p.m. daily.
Just before the show starts, out comes the tall, wavyhaired, bearded manager to cast an eye over the audience — full again so we can start the film.

Toldi
V. Bajcsy-Zsilinszky Endre út 36—39. T.: 131-8129.
10 p.m. daily. Fridays and Saturdays at 12 p.m. too.

Uránia
VIII. Rákóczi út 21. T.: 118-8955.
Friday and Saturday at 10 p.m.

Vörösmarty
VIII. Üllői út 4. T.: 133-8125.
10 p.m. daily.

OPEN-AIR CINEMAS

Budai Kertmozi
II. Bem rakpart 17. T.: 135-0993.
Advance booking is a must.

Csepel Parkmozi
XXI. Vasmunkás tér 12. T.: 114-7303.
25 minutes from the centre by car.

Petőfi Csarnok Kertmozi
Városliget, XIV. Zichy Mihály út 14. T.: 142-4327.

Vörösmarty Kertmozi
XIII. Margitsziget. T.: 112-5027.
Access. Bus 26

Twelve Hungarian Films

During the summer months some cinemas and clubs show recent Hungarian films with English subtitles. (Most of them can also be rented from Mokép Videotéka.) The following ones are not to be missed:

Miklós Jancsó: The confrontation
(Fényes szelek, 1969). A historical parable telling a story about the "revolutionary guardists" of the late forties, who start to disrupt the ancien régime with gusto, until they themselves are pushed off the scene. (Original title Fényes Szelek: "Shining Winds".)

Péter Bacsó: The witness
(A tanú, 1969). A hilarious comedy on the Hungary of the early fifties, when the authorities experimented even with growing cotton and lemons. Premiered in 1979. ("...a satirical comedy worthy to rank with Schweik" — The Times, London, 18. 2. 1982.)

Zoltán Huszárik: Szindbád
(1971). A sensuous, poetic film on the last days of an ageing hedonist, based on the writings of Gyula Krúdy, chronicler of small town fin de siéle. An exceptionally successfull common effort of director, cameraman, composer and actor. See also the introduction to EATING. ("A striking tour de force of visual technique and metaphysical imagery" — Films and Filming, Dec. 1981.)

Gyula Gazdag: The whistling cobblestone
(A sípoló macskakő, 1972). A philosophical satire set in a summer student work camp — on the perspectives of the post 68 generation. A feature film of documentarist technique. Amateur cast, black and white. ("...high-spirited and sly satire of government incompetence..." — Village Voice, 29. 10. 1979.)

Pál Sándor: Football of the good old days
(Régi idők focija, 1973). A very funny and moderately sentimental film about an impoverished laundry owner, who keeps on sponsoring a football team in the Budapest of the twenties (during the first low ebb of Hungarian football), because "There must be a team!". Starring Dezső Garas, the great comedian.

András Jeles: Little Valentino
(A kis Valentino, 1979). A young man runs away with some ten thousand forints and loiters through some of the most pessimistic Budapest neighbourhoods. A malicious, depressing, though

delightful film on values in the late seventies. Tells a lot about this city. (Black and white, amateur cast.)

Gábor Bódy: Psyché

(1980). A two-part, spectacular film-epic, an intellectual somewhat esoteric movie "relating" the adventures of a fictituous poetess from the 1790s up to now. The greatest effort of the avant-gard film-maker (1946—86), on the origins of new wave point of view. ("...a chronicle of seduction and depravity... in the experimental, avant-garde vein." — Variety, New York, 13. 5. 1981.)

István Szabó: Mephisto

(1981). A two-part, well-made, spectacular movie piece on the life of an actor in the Germany of early 20th century, on the limits of cooperation between the gifted and the powerful. Starring Klaus Maria Brandauer. (An Oscar-winning film based on the novel of Klaus Mann.)

Péter Gothár: Time stands still

(Megáll az idő, 1981). An irreverent, full-blooded "period piece", set in the Budapest of the sixties, about the struggles of teenagers. With impressionistic, highly original photography.

Amateur and professional actors. You couldn't say which was which.

Péter Timár: Healthy eroticism

(Egészséges erotika, 1986). A black and white black comedy, full of ingenious film tricks, on the working days of a factory making wooden boxes, somewhere, as Hungarian puts it, "behind the back of God". Humour occasionally worthy of Ionesco and Buster Keaton.

János Rózsa: Kiss, Mummy

(Csók, anyu, 1986). The days of an upper middle class family, in the witty, somewhat sentimental vein of recent American cinema. Provides insider's knowledge on present day Hungary. In the role of the overworked, amoral father the all-round personality of Hungarian film and cinema, Róbert Koltai.

Bereményi Géza: Eldorádó

(1988). A very funny and vivid, story of a market vendor and his struggle to survive in the dark fifties, his love for his grandson. Excellent fun plus authentic acting, even startling music. The story ends in 1956.
Starring Károly Eperjes, a marvellous actor — the Depardieu of the Hungarian cinema.

Radio and Television

For a foreigner in Budapest there are four Hungarian channels to listen to.

All-English-speaking **Radio Bridge** has news about Hungary every hour on the half, while has Voice of America news every hour on the hour. Plus a weather report after both. Plus a lot of music.

Bartók Rádió broadcasts a lot of classical music and some jazz in the evening. The problem is that it is on 69,38 MHz, you are unlikely to find it on your radio: it's Eastern standard FM.

Calypso 873 is a commercial channel with very pleasant oldies all day. And you are really fortunate not to understand the crap they speak in between. (873 KHz, hence the name.)

Danubius Radio is another commercial channel (Western standard FM), with German-speaking programs in daytime in the summer. (103,3 MHz).

Radio is now being used as background noise by most people. Apart from news and music programmes, the largest audiences are for a monthly variety show called "Rádiókabaré" and a soap called "Szabó család", the Szabó Family. The latter has been running since 1959, going out every Tuesday on **Kossuth Rádió**. It is written the week before and its script-writers pay heed to its large postbag.

The 1960 Olympics in Rome was when there were first a significant number of television sets in the country (the service had begun three years earlier). For years people would visit each other in order to watch television; sometimes up to fifteen people would be in front of a set. They brought their own chairs with them.

Now there is frequently more than one set per household and all broadcasts are in colour. Hungary uses the SECAM system, brought in from France. The proportion of colour sets is about 55% that of black and white sets.

Television was the arch propaganda medium of the late "party-state". (Until quite recently there was no broadcast on Monday, "to give the families some free time" — a feature envied by visiting German Chancellor Schmidt). The new President of the (only one and state-owned) Television, a remarkably youthful former sociologist, put forward reforms within weeks: among them to show **BBC News on Monday, Tuesday** and **Thursday, ZDF News on Wednesday** and **Antenne 2 News on Friday, always after 11 p. m., on Channel One**. (Original, uncut form, with Hungarian subtitles). The main newsprograms are at 7.30 and 9 p.m., on the two Channels, respectively.

Sport Events

Before the advent of television, sporting events were very well attended. True, Hungarian sportsmen were successful then too. (Still not very bad, after Seoul.) The best attended sports event now is undoubtedly the Hungarian Grand Prix for Formula One cars when the Hungaroring circuit, at the beginning of August (since 1986).

The national football team's setbacks at the Mexico World Cup in the same year brought a further fall in football attendances in their wake. (One headline after the 6-0 thrashing by the Soviet team simply read "Football Disaster with Hungarian Victims".) Hungary has done well at Olympiads, counting as one of the stronger countries, even though it is now a long time since our best result of 16 gold medals in the 1952 Olympics in Helsinki. At present Hungary still has a strong presence in the kayak, canoe, fencing, modern pentathlon and wrestling and water-polo competitions. Pesti Műsor does not list sports events; for information turn to Tourinform (117-9800). Here follows a list of the more important venues.

Népstadion
XIV. Stefánia út 3—5. Access: Second (Red) Metro; Trolleys 75, 80; Bus 55. T.: 251-1222.

Planned from the early days of the century, this stadium was finally built between 1948 and 1953 on the site of a horse-racing track. More than 50,000 people contributed their voluntary labour to the project designed by Károly Dávid and associates. As in the Colisseum in Rome, spectators reach their seats by going down gangways. The sight-lines are at more of an angle than is usual and the finishing-line can be seen clearly from every seat. The total area is almost 200,000 square metres and the capacity is 76,000 spectators. The Stalinist statuary ("sort of young proletars enjoying all kinds of sports") has to be seen to be believed.

Budapest Sportcsarnok
XIV. Stefánia út 2. Access: Second (Red) Metro line to Népstadion; Trolleys 75, 80; Buses 55, 95. T.: 251-1222

Circular, modern hall with a maximum capacity of 10,000. Hosts many indoor sports — from athletics to ice-hockey.

Also a very important venue for concerts, conferences and ballet. It was laid out so that it is in line with the Népstadion's north-south axis.

FTC
IX. Üllői út 129. Access: Third (blue) Metro to Népliget; Tram 23; Trolley 75; Bus 55. T.: 113-6025.

The best of the club stadia in Pest. After lean years the team again is a serious contender for the championship. The team is the only one to have always played in the top division.

They play in green and white and their matches are either on Saturdays or Sundays with the occasional Wednesday evening match.

Nowadays tends to be under sanction for some violence or other. If not, avoid it.

Hungaroring
Near Mogyoród, about 24 kilometre from Budapest, on the M3 motorway.

This purpose-built Formula One circuit was completed within one year. Hungary does not manufacture cars but the fifth largest bus factory in the world, called Ikarus, is Hungarian.

Komjádi Béla swimming-pool
II. Árpád fejedelem útja 8. On the Buda embankment between Margit híd and Árpád híd. Access: Tram 17; Buses 6, 60, 86. T.: 115-0639.

Venue for important swimming meets and water-polo matches. In summer the roof is opened.

Millenáris cycle track and icerink
XIV. Szabó József utca 1. Close to the Népstadion as the bird flies. Access: Trams 44, 67; Bus 7. T.: 251-1222.

The only cycling-track in the country, scene of the 1928 World Championships — under lights even then. It can hold 14,000. Bends are cambered at 36.6 and straights at 11.6 on the 412 m long track. Cycling used to be very big in Budapest. One of the great veterans can be seen in an old-fashioned bicycle shop whose window is virtually a museum display. (See *For the second time / Twelve old shops and workshops.*)

MTK stadium
VIII. Hungária körút 6. Access: Trams 28, 36; Trolley 75; Bus 55. T.: 133-6758.

Football stadium that is steeped in history. (The initials stand for the "Hungarian Physical Culture Circle".) Traditional rivals of FTC, their matches used to be called the "standing deciders".

Hajós Alfréd Sports Pool
XIII. Margitsziget. Access: Bus 26. Cars may not be driven onto the island but the pool is a five minute walk from the tram stop in the middle of Margit híd. T.: 111-4046.

The covered part was designed by Alfréd Hajós, who won two gold medals in swimming at the first modern Olympiad in Athens in 1896.

Horse Racing

Two forms of horse-racing exist in Hungary: *galopp* which is flat-racing and *ügető* which is trotting. Racing was introduced into Hungary in 1827 in imitation of English racing.

The present flat-racing track opened in 1925 and now bears the name of the legendary mare Kincsem (1874—1887) who won all her 54 races. Her statue is at the entrance. **Kincsem park** X. Albertirsai út 2. Access: Second (Red) Metro to Pillangó utca, then through the underpass to the end. Tram 29, Bus 100. T.: 252-0888.)

All races are handicaps; handicapping is based on the weight the horse has to carry. The season runs from Spring to Autumn on Sundays. Serious racegoers treat racing as a form of art. In a recent best-selling sociographic book one of the two authors left readers the following message: "If you have any further questions, I can be found on Saturday afternoons between 2 and 5 at the Trotting Track. On Sundays I am at the flat races but you are requested not to disturb me there — I take that seriously."

Trotting has been going since 1883. The track, built in 1933, is in town, at **Ügetőpálya** (VIII. Kerepesi út 9—11. Access: Trolley 80; Bus 95. T.: 134-2958).

Handicapping in trotting is not by weight but by distance. The track record was set here in 1972 by City, an American-bred trotter at 1:18.3. The convention is that all horses born in the same year bear names beginning with the same initial letter. Bets can be placed in some betting shops in town as well as at the course. All betting is Totaliser betting. There are three main types. The **helyfogadás** (place) is for the cautious who wish to try their luck: if your horse comes in first, second or third, you win a minimal amount. The **tétfogadás** (win) pays out on the winning horse only. The third is the **befutófogadás**, a form of forecast in which you have to nominate the winning horse and another which places. The first number you give when you call your bet at the window is for the winner and the second for the placing horse. For seven or fewer horses only second place counts, for more third place also counts. (This is the most popular form of bet at the course.) In addition there is another bet called the **hármasbefutó**, another form of forecast: here you have to call the first three horses in their order of finishing. Minimum stake for all the above bets is 10 Ft.

The race courses have a special atmosphere and they draw a combination of people which is unique in modern Hungary, perhaps the last remnant of the Bohemian society of the turn of the century. What is missing, as compared to some other countries, is the upper crust. All horses in training here belong to state or cooperative-owned stables; there are no private owners. There is an air of egalitarianism about racing here, such that well-known personalities are accosted for tips without any inhibition. The only faux-pas the visitor should take care to avoid is photographing his fellow race-goers. In general the feeling here is more like that of an Irish provincial course than of, say, Longchamps or Ascot.

An Australian firm has recently won the tender to modernize the tote.

BUDAPEST BESTS :: BUDAPEST BESTS

László Lugosi Lugo, photographer, chronicler of the Budapest art scene

What a fine thing it is to sit outside for lunch in those warm days of an Indian summer, in the garden of the **Ördögorom Csárda**. Especially when the sun is shining into the still warm valley. Above, if you turn left at the end of the road is a holiday area left behind by the sixties (XI. Edvi Illés utca) One of my grandfathers used to live near here.

The **Zöld Béka** (Green Frog) is another fine place to sit in during the summer. One of their starters is a fishroe pancake smothered in mayonnaise — delicious! You can watch home-made boats coming up and down the Soroksári arm of the Danube. Not easy to get to — the blue city buses don't run very close to it and I doubt if a taxi driver could find it unless it becomes a favoured tourist place. (XX. Horgász part).

When I have half a day free I wander around the second-hand bookshops seeking out books on the history of photography and photographic albums. The shops on Múzeum körút almost always are on my itinerary. To get there from home I tend to cross Gozsdu udvar, an arcade between Király utca and Dob utca, then I walk down Síp utca to Rákóczi út and then cross over to Puskin utca. Here I always peep into Trefort utca on the left — I went to school here — but I turn right and make a short cut throughout the garden of the Science faculty. (A short cut which perhaps only a real *budapesti* could find).

Here, almost opposite the Science Faculty garden, is the old passage leading from Múzeum körút to Magyar utca — the latter entrance is at number 2 Magyar utca. The passage is still paved with the old wooden cobbled blocks that were laid in the 60s of the last century.

In Buda the most beautiful street is **Orló utca** in the second district. This is a short lane with huge shade trees on both sides and, behind them, spacious gardens in which stand fine villas and houses. On any of my rare visits along Orló utca, I am always filled with serenity.

The only things wrong with **Rózsa beerhouse** in VI. Rózsa utca (at Wesselényi) is that they close early, at 10 p.m. and they don't open at the weekend. Wednesday is their fish day; otherwise their excellent menu is limited to the same thirteen dishes. It's a place where I go to treat myself or my friends. In fact I am slowly becoming a regular there, allowed to turn the lights on when I'm the first customer of the day.

For Children

Playground — Circus — Zoo — Amusement Park — Planetarium — Museums for Children — Boat Trips — Theatre, Cinema — Some Toy Shops — "Kidstown"

Budapest is one of the large cities were the presence of children can be felt. Yet not too many children are born, only one every 26 minutes. At that rate, the population will be on the decline, as everywhere else in the country.

Small children of the central area are brought to take the air to the Danube banks and to Városliget. In the housing estates, the phenomena of "catch-key children" has been noted — children with the house key on a string round their neck to let themselves in and out with while their parents are at work. (The vast majority of women work.)

The following list comprises the favourite places of my two daughters and myself.

Playgrounds

Városliget

Literally "town park". The playgrounds are in the southwest corner, with separate facilities for each age group. Forts, slides, swings made of wood. At the northern end of the Városligeti körút toys can be borrowed. In the vicinity of Petőfi Csarnok are the ball game areas and beside the Museum of Transport is the KRESZ PARK — from the acronym for the Highway Code — which is a bicycle track laid out with all the road signs, traffic lights and so on.

Margitsziget

Five minutes from Margit híd, to the left of the road.

Gellért Hill, South Side

A five minute climb on the side sloping towards Gellért baths. Slides.

Hajógyári-sziget — Shipyard Island

This Óbuda (III. district) park, in the north of the city can be reached by car from Mozaik utca across a single-lane bridge or by bus 142. It contains an adventure playground, the largest slides in Budapest at 15 metres with a 40% slope, a toboggan hill which is also perfect for kite flying. Official name: May 9 Park. No more ships made by the bankrupt firm. A Danish group will build a Club Med-like resort village. The playground will stay, I hope.

Vérmező

In the park between Déli railway station and the Castle Hill. (The name means "Blood Field", the Hungarian Jacobobinist conspirators of 1795 were executed here.) Has a giant dragonfly statue.

Népliget — People's Park

Large park easiest reached via Metro station of same name. The playground is at the north-east corner, which the 99 bus serves. A somewhat forgotten, underused asset of the town. No more motorcycle races!

Városmajor

Near the Terminus of the Cogwheel railway line. Playing areas and toys for borrowing at the end furthest from town. On foot from Moszkva tér.

Circus

A permanent circus was built on the traditional site for tented circuses in Városliget. This is the only circus in the capital.

Fővárosi Nagycirkusz
XIV. Állatkerti körút 7. Box-office telephone: 142-8300. Access: First (Yellow) Metro to Széchenyi-fürdő, Trolley 72. Shows are at 3 p.m. and 7 p.m. from Wednesday to Friday and at 10 a.m. and 3 p.m. on Saturday and Sunday. Closed on Mondays and Tuesdays, and from 1st September to mid-October.
Tickets near orchestra should be bought only if you have no other chance to see the show.

Zoo

Fővárosi Állat- és Növénykert
XIV. Állatkerti körút 6—12. Access: First (Yellow) Metro to Széchenyi-fürdő, Trolley 72. Open: 9 a.m. to 6 p.m.; Autumn to Winter closing at 4 p.m.
More than 3.000 animals in Art Nouveau buildings. The Pálmaház (Palm House) has an excellent collection of tropical plants and animals. There is a children's corner (**Állatóvoda** in Hungarian). The Oriental Elephant House and the recently restorated Bird House are two of the musts. Can be seen in three hours in all.

Amusement Park

XIV. Állatkerti körút 14—16. In Városliget. Access: First (Yellow) Metro to Széchenyi-fürdő; Trolleys 72, 74; Bus 1. Open: 10 a.m. to 8 p.m., from October to March not everything is open.
Very, very shabby, for description, see Walk Four. There is a separate section for children ages 3-5 with scaled-down rides.

Planetarium

In the Népliget, about 100 metres from Metro station of that name. (Third (Blue) Metro line.) Separate show for adults and children, starting at various times. For information, T.: 134-1164.
The Multimedia Studio's Laser Theatre (Lézerszínház in Hungarian) is also situated here.

Museums for Children

Hadtörténeti Múzeum — Military History Museum
I. Tóth Árpád sétány 40. Open: 9 a.m. to 5 p.m., Sunday 10 a.m. to 6 p.m. Closed on Monday. Up in the Castle District in the north-west corner. See Walk One for details.

Közlekedési Múzeum — Museum of Transport
XIV. Városligeti körút 11. Open: 10 a.m. to 6 p.m., except Monday. In the Városliget, on the Hungária körút side — old and new wing; the old used to be very richly decorated. See Entertainment/ Museums.

Postamúzeum — Museum of Postal Service
VI. Andrássy út 3. First floor. Open: 10 a.m. to 6 p.m., except Monday. See Fourth Walk.

Repüléstörténeti Múzeum — Museum of Aviation
XIV. Zichy Mihály út—in the building of Petőfi Csarnok. Open: 10 a.m. to 6 p.m., except Monday and Tuesday, but not between 1 November to 1 April, because there is no heating. A great collection of photos, models and real planes.

The underground railway museum
In the subway under Deák tér Open: 10 a.m. to 6 p.m. Closed on Monday. See Fourth Walk.

Boat Trips

Excursion boats depart at frequent intervals from Vigadó tér during the summer season. Time-tables are exhibited there (T.: 118-1223). Between 1 May and 1 September there is also a regular boat, one left of many:
Boráros tér—Pünkösdfürdő. From the Pest end of Petőfi híd to the northern boundary of Buda (64 minutes).

Theatre, Cinema

Állami Bábszínház —
National Puppet Theatre
VI. Andrássy út 69. T.: 142-2702, and VI. Jókai tér 10. T.: 112-0622.
Professional puppet theatre which has separate productions for adults and children. Tickets are hard to get.
In the basement of the Academy of Fine Arts - the site of a famous cabaret of the fin de siècle.

Arany János Színház —
Arany János Theatre
VI. Paulay Ede utca 35.
In a side-street, opposite the Opera. A rencently reorganized company puts on thoroughly modern productions,

directed at children. Biggest success so far has been **Oliver!** and **Emil and the Detectives**. Box office: 141-5626.
In a meticulously reconstructed Art Nouveau theatre building.

Bem cinema
II. Mártírok útja 5/b. T.: 115-8708.

Örökmozgó cinema
VII. Erzsébet körút 39. T.: 142-2167.
Films for children on Saturday and Sunday. Shows start around 10 a.m., 12 p.m. and 2 p.m.
See also Pesti Műsor's cinema section under **Gyermekeknek ajánlott** (For children).

Some Toy Shops

Märklin Játékbolt
V. Váci utca 71.
Mechanical and technical toys. The shop is on the southern end of Váci utca. Has been private all along the forty years. In these free business times it has lost its exlusivity.

Plüssjátékok boltja
XIII. Szt. Isván körút 12.
Specialises in textile toys and dolls.

Első Magyar Játékantikvárium
VII, Kazinczy utca 57.
"The First Hungarian Second Hand Toy Shop." Dolls, party games, model trains of all kinds and of all conditions. Pleasant atmosphere.

Burattino Játékbolt
IX. Rádai utca 47.
Wooden and textile toys designed by the proprietor who sells them at surprisingly low prices.

"Kidstown" (Kölyökvár)

VII. Almássy tér 6. This address houses one of the city's most go ahead leisure centres. Every Sunday between 10 a.m. and 1 p.m. they organize activities for children under this heading. The range of activities is staggering, covering everything from the computer club to drawing stories.
Music, theatre and films are also frequently included. Not organized from May to mid-October. Information from 142-4144.

Month by Month

Hungary is a small country, which has formed part of Europe for a thousand years. Geographically and politically it is central — there are no great extremes. The tourists most probably visit the country in summer but there are things happening here all during the year. This chapter will try to show something of the routine events that take place, highlighting those which may be of interest to the foreign visitor.

January

As almost anywhere, the first day of the month is a public holiday. It has to be, since most of the parties go on to 5 a.m. The quietest day in the capital until mid-afternoon. The government usually organize the days around New Year's Eve so that they make up a three day break. (It was only at the end of the seventies that the five-day week became the norm here.) Schools return after the first Sunday of the month. Traditionally the Christmas trees come down on January 6th, the feast of the Epiphany. Doorways all over the city seem to be filled with sorry-looking, bare trees.

Farsang, the ball season, also begins here and continues until Ash Wednesday. The large hotels are the venues for the balls organised by different professional groups and national minorities.

If there is heavy snow hundreds of street-cleaners are taken on — a traditional source of income for students.

February

Sometime around the beginning of the month, the snow-drop makes its appearance, indicating spring is not far away.

On the 2nd of the month the press descends on the Zoo to see if the bears will emerge from their caves. If they are fooled by sunshine and do so, chances are we are in for a long winter. University students finish their exams and the spring semester begins.

The ball season is still going strong. Even small cafés host their decorations. The biggest event is the annual presentation of new Hungarian feature films called **Filmszemle** concentrated into about a week and a half, at the Budapest Convention Centre. Usually the feature films produced annually used to amount to 20 or so. Less these days. Animated and documentary films are of a very high standard. Film lovers buy a subscription ticket in the form of a badge. Some don't leave the showroom by the day. People from the film distribution world have their annual meeting there also. It simply didn't take place in 1991 — to general disappointment.

March

The 15th is our national day. Everyone pins up red, white and green ribbons to commemorate the 1848 Revolution. (The cockades have to be made at home — it is not done to buy them in a tobacconist's.) There is always a commemorative gathering at the statue of Petőfi and at the National Museum — the man and the place closely associated with the beginning of the revolution. Normally spring is here by then. It is a school holiday, and a public holiday from 1989 as well.

Between the 20th and the 28th usually falls the **Budapest Spring Festival**. Huge posters are up everywhere ("10 days, 100 places, 1000 events") Tickets for the outstanding performances are incredibly difficult to obtain. The **Central Office of the Festival** is usually at **Vörösmarty tér 1.**, the large building on the west side of the square. Music and theatre events are especially attractive. During the Festival concerts are also held in a number of places of worship, such as the Church in Kálvin tér or the Great Synagogue.

Pop concerts take place in Petőfi Csarnok. On the International Fair site is held the **UTAZÁS** (Travelling) exhibition, which is becoming a sort of popular festival, where not only the travel agencies present themselves but every sort of leisure activity club is on display, from the naturalists to the marathon runners. Young roller-skaters hand out leaflets, miners' orchestras play, drum majorettes twirl, the voices of country folk-choirs ring out. Food from every Hungarian region can be tasted and all kinds of holidays can be bought at a reduced price.

Into the sweet shops arrive chocolate bunnies and eggs as Easter is approaching. The second half of the month, depending on the weather, sees the beginning of the Flat season — and that Sunday is the beginning of Spring.

All during Spring, street by street takes its turn at what we call "the clearout": on the assigned days every household can dump its unwanted possessions onto the pavement outside to await collection by the council. It is a time for the young, the poor and the magpies to rummage for what might come in handy. (Certain streets have a reputation for being a happy hunting ground and are descended on by treasure-seekers in cars.)

Summer time begins on the morning following the last Saturday in March. Clocks in the street are put forward a day or two in advance, just to make life a little more interesting.

April

As a traditionally Catholic country, Hungary celebrates Easter as an important holiday. **Easter Monday** is a public holiday. One special tradition, though under threat, is the **locsolkodás** (the splashing). Men and boys call on all the girls and women they know and spray them with cologne. In return is given a red-painted egg, and to younger children, some money.

April 4th was a big public holiday for forty years: it was supposed to commemorate the day the Second World War ended in Hungary, with the driving out of the last German forces. (As with many other "facts", this date turns out to have been invented.) Before April 4 annual bonuses were handed out, arts prizes were announced just then. A selection board for each branch of the arts made these awards, which had the titles of "Excellent Artist" or "Outstanding Artist" for a successful career.

Schools take a one week break in early April. Around now class photographs are added to the city shopwindows; all secondary schools have a photograph of their final year classes and their teachers taken and displayed — the size and the layout say much about the school's spirit. Especially where the teachers' photos are bigger than the students'.

May

May 1st is a public holiday. But there is no more May Day parade in Felvonulási tér. (Employees used to assemble in company groups in the sidestreets and in a prescribed sequence joined in. Their placards reflected the company business. The parade filed past the country's leading figures. They were jovially waving to the crowd from a marble podium the site of which has recently been "sprinkled with salt", in the Roman manner.)

The weather is now normally warm and sunny. Around now, as soon as the weather settles, the Budapest strands open. (See *Day by Day*)

The Budapest Spring International Fair opens on the Friday nearest the 20th. (A show of non-consumer goods.)

The final week of May is now **Book Week** and everywhere in the city sprout bookstalls selling the season's new books. Authors are on hand to autograph and dedicate their work. Vörösmarty tér and Váci utca have something of a

Carnival atmosphere, which fine weather can heighten, spring showers never dampen. (A few years back an English publisher reacted to one showery day with an awe-struck "People queueing in the rain to buy books!")

Different types of readers quickly establish the best-selling books within days. And there are many new publishers fighting for survival — most with horrendous trash.

This is when three annuals appear, **Körkép** for short stories, **Szép versek** for poetry and **Rivalda** for drama. Book prices have gone up in the recent past, since no more subsidies are given to books.

June

High summer with dusk falling around 9 o'clock. The city empties at the week-ends. June 8th is Medárd Day, which has a tradition identical to that of St Swithin's Day (July 15th) in England. (If it rains, forty days of rain will follow.) Rain or no rain, Friday sees bumper to bumper traffic heading for Lake Balaton and to weekend houses. Our summer holidaying season is by no means limited to a single month. Schools break up on the third week of June. Theatres close, open-air cinemas and open-air theatres start opening. The latter put on light drama, musicals and revues, often from as far afield as Martinique. (See *Entertainment*.)

July/August

Most families aim to take part of their annual holidays during these months. (Paid holidays are between 2 to 4 weeks depending on the number of years in employment.) Many companies and trade unions have resorts — **üdülő** in Hungarian, you will see the sign everywhere along the Balaton shore — where employees can have a two week holiday at literally a fraction of the cost of a stay in a hotel. (A perk the future of which is quite uncertain.) These holidays run from a Thursday morning to a Wednesday evening. These are times to avoid travelling in the wrong direction on the Balaton motorway.

The most important race on the calendar, the **Hungarian Derby**, is run on the second or third Sunday of July at Kincsem Park (See *Entertainment / Horse Racing*).

The **Formula One** race is usually held in the first half of August.

Major summer concerts are held in the air-conditioned Budapest Convention Centre, and the ever-cool Mátyás church. Concert series are in two places near Budapest, in Martonvásár, 30 kilometres south-west (which Beethoven often visited, hence his works fill the programmes), and Vácrátót, 33 kilometres to the north. (Tickets from Central Ticket Office: V. Vörösmarty tér 1. T.: 117-6222.)

The 20th is the feast of the founder of the Hungarian state, King Saint Stephen I. This day is also celebrated as the festival of the new bread. There is a **Corpus Christi procession**, and the Holy Right Hand is on display at St. Stephen Church. (q.v.) There is a 2-day "**Craftsmen's Fair**" in the Castle District, a curious cross between a show of traditional crafts and a tourist attraction. The thrilling part of the evening comes at 9 p.m. with a 30 minute, gigantic **fire-work display**. The area on the Pest side around Erzsébet híd is jampacked, but there are many other good vantage points to see the spectacle coming from Gellért Hill. The traffic jam that follows is more than gigantic. (Check Tourinform to find out the traffic restrictions in force T.: 117-9800.) This is our only public holiday in high summer. Few Budapest people are present — most of them can be spotted in downtown Vienna, doing shopping. This is not a holiday in Austria, of course.

September

Schools go back on the 1st, universities two or three weeks later. September is generally fine, too. During an "old women's summer" — for that's what we call Indian summer — Budapest is a marvellous place to be. On the Friday of the third week, the **Budapest Autumn International Fair** opens its doors on a display of consumer goods.

Theatres re-open, usually with the previous season's hit. On September 25th, the anniversary of Bartók's birth, the most important series of arts events commences — the **Budapest Arts Weeks**. These include music, theatre, dance and fine arts events and go on to the end of October. Tickets, information: A SZÍNHÁZAK KÖZPONTI JEGYIRODÁJA VI. Andrássy út 18. T.: 112-0000. — Central Ticket Office: V. Vörösmarty tér 1.

The clocks go back on the last Sunday of the month. This is a very sudden, dramatic change.

On one Sunday there is a **"Dog Fair in Buda"** held in II. Marczibányi tér. The name goes back to the great and "just" King Matthias, who often mixed with his subjects in disguise, and who once helped a poor man telling him to catch a couple of mongrels and to go and sell them at Buda. But the rich neighbour, who wanted to try the same, was turned down with the remark (also the punch line of the tale:) "Alas, there was a dog-fair only once under Buda!" (Egyszer volt Budán kutyavásár!) The event is not very spectacular, just a show of all kinds of dogs popular in Hungary — and a show of the owners. (These are not the ones who get rid of the dogs every time the tax on dogs is raised. By the way. This is the only one that hasn't been, for years.)

Also a two-day **"Cultural Fair"** is in III. Fő tér at the weekend around the 20th. Patterned on the Amsterdam example, theatres, publishers, periodicals, orchestras, dance groups advertise their next season activities. (You can have a look at the high-brow literary and social monthly I co-own and co-edit, called 2000, and buy a gift subscription for yourself or for a Hungarian library in a school).

October

The continuation of the **Arts Weeks**. At the beginning of the month the **Korunk Zenéje (Music of Our Age)** series starts, which brings guest performers of high renown from all over the world. Many premières, electronic and repetitive music.

The weather changes and gets wetter.

This is when the museums organise their special month and many new items and acquisitions are put on display.

The second half of the month sees the **Hungaroton Record Weeks**. The recording company presents its new records (around ten) in a context that can include live performances. Records (other than CD records) are sold at a substantial discount on a price which is already very cheap. Hopefully, the new, pro-government management doesn't break this tradition. Gellért Hill goes brown, red, ginger, orange and every conceivable colour. Otherwise a depressing month in Budapest.

Unconceivable a few years back: **October 23**, the anniversary of the 1956 revolution, a secret, intimate holiday for everyone, is now a public one. (Even the power cords of xerox machines were ordered to be disconnected and locked in safes a day before that day, in order to make copying of leaflets impossible.) On that day in 1989 Hungary was declared a Republic again (as opposed to People's Republic), from the balcony of the Houses of Parliament. This, after 1918 and 1946, could be called The Third Republic, but nobody calls it that way.

November

The weather takes a definite turn for the worse, the sun disappears as do tourists from the Castle district. November 7th is of course no more a public holiday. For forty years this was made one of the most important days in the year, by giving out bonuses, thirteenth month's salaries (where it could be afforded). Schoolkids were forced to attend some Soviet-made war film (not in the last years, though.)

For my generation this day will always be a "gesunkenes Kulturgut", a sort of "sunken cultural goods" — a conspicuous absentee.

Sweetshops start selling the red-wrapped chocolate Santa Clauses (**Mikulás** in Hungarian).

The press doesn't deplore the practice of the "end-of-the-year-campaign" any longer. (State-owned companies may still make a last effort to improve the year's figures — with week-end shifts and moonlighting. But private firms work like hell all year round.)

Time to start worrying about Christmas shopping.

December

On the eve of the 6th children put their boots into the window and *Santa Claus* fills them with chocolates, oranges and other goodies. (At Christmas it is not him, but "little Jesus", or Jézuska, who brings kids presents.)

Christmas trees appear for sale everywhere. They go up everywhere — at work, in schools and in shops. The two Sundays before Christmas, called Silver and Gold ones respectively, see virtually all the shops open. (Recently some shops have added "Bronze Sunday", three weeks before Christmas.) All along the Nagykörút stalls are selling decorations, candles, sparklers.

The traditional family dish on Christmas Eve is jellied carp, turkey or stuffed cabbage. Housewives bake poppyseed and nut "beigli" — as much part of a Hungarian Christmas as mince-pies are of an English. Many go to midnight mass. The most impressive one, from Mátyás Church was televised in 1987 for the first time. Although only two days are public holidays, life does not really get back to normal until after New Year. Many take up part of their annual holidays and a few factories simply shut down for the duration.

The build-up for New Year's Eve starts immediately and in the days before the noise of paper-trumpets — the bigger the trumpet, the smaller the child at the end of it — starts to dominate the city. Although the 31st is a working day, celebrations start at work. Policemen on traffic-duty are given small presents; the noise of trumpets starts towards its crescendo, an impromptu Carnival forms on the Nagykörút, a trumpet battle takes place where the Nagykörút meets Rákóczi út.

Earlier the **Szilveszteri Műsor (New Year's Eve Show)** had the biggest viewing figures. Political cabaret has lost a great deal of its importance, as with the reintroduction of democracy, there is not only one but 365 days of irreverence towards the government. After the hour strikes, both radio and television give out the mournful strains of the Hungarian national anthem, which many people sing the words to.

During the New Year's Eve party there has to be at least one funny guy, who cracks the old joke:

"Do you know what year this year will be?"

"???"

"An average one. Worse than last year, but better than next year."

Reading

Twelve good books — Twelve good bookshops — From bookshops — From antiquarian and second hand bookshops — From libraries

Friends of mine from Western Europe remark with surprise on the number of books in peoples' homes here in Budapest. Because of a high level of state subsidy, books were very cheap compared to many others in the seventies and early eighties. Then came a running debate in the press as to whether "culture is a commodity". The answer was both Yes and No. The monopoly held by several state publishers went and some 400 (!) small publishers sprang up.

Anyone can publish a book in Hungary out of his own pocket, the proviso being the necessary license has to be obtained. Books are sold in all sorts of places, including the streets, pedestrian subways and supermarkets — which is quite a recent development too.

Twelve Good Books

Lukacs, John: Budapest 1900. (A Historical Portrait of a City and Its Culture.)
Weidenfeld and Nicholson, New York, 1988.

An intimate and engaging story - an unusual one. Budapest experienced a remarkable "exfoliation" at the third third of the last century. It was one of the most promising metropolitan centres of Europe, both expansion-wise and exuberance-wise. This is a scholarly, yet very readable book, by a Budapest born American historian.

Not on sale in Budapest.

Budapest, anno...
Corvina, 1979. Second Edition 1982.

This is a selection of the work of György Klösz and court photographers. A major photographer of the nineteenth century and his work which provides many scenes which have changed little since, many contemporary advertisements too. Foreign language versions are in English, French and German. Turns up in second-hand shops from time to time.

Also to be had is a folder containing a booklet and 12 postcards, available at stationers as well as bookshops.

Gundel's Hungarian Cookbook
Corvina, 1986.

The name Gundel is to Budapest as Sacher is to Vienna and Horcher to Madrid. Károly Gundel first published this book in 1934 and it has since gone through more than 30 editions. He is the great figure in Hungarian cooking. The two of his thirteen children who followed in his footsteps have compiled this present edition.

Present Continuous
Corvina, 1985.

An anthology of Post-War Hungarian short stories. The first part (Past Time) is devoted to older writing, the second (Present Time) to contemporary. Quite a few of the selections give an idea of the tart, self-deprecating humour which we like to consider our own. In English only.

100 + 1 éves a magyar plakát (100 + 1 Years of Hungarian Posters)

Large, delightful catalogue of a major (1986) exhibition. Many reproductions in colour, detailed presentation of periods. Text in Hungarian and English. Available from kiosk in foyer of Műcsarnok (XIV. Hősök tere — See Walk Four).

Four seasons at the Golden Dragon Inn (Spring—Summer—Autumn—Winter)
Corvina, 1987. (Also in German.)
This series of four cookery books is linked to the Aranysárkány (Golden Dragon) restaurant in Szentendre, a picturesque and historic town near Budapest. The restaurant is one of those which have contributed to the revival of Hungarian cooking — see introduction to Eating. The four volumes are in hardback and each dish is illustrated with a full page in colour. Béla Licsinszky, chef de cuisine, wrote the recipes for this deservedly successful restaurant, cooked all the dishes and took all the photographs.

Kosztolányi Dezső: Darker Muses (Nero)
Corvina, 1990.
A historical novel by the great master of twentieth century Hungarian prose.

Féner, Tamás — Scheiber, Sándor: ...And you shall tell your son
Corvina, 1984.
The compilers are respectively a leading photographer and recently deceased Rabbi. This warm album documents the vanishing traditions of Hungarian Jews.

Gerő, András: Heroes' Square, Budapest
(Hungary's History in Stone and Bronze.) *Corvina, 1990.*
A fascinating story of a monument about Hungarian history. About how it was designed and built, how it was changed by the specific regimes that happened to rule in Hungary. Very well written, with superb colour and black and white pictures. Also in German.

Csontváry album
Corvina, 1988.
The stunning great original of Hungarian painting, Csontváry flashed across Hungarian art like a gigantic comet. Sudden inspiration led him to take up art as an adult and the results, enormous bewitching canvesses, are to be seen in the Nemzeti Galéria and in the Csontváry Múzeum in the town of Pécs. See our First Walk. Better still, see the paintings.

Leletek (Finds)
Gondolat, 1983.
Unique album of photographs, taken not so much by the great names but by those who at various times managed to capture the interesting moment for eternity. The man behind the camera can equally be an artist, a commercial photographer or an (unknown) amateur. Available from Képesbolt (VI. Deák Ferenc tér 6.) and Poszterház (V. Bajcsy-Zsilinszky út 52.). Frequently to be found in second-hand shops.

K. Pintér Tamás: Budapest Architectura 1900. (Budapest Buildings at the Turn of the Century)
Magyar Építőművészek Szövetsége, 1987.
An excellent architectural guide on 101 buildings. In English and German.

Twelve Good Bookshops

Bookshops are generally open on weekdays between 10 a.m. and 6 p.m., Saturdays 9 a.m. to 1 p.m. In the list that follows, opening hours are only given when they differ from these. During the Book Week at the end of May/beginning of June, the stalls that sprout up everywhere trade on Sundays too.

Fókusz
VII. Rákóczi út 14.
Occupying two large floors, this is the biggest bookshop in the country. Maps, records and Hungarian books in translation all available. Remaindered books are to be found on the first floor.

Stúdium
V. Váci utca 22.
Pleasant, elegant bookshop right next to the Taverna Hotel. Academic books on first floor and leather easy-chairs by the window. Hungarian books in translation on the ground floor to the left.

Corvina
V. Kossuth Lajos utca 6.
Full selection of Hungarian books in foreign languages to the left on entry, sheet music and records to the right.

Libri
V. Váci utca 32.
Foreign language books only, from both Hungarian and foreign publishers — these include travel books and guides. Busy but helpful assistants are competent in many languages, a feature sadly uncommon in our bookshops.

Erkel
VII. Erzsébet körút 52.
Opposite Royal Hotel, with three display rooms. Large selection of sheet music and records too. The latter are on first floor and a stiff cardboard record sleeve is happily supplied on request to protect purchases. Catalogue availabe.

Könyvértéka
V. Honvéd utca 5.
Not far from Parliament and on our Second Walk, this large, well-designed bookshop has two floors. The upper floor stocks in many foreign languages, Hungarian computer software and videocassettes.

Könyvesház
XIII. Váci út 19.
One of the larger book wholesalers recently acquired this former factory. The larger part of their space is devoted to remaindered books, records and cassettes, the smaller to new. Self service here as, indeed, in almost all bookshops.

Litea
I. Hess András tér 4. Opposite Hotel Hilton — in the courtyard.
The name comes from the merge of two words: Literature + Tea, both of which is available there, a really choice selection of both. A singularly pleasant, recently built pavilion. A full range of foreign language Hungarian books. Catalogues. They also send books abroad: above 800 forint's worth no mailing costs. Ice tea. Irish Coffee. Grog. Portuguese tea.

Zenei Antikvárium — Second Hand Music Bookshop
V. Múzeum körút 17.
Virtually opposite the Nemzeti Múzeum, with a huge selection of books on music and of sheet music. Occcasionally amazing older East-European scores and records in good condition are to be found.

Központi Antikvárium
V. Múzeum körút 15.
The largest of the second hand and antiquarian bookshops and on our Third Walk. The few Hungarian books in translation are to be found on the shelves just to the right of the door as you leave. Shopping baskets required — collect one on going in.

Bookshop
I. Hess András tér 3. In the Red Hedgehog House
The medieval building mentioned in the First Walk. Formerly an inn, the façade is decorated with a hedgehog who observes everything that is happening in the street. The shop is small but the selection large and the ambiance is exceptional. The friendly and helpful manageress knows everything there is to be known about Hungarian horses.

Láng Téka
XIII. Pozsonyi 9.
Open 11 a.m. to 11 p.m.
It's also a video rental outlet, that's why it closes so late. Also records and cassettes.

From Bookshops.

Entz, Géza: The Mathias Church and Fishermen's Bastion. With 90 colour photos and summaries in 5 languages. Képzőművészeti Kiadó, 1985.

Csalog, Zsolt: M. Lajos, 45 éves / M. Lajos, Aged 45. A classic, moving Gulag story, originally a celebrated samizdat, by a leading sociographer. In English and in Hungarian. Maecenas, Budapest, 1989.

[Ed. Csorba, Géza]: Twentieth century Hungarian painting and sculpture. The catalogue of the permanent exhibition in the National Gallery. In four languages, colour and black and white photographs. Képzőművészeti Kiadó, 1986.

Katona, József: A Guide to Hungarian Wines. Corvina, 1988.

Moravánszky, Ákos: Die Erneuerung der Baukunst—Architekturströmungen der Österreichisch—Ungarischen Monarchie, 1867—1918. With 250 photos. Corvina/Ernst Sohn, 1988.

Pamer, Nóra: Magyar építészet a két világháború között. ("Hungarian Architecture Between the Two World Wars".) With black and white photographs. Műszaki Könyvkiadó, 1986. In Hungarian.

Rohonyi, Katalin — Marót, Miklós: Walking round Budapest. Corvina, 1981.

Szabóky, Zsolt — Száraz, György: Budapest. An essay, full of data and even more sentiments, with matching colour photos. Corvina, 1982.

Wellner, István: Sightseeing Budapest. Panoráma, 1983.

Wellner, István: Budapest. A complete guide. Corvina, 1987.

From Antiquarian and Second Hand Bookshops.

Biczkó, Tamás: Budapest egykor és ma ("Budapest, Then and Now") Panoráma, Budapest, 1979.

[Ed. Ságvári, Ágnes]: The history of a capital. With documents and 90 photos. Corvina, 1973. (Also in German.)

Gáll, Imre dr.: A Budapesti Duna-hidak. ("The Bridges on the Danube at Budapest".) With more than a hundred pictures and drawings. Műszaki Könyvkiadó, 1984.

Jékely, Zsolt — Sódor, Alajos: Budapest építészete a XX. században. ("Budapest Architecture in the 20th Century".) With hundreds of stamp-sized but clear photos. Budapest, 1980.

Kaiser, Anna — Póczy, Klára: Budapest római öröksége. ("Budapest: The Roman Heritage.") Corvina, 1985.

Kollin, Ferenc: Budapesti üdvözlet ("Greetings from Budapest"). 259 old postcards reproduced, together with the facsimile of a map from 1896. Helikon, 1983.

[Ed. by Pereházy, Károly]: Régi Házak Pest-Budán. ("Old Houses in Pest-Buda".) Last century buildings preserved. With photos and drawings, and a summary of principles in English and German. Műszaki Könyvkiadó, 1976.

From Libraries

Borsos, Béla — Sódor, Alajos — Zádor, Mihály: Budapest építészettörténete, városképei és műemlékei. ("History of Budapest Architecture, its Landscape and Monuments".) A very great effort, with very good black and white photos. All captions in four languages. With a complete list of monuments. Műszaki Könyvkiadó, 1959.

[Ed. by Bernát, Tivadar — Viszkei, Mihály]: Budapest társadalmának és gazdaságának 100 éve. ("A Hundred Years of Budapest Society and Its Economy".) With over a hundred diagrams, all with Hungarian—English captions. Közgazdasági és Jogi/Kossuth, 1972.

[Ed. by Ságvári, Ágnes]: European capitals: the sources in history of architecture. With a 25 page, very thorough and clear sketch on Budapest. With further reading. Comparative statistics at the end of the book. Corvina, 1980.

Robertson, Anthony — White, Bruce: Architecture and Ornament. A Visual Guide. Studio Vista, London, 1990.

Scruton, Roger: The Aesthetics of Architecture. Princeton University Press, 1980.

[Ed. by Tóth-Epstein, Elizabeth]: Historische Enzyklopädie von Budapest (Only in German.) Corvina, 1974.

Index

Budapest Bests

Richard Baltimore, Deputy Chief of Mission, US Embassy, 148
Ferenc Bodor, gallery director, coloumnist, a fine judge of pubs, 37
Peter Doherty, Dubliner, translator, teacher, virtuoso of English, 64
András Kepes, television talkshow host, 155
Péter Lengyel, reclusive novelist, short story writer, a living classic, 34
László Lugosi Lugo, photographer, chronicler of the Budapest
    art scene, 189
Péter Molnár Gál, aka MGP, a wit and a theatre critic, the wickedest
    pen, 84
András Nyerges, language teacher, editor, a Budapest freak, 118
István Rév, historian, maverick political scientist, a true son
    of Buda, 142